George & Darril Fosty's

BLACK ICE

THE LOST HISTORY OF THE COLORED HOCKEY LEAGUE OF THE MARITIMES 1895-1925

NIMBUS
PUBLISHING

Nimbus Publishing Limited
PO Box 9166, Halifax, NS B3K 5M8
(902) 455-4286
www.nimbus.ca

Printed and bound in Canada

Front Cover: c.1904 Colored Hockey League Champion Halifax Eurekas.
Cover design: Steve Klinkel, www.vonklink.com
First published in the United States by Stryker-Indigo New York. A division of Stryker-Indigo Publishing Company, Inc., New York.

Library and Archives Canada Cataloguing in Publication

Fosty, George Robert
Black ice : the lost history of the
Colored Hockey League of the Maritimes,
1895-1925 / George Fosty, Darril Fosty.
Includes bibliographical references and index.
ISBN 978-1-55109-695-7

1. Colored Hockey League—History. 2. Black Canadian hockey players—Maritime Provinces—History. 3. Hockey—Maritime Provinces—History. 4. Black Canadians—Maritime Provinces—History. I. Fosty, Darril, 1968- II. Title.

GV847.8.C65F68 2008   796.962089'960715   C2008-902752-3

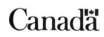  

We acknowledge the financial support of the Government of Canada through the Book Publishing Industry Development Program (BPIDP) and the Canada Council, and of the Province of Nova Scotia through the Department of Tourism, Culture and Heritage for our publishing activities.

This book is dedicated to the memory of
Stan "Chook" Maxwell and Duane A. Snipe.

TIMELINE

NOTABLE DATES IN BLACK CANADIAN HISTORY

1600-1749	1750-1784	1785-1799	1800-1824
1603: Samuel de Champlain exploration and founding of New France	November 7, 1775: John Murray, Earl of Dunmore, British Governor of Virginia, issues a proclamation of freedom for Loyalist slaves	1791: establishment of Upper and Lower Canada as provinces of the British Crown	War of 1812 & mass exodus of runaway Blacks from America into the Canadian borderlands
1608: Pierre du Gua de Monts exploration of Nova Scotia	Ethiopian Regiment & the Battle of Great Bridge, Virginia December 9, 1775	1791: British Government offers free passage to Blacks willing to relocate to the British colony of Sierra Leone	1815:The Year-of-the-Mice First accounts of hockey on the Northwest Arm
1749: Governor Edward Cornwallis founded the City of Halifax	September 1776: the British capture New York City	1793: John Graves Simcoe lobbies to have a law passed forbidding the import of slaves into Upper Canada	1816: The Year-of-No-Summer Halifax Green Market Riots
1749: British military diary explains fusion of shinny and Mi'kmaq hockey	1783: the end of the American Revolution & the first large influx of free Blacks to Canada. Colonel Stephen Blucke, Est. Birchtown	1796: second-influx of Blacks, with the arrival of the Maroons from Jamaica in Halifax; Africville established	By 1820: the Underground Railroad, a secret network of anti-slavery, comes into existence

TIMELINE

1825-1849	1850-1899	1900-1910	1911-1920
1820's – 1840's: first Black Canadians begin playing early form of ice hockey	July 29, 1870: Boxer George "Little Chocolate" Dixon born in Africville	1900: West End Rangers played their first *official* game on New Year's Day	March 25, 1911: Henry Sylvester Williams dies at age 42
June 9, 1844: founding of the African Baptist Church in Dartmouth, N.S.	1892: Lord Stanley purchases trophy as annual challenge cup awarded to Canadian Amateur Champions	1900: Pan-African Conference held in London, England	1915: James Robinson Johnston murdered by his brother-in-law
1848: land records show the first property to be purchased in Africville by William Brown Sr.	1893: Henry Sylvester Williams enrolls at Dalhousie University in Halifax	1904: last year the Colored Hockey League as a major entity	December 6, 1917: at 8:45 am, the *Imo* collides with the French munitions ship, *Mont Blanc*, in Halifax Harbour (Halifax Explosion)
The Campbell Road Church (Africville Baptist Church) established	1895: Acadian Recorder Newspaper reports on the first official Black hockey league	From 1901 to 1905 Mackenzie, Mann & Company worked to buy up all the independent railroads across Nova Scotia	January 12, 1912: the Herald Newspaper Building, the Cragg Building & the Barnstead and the Sutherland Buildings go up in flames

TIMELINE

1921-1925	1926-1940	1941-1954	1955-1970
1916: WWI Black Battalion	1929: Stock Market Crash signaling the Great Depression	1947: former West End Rangers star Jack Mills dies	1962: Jamaica given its independence
1921: Orphanage for Colored Children opened by James Kinney	1933: Gordon T. C. Jemmott, former star and coach of the Africville Brown Bombers, became the new headmaster at the Africville School	1953: Africville School closes	1968: Portia White dies at the age of 57
1921: sparse coverage of the colored teams would once again appear in the local newspapers	1939: Outbreak of World War II; Canada declares War on Germany	1956: report recommending the annex of Africville land by City of Halifax	1969: City of Halifax begins to bulldoze Africville
1922: last recorded game of the Africville Sea- Sides (v. Halifax All- Stars)	October 1940: Kinney dies at age 61	1958: Willie O'Ree becomes first Black hockey player in the National Hockey League	January 2, 1970: Aaron "Pa" Carvery last man standing at Africville

TABLE OF CONTENTS

Behold ye among the heathen, and
regard, and wonder marvelously: for
I will work a work in your days,
which ye will not believe, though it be told you.

The Book of Habakkuk
Chapter 1, Verse 5

To every thing there is a season, and a time to every purpose
under the heaven:
A time to be born, and a time to die;
A time to plant, and a time pluck up that which is planted;
A time to kill, and a time to heal;
A time to break down, and a time to build up;
A time to weep, and a time to laugh;
A time to mourn, and time to dance;
A time to cast away stone, and a time to gather stones together;
A time to embrace, and a time to refrain from embracing;
A time to get, and a time to lose;
A time to keep, and a time to cast away;
A time to rend, and a time to sew;
A time to keep silent, and a time to speak;
A time to love, and time to hate;
A time of war, and a time of peace.

Ecclesiastes
Chapter 3, verses 1-8

How About "Black" Hockey - Say What?

Do you like ice hockey? Whether the answer is yes or no, after reading this book *Black Ice: The Lost History of the Colored Hockey League of the Maritimes 1895-1925* by brothers George and Darril Fosty you'll form a new perspective on this team sport! Tremendous research and expertise in authorship provides previously undisclosed and detailed information on this remarkable history of the "Black Struggle" in hockey.

It is a book loaded with first hand accounts and fascinating facts about Black hockey teams and players in Canada's Maritime Provinces of Nova Scotia, New Brunswick and Prince Edward Island. It is a story that chronicles how they were able to overcome the tribulation of racism with strong bodies and strong wills.

In the annals of history a great deal has been achieved by athletes and their fight in the arenas of politics and economics for equality! You'll enjoy an up close and personal glimpse of the impact on the individuals involved.

In order to fully appreciate and understand the occurrences presented in this story one must sensitize oneself. Black hockey has a long history, one which is relatively new to the common person. This scholarly record seeks to change that predicament.

Considered by many as being superior in ability to many of their White counterparts, you will find out the who, the what, the where, the when and the why at the time.   Given rise to the intrigue, the mystery and the fascination of *"Black"* men playing hockey - Canada's National sport.   These forgotten heroes on ice will set the record straight on topics such as origins, migrations, religion and education while presenting interesting and intriguing material on other sports that influenced hockey.

Most remarkable are the team name concepts. With each team being comprised of various individuals from specific Black locations, each team's name was derived on the historical Black Heritage of a particular area. For example, the *Mossbacks* from Hammond Plains, Nova Scotia's team name originates from the Underground Railroad's secret code for moss growing on the tree bark to indicate the direction to Canada. This is because moss grows on the north side of trees.

All of these teams had affiliations with organizations, businesses or church denominations. Although no known film documentation exists of the games, there is little doubt that this was some of the best grass roots hockey in the world.

The book's title, *Black Ice*, is appropriate in the context of Black Culture. It has indeed been brilliantly conceived for its dual meaning. In this geographical part of North America called Nova Scotia, it refers to winter driving conditions that exists when a thin invisible layer of ice covers the road which make driving extremely treacherous. But in this case it could and should also stand for *Black hockey's* state of affairs as being physically dangerous along with formidability of the teams themselves.

Eventually this story had to be told and now here it is, taking its rightful place on the bookshelves. *Black Ice* is an outstanding tribute to Black people, their places and their perseverance. This literary gem of a product captivates and delivers the passion, the pain, the power and the purpose of Black ice hockey in the Maritimes. *Black Ice: The Lost History of the Colored Hockey League of the Maritimes* is indeed the greatest hockey story ever told!

Peace & Enjoy,
Dr. Henry Bishop
Editorial Consultant
Black Cultural Centre for Nova Scotia

SOUL OF A PEOPLE

It is claimed that the freedman cannot endure a Northern and Western climate, that the winters are too severe for him. Never was a greater mistake. While it is true the coloured man, as he goes North into colder regions, adapts himself with ease to the climate. In no part of our country does he show more robust health, finer physical development and endurance, and consequent longevity, than in the Western and Northern portion of our country.

A New Negro For A New Century: An Accurate and Up-to-Date Record of the Upward Struggles of the Negro Race.

Booker T. Washington, 1899.

Nova Scotia is considered the birthplace of modern ice hockey. The quantity and convenience of natural ponds, ideal for skating, combined with the British tradition of shinny, bandy and hurley, along with the local Mi'kmaq Indian version of the game, helped facilitate the geographic and social conditions necessary for the development and creation of the game we now know as Canadian hockey. Citing a British military diary from the 18th Century, author Thomas H. Raddall explains this unique fusion in his book *Warden of the North*. He writes:

It is a fact little known in Canada, but a fact none the less, that ice hockey, Canada's national game, began on

1

the Dartmouth Lakes in the eighteenth century. Here the garrison officers found the Indians playing a primitive form of hockey on the ice, adopted and adapted it, and later put the game on skates. When they were transferred to military posts along the St. Lawrence and the Great Lakes they took the game with them.

Our knowledge of the roots of Canadian hockey have been based almost solely on the historical records maintained by early White historians. Because of this, the misconception that hockey is a White man's invention has persisted. We know today, such an assumption could not be further from historical fact. The ancient roots of early Canadian hockey originate with the North American Indians. The roots of modern Canadian hockey originate, in large part, from the influence of an even more surprising source, that of early African-Canadian hockey. For it was Black hockey players in the later half of the nineteenth century whose style of play and innovations helped shape the sport, effectively changing the game of hockey forever.

The earliest recorded evidence of organized modern Canadian hockey games dates from c.1802 in and around the area known as Long Pond near King's College School in Windsor, Nova Scotia. Though the historical record is sketchy, it appears quite possible that the Mi'kmaqs and their subsequent European-Canadian counterparts were not the only Nova Scotians who enjoyed the sport.

With certainty, we can only date Black hockey to the early 1870's, yet we know that hockey and Black history in Nova Scotia have parallel roots, going back almost 100 years.[1] Among

---

[1] It is of interest to note that among the first Europeans to arrive in what is known today as the Canadian Province of Nova Scotia, was a former Portuguese Black slave named Mathieu Da Costa. Serving as an Indian translator for the French explorer Pierre du Gua de Monts expedition in 1608, Da Costa is one of the first known Black men to have explored eastern North America. Previously, in 1603, Samuel de Champlain had visited the region during his attempt to establish a French colony in the area. Like de Monts, Champlain had solicited the help of the local Mi'kmaqs to aid as guides in his exploration of the St. Lawrence River.

the first reports of hockey being played occur in 1815 along the isolated Northwest Arm, south of Halifax. The date is important for the simple fact that as late as October 1815 the region was not home to a large White settlement but was instead the site of a small Black enclave. Four Black families originally from the Chesapeake Bay area, with a total of fifteen children, had relocated and settled on the Arm. It is reported that these families, Couney, Williams, Munro and Leale, received adequate food, lodging and employment implying that their children were healthy and would have been able to play hockey during the winter months when the Arm was frozen and suitable for skating. Were these children among the first Canadians to play the game of hockey? We do not know. All we can say is that the coincidence between the date of the Northwest Arm's Black settlement and the first records of hockey being played in the area are worthy of reflection.

As early as 1828 hockey had been reportedly played on Dartmouth, Nova Scotia's Lake Banook, an area inhabited by poor Whites and Blacks. Overall, the Dartmouth area consisted of a chain of twenty-three lakes used for centuries as a major navigational route by the Mi'kmaqs. It was a place where thousands came to skate and a perfect place for Canadian hockey to develop. At the time it was considered the most popular place where people, regardless of race, could come to skate and to play hockey. At the Shubenacadie Canal, where it entered Lake Banook, and the adjacent Sullivan's Pond, hockey was becoming a common winter activity. This implied evidence suggests that Black Canadians, some of who only a few years earlier settled in Canada as runaway slaves, had been playing organized hockey, in non-segregated pick-up games on frozen ponds and lakes throughout Nova Scotia, as far back as the 1820's. At the time, given the lack of communications and written sources, few would have placed any importance to the games, as they simply were a form of entertainment to occupy the long drawn out season that was typically a Canadian winter.

It was said that accompanying Champlain on his campaign was a Black man; likely Da Costa.

By the mid-1850's, ice hockey had evolved in popularity to a point where it was common throughout Nova Scotia. In 1861, John Forbes developed a skate that could be adjusted with single lever, eliminating the need for screws and plates. Produced by the Dartmouth based Starr Skates Manufacturing Company, the invention and mass production of the skate insured that by 1863 skates were instantly accessible and affordable to the general public. From 1863 to 1939, aside from the demand in Nova Scotia, Starr would ship over 11 million skates worldwide.

In Canada artificial ice arenas sprang up and hockey began to develop a national following. In 1863, the same year Forbes revolutionized the skate, the first covered rink built in Canada was constructed on the grounds of the Halifax Horticultural Garden. With the first rinks, the evolution of hockey in Nova Scotia took a turn that would forever change the direction of the game and the way it was played.

So popular was the game in and around Halifax that the first "official" Canadian rules, known simply as "The Halifax Rules" were published in order to standardize play. These rules would define Canadian hockey for generations. In a race to claim credit for the rules and the origin of the game of hockey, a number of socially conscious individuals announced themselves as the game's originators. Some of them went so far as to write and publish their own versions of the "official rules" in order to aid in their declarations. Due to social standings, many would be credited with their false declarations, falsehoods that exist to this day.

From the 1880's to the mid-1890's, hockey continued to spread across Canada yet no evidence exists to indicate that Black hockey players had been allowed to join White teams. Not a single Black name appears on known championship rosters of the time inferring that they remained separate of the mainstream. Given the skills of the players, had they been allowed access to White leagues many would have surely emerged as some of the so-called "best" players of their regions.

Unfortunately, in keeping with the elitism of the day, only the games and influences of the upper classes, and their teams and leagues, were recorded for posterity. It was the Englishman, Lord Stanley of Preston the sixth Governor General of Canada and 16th Earl of Derby, who gave the game its most sought after prize. In 1892 Lord Stanley sent his aide, Captain Charles Colville, to England to purchase a trophy envisioned as being an annual challenge cup awarded to the recognized amateur champions of Canada.

For a mere ten pounds, Colville purchased what has become the oldest and most prestigious trophy in North American sports. Within a season, the first Challenge Cup Championships, later nicknamed the Stanley Cup, would take place in Canada. Lord Stanley's concepts on sport were in keeping with his time. During the nineteenth century, it had been the English who had introduced the concept of competitive sports to much of the world. In an age of the Victorians and Victorian ideals, sports were regarded as models of teamwork and fair play. Many believed that sports could raise the lower classes and non-White races to a higher level of civilization and social development. All was well, the theory held as long as White men continued to win at whatever sport they played. Hockey was no different.

By recognizing Canadian hockey Stanley had accomplished something more. He has given the game "royal acceptance" removing its status as a game of the lowly masses and creating a tiered sport based on club elitism and commercialism. It is no secret that the Stanley Cup was only to be competed for by select teams within Canada. At the time of its presentation, it was a symbol for self-promotion all the while serving a "supposed need". In time, those who controlled the Challenge Cup controlled hockey, effectively creating a "bourgeoisie" sport. A sport that now, by its very nature, would exclude and fail to recognize Black contributions.

In the early 1880's, within Nova Scotia and the other Canadian Maritime Provinces urbanized Black communities formed separate sporting clubs. Semi-professional Black Baseball Teams began touring the region playing exhibition matches against other rural African-Canadian clubs. By the 1890's, with the newfound interest in sports sweeping Canadian Society, "all-Black" baseball sports clubs were well established throughout the province of Nova Scotia as well as other parts of Eastern Canada. By 1900, All-Black Maritime Baseball Championship was being held. In many areas of the country, scheduled leagues were in play as so-called "barn-storming" Black teams toured the Canadian countryside competing against each other and local White clubs.

By the mid-1890's these all-Black sports clubs functioned year-round, as these same baseball players turned their attention to the winter sport of hockey. In an era when many believed Blacks could not endure cold, possessed ankles too weak to effectively skate, and lacked the intelligence for organized sport, these men defied defined myths. Segregated from their White counterparts Black Canadians would create their own hockey league. Their style of hockey was revolutionary. It was fast moving, tough, acrobatic, exciting and entertaining. Athleticism and skill were the hallmarks of the teams and their fast flowing and skilled style of hockey would, years later, be reputed to have been forty years ahead of its time.

The first recorded mention of all-Black hockey teams appears in 1895. Games between Black club teams were arranged by formal invitation. Following the matches, the host teams often entertained the visiting squad with an after game dinner. By 1900, The Colored Hockey League of the Maritimes had been created, headquartered in Halifax, Nova Scotia. Despite hardships and prejudice, the league would exist until the mid-1920s.

Historically speaking, The Colored Hockey League was like no other hockey or sports league before or since. Primarily located in a province, reputed to be the birthplace of Canadian hockey, the league would in time produce a quality of player and athlete that would rival the best of White Canada. Such was the skill of the teams that they would be seen by as worthy candidates for local representation in the annual national quest for Canadian hockey's ultimate prize - the Stanley Cup.

Twenty-five years before the Negro Baseball Leagues in the United States, and twenty-two years before the birth of the National Hockey League, Black Canadians helped pioneer the sport of ice hockey changing this winter game from the primitive "gentleman's past-time" of the nineteenth century to the modern fast moving game of today. Led by skilled and educated leadership, the Colored League would emerge as a premier force in Canadian hockey and supply the resilience necessary to preserve a unique culture; a culture that exists to this day. Unfortunately, such was their fate, that their contributions were conveniently ignored, or simply stolen, as White teams and hockey officials copied elements of the Black style or sought to take self-credit for Black hockey innovations.

The Colored Hockey League was one of the most complex sports organizations ever created. It was a league led by Baptist Ministers and Church Laymen. Natural leaders and proponents of Black Pride, these men represented a concept in sports never before seen. Their Rule Book was *The Bible*. Their Game Book, the words, oral history, and lessons derived from the experiences of the Black struggle and the Underground Railroad. Their strategy, the principles and teachings of the American Black leader Booker T. Washington the founder of the Tuskegee Institute and a believer in the concept of racial equality through racial separation. The Colored Hockey League of the Maritimes was a league built on religious beliefs that were cornerstone of the Baptist religion. A league comprised of determined Black athletes and organizers who would be the personification of athletic and spiritual excellence. *The Baptist Articles of Faith*, a 17-point declaration, was for many their unofficial *Oath of Allegiance*. An allegiance understood and upheld by all who wore the team uniforms. An allegiance rooted in faith and hope and one that spoke of a bright tomorrow and the promise of a new world to come. Seventeen points designed to guide the human soul and to serve as a foundation of belief. A declaration of faith and covenant that declares among other points that there is *"but one living and true God."*

CHAPTER ONE

BLACK LOYALISTS

More than an outpost on a distant shoreline, it was a daunting symbol of France's New World aspirations and might; a beacon of French colonial power on the East Coast of North America. Ordered built by King Louis XIV in 1713, the Fortress of Louisbourg on Cape Breton Island, in Nova Scotia, was the largest fort in North America and thought to be impregnable. A quarter century to construct, Louisbourg not only guarded the entrance to the St. Lawrence River - the gateway to New France, but it protected the region's French Acadian settlers against their English colonial adversaries. It was here at this military outpost where the first recorded accounts of slavery in Canada occurred.

Its fall to the hands of the British in 1745 jeopardized one hundred and forty years of French North American interests and was considered as much an embarrassment to France's national psyche as it was a blow to their empirical goals. The conquest of Louisbourg led to an unprecedented military effort by France designed to reassert French influence and control in North America.

The French plan was to send an overwhelmingly large naval armada to Nova Scotia in order to force the British out of the region. This was to be followed by a series of attacks on British North American interests along the Eastern Seaboard, all the way to the West Indies. It was believed that this bold aggression would act as a deterrent against English colonists who may have been considering future attacks on New France (Quebec).

Led by the French Commander Duc d'Anville, over seventy ships and 13,000 men, believed to be the largest naval fleet ever to sail to the North American colonies, departed France on June 22, 1746. Plagued by a series of delays, the fleet's supplies had already began to diminish before the French coastline had even disappeared over the horizon. Later, ravaged by Atlantic gales, almost half of the ships were forced back to France for repair. Of the ships that did continue, smallpox and scurvy devastated their crewmen and roughly 1,300 fatally succumbing to illness. Their dead, diseased bodies, placed in white body-bags weighted with cannon balls, were dumped into the ocean's abyss before even reaching the shores of Nova Scotia. Given these fantastic hardships, many in the fleet felt that the ships been cursed.

Three months after leaving France, d'Anville, along with eight ships, would be the first to reach Bedford Basin (then known as Chebucto Bay). While the ships lay waiting for reinforcements, their French crewmen and soldiers would continue to fall victim to smallpox, including d'Anville himself. On September 27th, six days after the commander's arrival, Vice-Admiral d'Estournelle, along with four ships, reached Bedford Basin only to bear witness to d'Anville's body being rowed to tiny George's Island for burial. With the death of d'Anville, the Vice-Admiral now found himself in command. D'Estournelle immediately ordered the fleets return to France.

To overcome such adversity, to suffer such enormous losses, to reach the North American continent only to turn back without firing a single shot, were conditions the other French officers would not accept. If they did as the Vice-Admiral commanded, not only would the return to France be a humiliating and a demoralizing journey but also to be associated with such a resounding failure would have effectively ended many officers' future career aspirations. For to many, the order to return was unacceptable.

After a heated debate, the newly promoted second-in-command Jonquière and the officers overruled the Vice-Admirals decision. It is unclear if d'Estournelle committed suicide or was murdered, but what is clear is that he was impaled with his own sword. Officially his death was recorded an act of insanity, caused from seeing his beloved Commander d'Anville's body being rowed to George's Island, conveniently clearing Jonquière and the officers of treason.

Jonquière decided to stay in the harbor and receive aid from the local area Mi'kmaq Indians and Acadians settlers until the soldiers and crewmen were ready to proceed. The sick were isolated on five ships used as floating hospitals yet, despite these measures; the men continued dying at a rate of almost fifty-a-day. In total, 1,130 men would die in the three weeks the armada assembled and waited in Bedford Basin. Many of the natives who had helped bring the French provisions also became afflicted resulting in smallpox killing over one-third of the entire Mi'kmaq nation.

During their short time in Bedford Basin, a French military ship patrolling the coastline intercepted a British vessel carrying a dispatch advising that a fleet of eighteen British warships was due to arrive off the Nova Scotian coast. It was noted that the British controlled Louisbourg and the Nova Scotian colony of Annapolis Royal had been considerably strengthened with British troops. Realizing the British had become aware of the French fleets arrival, and not wanting them to learn the terrible state of the men, a decision was made to dress many of the dead in military uniforms and to deposit them with rifles on shore, propped-up against trees. This gave the impression that the force was encamped and on guard against hostile attack.

Overall, many of the dead came from two of the largest warships, the 54-gun *Parfait* and the 60-gun *Caribou*. With their crews virtually annihilated, the surviving men refused to board the ships believing them cursed. According to official French records, the two warships *accidentally* caught fire and burnt in the harbor. In all likelihood, the refusal of the men to board these two mighty warships meant the vessels, along with others, were intentionally scuttled in order to keep them from falling into the hands of the British.

With a dwindling force and fearful of attack, Jonquière decided to gather the men and launch an offensive. Rather than the ambitious battle plan that had first been proposed, Jonquière set his sight on attacking Annapolis Royal. On October 13th, with only twenty-five ships, of which five were still being used as hospitals, Jonquière and his men set sail from Bedford Basin.

At Cape Sable the fleet encountered another severe storm, damaging many of the ships and forcing what was left of the armada to return to France.

In a 1749 peace treaty between England and France, the Fortress of Louisbourg was given back to the French. That year, as a direct result of relinquishing the fort, Governor Edward Cornwallis established the British military outpost of Halifax, later to become the provincial capital of Nova Scotia. In William R. Bird's book, *This is Nova Scotia,* he writes:

> *When the settlers who founded Halifax arrived, they found countless skeletons among the trees along the Basin. French muskets were leaned against the trees and French uniforms were moldering on the moss. In the Basin they could see the Blackened hulls of the ships the luckless Frenchmen had burned because there were not men enough to form crews for them. Small wonder, then, that there are tales of French ghosts along the Rockingham shore or that residents there move about nervously in their gardens at dusk, dreading they may see a grinning skull beneath one of the trees on the hillside.*

It is said that as late as the 1850's the remains of the *Parfait* and the *Caribou* were still visible beneath the surface, acting as an eerie reminder for many of the horrifying history of the area.

Although its proximity to Halifax and the water made the land a prime location, the stories of French ghost-soldiers walking the hills and the disturbing history of widespread death would make the region the least desirable location for settlement along the harbour. For many it was an area to avoid. Especially at night, when it was said that the trees would come alive with the souls of the dead allowing the eyes of those trapped inside the covering tree bark to peer out at the living. Fifty years later, this unofficial French military graveyard would become the site of the first permanent *Black* settlement in Canada.

During the two years Halifax was under construction, skilled Black craftsmen worked on the fortifications and structures. At the end of their service these Blacks were herded onto an English naval ship and transported south to the city of Boston, where they were sold into slavery. *The Boston Evening Post* newspaper in 1751 recorded:

> *Just arrived from Halifax and to be sold, ten strong, heavy Negro men, mostly tradesmen, such as caulkers, carpenters, sailmakers and ropers. Any person willing to purchase may inquire of Benjamin Hallowell of Boston.*

Although records of a Canadian slave tradition are numerous, modern Canadian historians have often downplayed its existence.[2] Instead they have argued that the practice was not as widespread, or as brutal, as the form which existed in the United States.[3] This attempt to mask the brutality of the historic record is nothing less than a deliberate effort to rewrite history. The reason why slavery was not as economically developed in early Canada was not so much due to the attitude of the people, but rather, due to the short growing season and the rugged lifestyle of the Canadian homestead experience. The costs of maintaining a slave in Canada exceeded the costs of maintaining a slave in the American South. Slavery was not economically viable on a large scale therefore it was never permitted to expand in the manner to which it had in the United States.[4]

In order to divide American unity during the Revolution, the British attempted to pit Southern slave owners against non-slave

---

[2] Official records indicate there were 1,132 Black slaves held in servitude in New France in 1759.

[3] It was reported that in 1734, in Montreal, a Black slave woman named Marie-Joseph Angelique set fire to her owner's house after she learned she was about to be sold elsewhere. The fire spread, destroying 46 homes. When Angelique was caught, one of her hands was cut off and she was hanged.

[4] By 1767 the total number of Black slaves in Nova Scotia was recorded at 104 among a total provincial population of 13,374. These numbers increased substantially with the arrival of British Loyalists from the American Colonies who subsequently brought approximately 2,500 slaves into Canada the days following the American Revolution.

owning Northerners. On November 7, 1775 John Murray, Earl of Dunmore, British Governor of Virginia, issued a proclamation stating that all Colonists not coming to the aid of the Crown were traitors, and declaring that all indentured servants, Negroes and others able and willing to bear arms, as freemen. Following Dunmore's lead, Sir William Howe, the British Commander at New York, and Sir Henry Clinton, the British Commander-in-Chief, both issued similar proclamations.

Within a week of the Lord Dunmore proclamation over 300 Blacks had volunteered for a newly formed British *Ethiopian Regiment* and were given shirts with *"Liberty to Slaves"* written across the banner on their uniforms. Despite the assurances of being released from slavery for their service to the Empire, a large number of Blacks would not take the opportunity to flee to British lines. Ironically, a great many would fight on the side of the American Revolutionary Army. By some accounts, as many as 5,000 Blacks chose to fight for the American Colonists, many believing they would gain freedom for their service.

For the slaves who did take the opportunity to fight alongside the British they received immediate training in marching and musketry. In the case of the Ethiopian Regiment, their first military action would occur at Kempsville, in Princess Anne County, Virginia when they intercepted North Carolina Colonialists en route to join the Virginians. The Regiment would win an easy victory over the disorganized Colonial forces including the capture of the North Carolina military leaders.

Following this victory, the Black troops were engaged in a series of short skirmishes near Great Bridge, Virginia, in which the Americans decimated the attacking force. Later on January 1, 1776, after failing to hold Norfolk, the British Army and their Ethiopian Regiment counterparts were evacuated by ship. The British Fleet sailed north to Gwynn's Island at the mouth of the Piankatank River in Virginia. There they endured a winter of severe weather and illness. An estimated 500 Blacks died and their bodies were simply dumped overboard.

For five months Lord Dunmore and his Ethiopian Regiment stayed aboard the British Fleet sailing the coastal waters in an attempt to maintain a presence in the colony. Finally, Dunmore's forces sailed north to New York City in an attempt to link up with forces under the Command of the British General Howe, arriving at Staten Island on August 13, 1776. By now only about one hundred men remained of the Ethiopian Regiment and, while on Staten Island, these Black soldiers were housed with other refugee Blacks.

By 1778 lower New York City had become a large Loyalist military base housing over three thousand escaped slaves. In the book, *From Slavery to Freetown Black Loyalist After the American Revolution,* Mary Louise Clifford writes:

> *The British had captured New York in September 1776 and used it as a central base from which to patrol the Atlantic coast . . . Before the revolution, the city was dominated by merchants, shopkeepers, tradesmen and artisans. Those who wanted greater economic independence from Great Britain to increase their success had sided with the patriots and fled the city when Howe occupied New York. As many as 15,000 may have departed, leaving perhaps 5,000 loyalists behind. Refugee White Loyalists quickly swarmed into the homes abandoned by patriots and were given pensions, free fuel, and candles.*

By 1781, in what was by then the final days of the American Revolution, the British Loyalist population in New York had climbed to 40,000, including 5,000 Black soldiers and their families. It was this group of individuals that made up the bulk of the White and Black Loyalists who, upon the British surrender of New York City, sailed north to the shores of Nova Scotia. American history has always promoted the myth of the original thirteen colonies. In truth, at the time of the American Revolution, there was no such thing as thirteen colonies. There were actually nineteen - six of those colonies did not agree with the Revolution. Those colonies became Canada.

Following the end of the American Revolution in 1783, an estimated 100,000 British Loyalists were forced to flee the United States moving north into the territories of Canada. During the surrender negotiations with the British in New York, American General George Washington demanded that all Blacks be turned over to the Americans. Washington argued that these Black Loyalists and their families were all runaway slaves and as such they were the property of Americans. Washington even went so far as to proclaim that some of his own runaway slaves were in lower New York, although he felt that they had changed their names to avoid detection. The British government would not capitulate to General Washington's demands.

In May 1783, the first large influx of Black Loyalists (nine hundred and thirty-six in number) arrived at the Loyalist stronghold of Shelburne, Nova Scotia. Three months later, an even larger contingent of Black Loyalists arrived to join them. In total approximately 3,550 Blacks had boarded ships to Nova Scotia. Of these 1,232 were slaves, owned by White Loyalists, escaping from the war. The remaining 2,318 were free Blacks.

Though they believed that their loyalty to the British Crown had given them the same rights as their White counterparts, the free Blacks were quickly reminded that their freedoms had limitations. Inundated by the arrival of White and Black refugees, the Nova Scotia authorities had placed their priorities on the resettling of Whites, many of which were displaced upper class citizenry of the former American colonies. At the time, all Loyalist families were promised 100 acres of land each and an additional 900 more if they could cultivate it. Governor John Parr was given the task of land and provision distribution. Land was dispersed on the principle of those that lost the most would be compensated first. This meant that wealthy White landowners received the best available lands. On average, Black Loyalists received one-third the granted land of which they were promised.

At the British port of Halifax, a large group of Black Loyalists were resettled. As early as 1784 Black loyalist families had been granted 388 land parcels at the township of Preston near Dartmouth. In his 1829 book, *An Historical and Statistical Account of Nova Scotia: in two Volumes,* Thomas Chandler Halliburton writes:

The Blacks in general were industrious and thrifty; furnishing a large supply of butter, eggs, poultry and vegetables, for the Halifax market, and by their

*preserving industry, procured a comfortable existence . .
. The land in this township is stony, but its proximity to
Halifax, to which the inhabitants can with great ease
carry their produce and return the same day, given it a
value which it does not intrinsically possess.*

Many of these Blacks had taken up jobs as servants and
tradesmen in and around the community in an effort to obtain
economic funds to assist in their resettlement. Even so, it would
be the Halifax Green Market that would become the cornerstone
of the region's Black economy. For over one hundred years
Black Loyalist families and their descendants from Preston and
other Black enclaves would subsequently supply farm produce
and goods to the Halifax Green Market creating a cottage
industry that helped the families sustain themselves financially
through a long Nova Scotia winter.

On September 3, 1783, led by the dynamic and flamboyant
Black Loyalist, Colonel Stephen Blucke, a free man originally
from Barbados, Black settlers established the community of
Birchtown, Nova Scotia. Encompassing nearly four hundred
acres in area, and home to nearly two thousand disciplined,
highly skilled, well led, and heavily armed Blacks, Birchtown
was the largest free Black settlement in North America. Its
occupants were fiercely anti-American. Many of the Blacks had
served in Dunmore's Ethiopian Regiment as well as the much-
feared unit known as *Butler's Rangers*.

Formed in 1777 and led by the former New York Militia
Lieutenant Colonel John Butler, the Rangers were considered the
most active and successful Provincial Corps in the British
Northern Command. Headquartered at Fort Niagara in
Youngstown, New York, Butler's force of over 800 men
included many Black Loyalists. The Rangers success was
largely due to their close co-operation with, and recruitment of,
The Six Nations Indian tribesmen from the Great Lake region.
Due to their use of guerrilla tactics, Butler's Rangers were not
just feared by the Americans, they were also hated. This Corps
would fight on the frontiers of Michigan, New York,
Pennsylvania, West Virginia, Ohio, and Kentucky, a remarkable
feat given the men traveled largely on foot and in canoes. At the

end of the American Revolution, the Rangers would be disbanded as part of the British army's general reduction of forces in British North America.

By its very existence, Birchtown raised fears and anxieties in the former British Colonies not only for what it stood for, but also because of its potential military threat. Birchtown was only a day's sail from Boston. According to the *1899 Collections of the Nova Scotia Historical Society:*

> *The arrival of so many freed Blacks, however, complicated the situation for slaveholders because they could no longer tell who was in bondage and who was free . . . Birchtown became a haven to which slaves fled from all over the province knowing that the free Blacks would hide them . . .*

For Colonel Blucke and his followers, the task of establishing the community, creating adequate lodging and sufficient food stocks before the onset of winter was daunting. Located on non-fertile, barren soil, Birchtown would enter its first winter of existence ill-prepared for the subsequent long months of struggle and human suffering. William Dyott, a resident of Birchtown, would write in 1784:

> *. . . beyond description wretched, situated on the coast in the middle of barren rocks, and partly surrounded by a thick impenetrable wood. Their huts miserable to guard against the inclemency of a Nova Scotian winter, and their existence almost depending on what they could lay up in summer. I think I never saw wretchedness and poverty so strongly perceptible in the garb and countenance of the human species as in these miserable outcasts.*

By 1784, tensions between the loyalist Whites and Blacks had increased as the hardships and the reality of scraping an existence from the Nova Scotia frontier began to set in. In that year, a mob of angry Whites, desperate for work, and fearful of Black labor, went on a rampage attacking any Black man, woman or child unfortunate enough to cross their path. When the melee was over, all Blacks formerly in the community of Shelburne had been evicted and forced to relocate to Birchtown. Though many of the Whites believed that the forced exodus of Blacks would improve their plight, in truth, it only made things worse. The Blacks were some of the most skilled of the regional laborers. By denying them access to employment, the town of Shelburne quickly discovered that it lacked the necessary skills to sustain its long-term growth. As for the Blacks of Birchtown, the lack of employment opportunities ensured that they too would be denied the necessary economic funds required to feed their families and improve their situation.

So difficult were the first few years of resettlement in Nova Scotia that in 1791, the British Government offered free passage to any Black willing to leave Nova Scotia and relocate to the British West African colony of Sierra Leone. Twelve hundred Black Loyalists and their families, half the areas Black population, abandoned Birchtown – marking the first large-scale return of former slaves from North America to the African shores. Following the loss of such a large number of Blacks from Birchtown the community faded from existence. For the remaining Blacks, the decades to follow were ones of struggle and little respite.

As a direct result of the large Loyalist influx into Canada, the British moved to grant the regions inhabitants limited government. In 1793, Upper Canada (present-day Ontario) became the first colony in the British Empire to outlaw slavery. This action meant that Upper Canada was now a haven for slaves - the first of its kind both in the North American continent as well as in the British Empire.

As a result of the Upper Canada legislation, slaveholders in the United States helped create a myth that Canada was, climatically speaking, a land of ice and snow and an inhospitable land for slaves to resettle in. This misconception of Canada has remained a part of popular American culture to this day.

CHAPTER TWO

THE MAROON COLONY

Prior to the British conquest of Jamaica in 1660 the island had been under the control of the Spanish. With a force of 38 ships and 8,000 men, the British, along with a contingent of Black soldiers under the command of Juan De Bolas (a runaway slave), had attacked the Spanish garrison in an attempt to seize the island. Though the Spanish were outnumbered they fought well and had it not been for the remarkable fighting abilities of De Bolas and his Black regiment, the British could have easily lost the campaign. Instead, they overcame the Spanish and were able to claim Jamaica as a territory of England. In exchange for their service, De Bolas and his men, along with hundreds of runaway Jamaican slaves known as *Maroons*, were given their freedom and "promised lands" in the interior of the island. The term *"promised land"* historically refers to the lands awarded to former British soldiers who had performed military service and were thus eligible for land allotments.

The British wasted no time in exploiting Jamaica and its resources. Within a few decades more than a million slaves were transported by British ships from West Africa to the island and put to work on massive sugar plantations owned by Whites. The life span of the average slave, if he or she were fortunate enough to survive the Atlantic crossing, was only months due to the harshness of the living conditions and the brutality of the slave owners. Yet, so lucrative was the Jamaican sugar business that tens of millions poured into the coffers of English Aristocrats in

Kingston and London. So much so that by some estimates the Jamaican sugar cane business is credited with being the financial force behind the British Industrial Revolution. As the demand for plantations and land increased White-run slave farms were established away from the coast, inland into the swamplands of the interior, eventually encroaching upon the isolated free Black communities of the Maroons and De Bolas factions.

As the demand for good land increased, the Black slaves hauled soil inland to the swamps in order to fill them in. Thousands of Blacks died, their bodies thrown into the swamps as a way of filling in the landscape. The brutality of these plantations created tensions between the Whites and their free Black neighbors. Subsequently, in 1730, this tension resulted in the Maroon and De Bolas factions attacking the plantations in an attempt to free the slaves. The White farmers pleaded with the English Government to send troops to the island in order to suppress all resistance. For the next nine years the British and Maroon-led forces battled each other across the interior of Jamaica. The history books would record the events as the *First Maroon War*.

The British failed to defeat the Maroon forces despite doing everything in their power. In 1739 the British proposed a treaty between themselves and the Blacks effectively allowing the Maroons to live free and in peace. In exchange, the Maroons agreed to stop their raids on White plantations and to aid the British in the defense of the island should it be attacked by a hostile European power. For fifty-six years an uneasy peace prevailed across Jamaica.

In 1795 all hell again broke loose following the attempts of some White plantation owners to seize Maroon families and force them into slavery. The Maroon township of Trelawny Town found itself front and center in the controversy and the community armed itself in order to defend the Black citizenry and their families against the British and White plantation owner's onslaught. Determined to strike first, the Maroons attacked the nearby British plantations and attempted to free the Blacks. So vicious were the Maroon attacks that fear gripped the Island and the British were forced to rush thousands of heavily armed soldiers and militiamen to the region in order to crush the rebellion. We call this chapter of history the *Second Maroon War*.

Forced inland from Trelawny Town, the Maroon forces attempted to regroup in the interior. In an effort to flush them out, the British imported one hundred Cuban bloodhounds - animals so vicious that they were known to tear their victims to pieces. Faced with the possibility of having their wives and children attacked by packs of dogs the Maroons agreed to a truce. In exchange for peace, the British agreed to relocate the Maroons to Nova Scotia and allow them the opportunity to establish their own self-governed colony. In exchange for promised resettlement and lands in Nova Scotia all Maroon lands located near Trelawny Town were to be given to the British. In return, Maroon families would be given comparable parcels of land in Nova Scotia, effectively creating a land-swap scenario.

In June 1796 five hundred and sixty-eight Maroon men, women and children boarded British slave ships at Kingston harbour and sailed north towards Canada. They would represent the second largest influx of free Blacks to Nova Scotia. Upon arrival at Halifax, the Maroons would be contracted to build the defenses at the Halifax Citadel and to also serve as militia in the fortresses defense against French Marauders. In her 1893 book, *The History of the Townships of Dartmouth, Preston and Lawrencetown, Halifax County, Nova Scotia*, Mrs. William Lawson, with a certain degree of English bias, writes:

> When they were once fairly captured, the government decided to remove them all from Jamaica. Accordingly in June 1796, three transports, the Dover, the Mary and the Anne, having on board six hundred Maroons, sailed for Halifax, Nova Scotia. They arrived at the port on 22nd or 23rd July, after a voyage of six weeks from the West Indies. They were well provisioned and had abundant clothing. William Dawes Quarrell, Esq. came from Jamaica in charge of them. An allowance of twenty-five thousand pounds was given by the government of Jamaica for the purpose of settling the negroes in Nova Scotia . . . The Maroons were first quartered two miles from Halifax; and several estates in

21

Preston, about five miles from the town, were purchased for their settlement. The cost of these lands and the buildings required, was estimated at three thousand pounds sterling. The title was vested in the government of Jamaica. Sir John Wentworth suggested the escheat of another large tract of land - 16,000 or 18,000 acres - about four miles further in the country, in order to grant it for use of the Maroons.[5]

What makes this statement remarkable is the references to the distances of the Maroon settlements in relation to Halifax. The first reference to a settlement two miles from the outer edges of Halifax would place the Maroon settlement right square at Africville - a settlement some historians and government land officials in Halifax have long claimed was not inhabited until the late 1830's. This reference also validates Black claims of pre-1830's Black occupation of the area. The second reference to lands four miles beyond the first settlement would place the location at Bedford the area in and around the Wentworth Estate once again validating Black claims of area habitation. The third glaring element of the Lawson account is the reference to the land title deeds being *"vested in the government of Jamaica"* effectively explaining why it was that Wentworth, as Governor of Nova Scotia, did not give the Blacks land titles, and explaining why some families could not produce land title registrations when the ownership of their land came under question. No one has taken the time to search the archives of Jamaica for land titles pertinent to Halifax. Such an undertaking would have been farthest from anyone's mind.

Most importantly however is the notion that the lands around Africville, Bedford and parts of Preston were not owned or deeded to the colony of Nova Scotia but were in effect the property and jurisdiction of Jamaica. At the time of the

---

[5] These points are important as they prove that Africville was a Black settlement predating the dates cited by the City of Halifax at the time of the Africville takeover in the 1960's. In addition, the passages show clearly that the Government of Jamaica held the deeds to the land in trust. This explains why some of the Black families at Africville could not prove ownership.

relocation of the Maroons to Nova Scotia the legislature of Jamaica had paid the Colony of Nova Scotia twenty-five thousand pounds to be used for resettlement. In his book, *An Historical and Statistical Account of Nova Scotia: In Two Volumes*, written in 1829, Thomas Chandler Haliburton, a Nova Scotia Judge and Historian writes of the Maroons:

> *They had been provided with all manner of necessities, as well for their accommodation at sea, as for the change of climate, and were accompanied by William Dawes Quarrel, Esq. who had been appointed Commissary General (of Jamaica), with instructions to purchase lands in Nova-Scotia, or elsewhere, for their future establishment and subsistence as a free people.*

Haliburton goes on to make a key point. He identifies individuals deemed to be among the leaders of the Maroons and points to the fact that efforts were being made to create a separate colony for these people near Halifax. He states:

> *His Excellency Sir John Wentworth, having received instructions from his Grace the Duke of Portland, to settle the Maroons in Nova-Scotia if it could be done without injury to the Colony, purchased lands for them in the township of Preston, and by the month of October they were all removed thither. At this time an alarm was felt at Halifax, on account of a French squadron hovering on the coast, under the command of Admiral Richery, and they were enrolled as militia. Montague and Johnston, two of their chiefs, were appointed Colonels, and Jarrat and Bailey, Majors, while others were complimented with the Commissions of Captains and Lieutenants.*

Among the names mentioned were the Johnston's and Bailey's two of the original families said to have settled at Africville. This Chieftain status would also explain why these two families, years later, would be seen as the so-called *"elite Blacks"* of Halifax. Haliburton does not give the names of the

23

Maroon Captains and Lieutenants however it is possible to argue, based on historic records and the simple process of elimination that one of these unnamed officers would have had the surname Carvery.

This means that Maroon families and their heirs were not bound to the laws of Nova Scotia or *any* of its governments (including, later, the City of Halifax) as these families enjoyed the status of residents of a foreign territory or reserve. This meant they could not be lawfully taxed, nor their land confiscated in any manner without the consent of the Jamaican or British Governments effectively making Africville, Bedford, and parts of Preston territorial extensions of Jamaica.

This would also explain why, whenever a Maroon was tried in Nova Scotia for a crime, it was necessary to have seated on the court, three Maroon Captains (officials) as the Maroons were considered citizens of a foreign territory and as such could only be tried using authorized foreign representatives. Finally, these facts would also explain why, at the time of the Maroon resettlement, Halifax officials wanted the settlements to be some distance from the Nova Scotian colony, as to not impact on the Nova Scotia residents. As the difficulties of having two distinct jurisdictional territories within close proximity of each other would at times create a question of legal jurisdiction.

The English never defeated the Maroons and because of this, the Maroons were allowed to establish their own free semi-autonomous self-governing settlements not considered part of the Crown. No one realized that within fifty years Halifax would grow beyond its military boundaries and in effect reach the territorial borders of the Maroon *Colony*.

CHAPTER THREE

NORTHERN TERMINALS

A year after Napoleon Bonaparte's forces were defeated at the *Battle of Trafalgar* in 1805, the French leader would initiate an 'economic battle' against the English. With the creation of *"Fortress Europe,"* Napoleon would stop the sale of British goods from being sold in Continental Europe. As a result, a neutral United States would find itself in the middle of the conflict.

Although the British lost the Revolutionary War, they still had not recognized an independent America. As a response to Napoleon's economic embargo, the British began forcefully blockading American goods bound for France, seizing American ships and crewmen. This, in addition to England's backing of Native Indian interests over the U.S. interests on the American frontier and their refusal to withdraw troops from American territory along the Great Lakes, would ultimately lead to America's decision to attack British colonial possessions.

By the turn of the century, British North America, as Canada was referred to at the time, was beginning to develop a character of its own. The first permanent churches, schools, and universities were appearing within the smaller towns and settlements. Roads, lines of communication, and trade within the region were increasing as communities, once isolated, began to experience the first vestiges of outside civilization. Lessons learned through years of struggle, with the adoption of Native Indian survival practices, helped the settlers to this new land forge an existence from the wilderness. These lessons of survival would also help them forge a successful defense of the country during the *War of 1812*.

Thinking they could quickly overrun the British Colony, the United States would launch a three front attack, assembling their largest force in the Niagara region of New York State. On October 13, 1812 six thousand American troops launched a surprise assault on the town of Queenston, Upper Canada (Ontario). Outnumbered six to one, the British and Canadian forces held the town forcing the American invaders back over the border. The victory would have a unifying effect on the people of Canada while denying the United States an easy victory. Part of the forces who fought the United States at Queenston Heights was a unit known as *Captain Runchey's Company of Colored Men.*

Fearing an American victory would mean a return to slavery, Richard Pierpoint, a veteran who served in the Butler's Rangers, petitioned the government to create a *Corps of Colored Men.* Retired British lieutenant and tavern owner, Robert Runchey, would be selected to lead the newly formed outfit and was promoted to captain. The unit would initially consist of thirty Blacks from the Niagara Falls basin area, including Pierpoint, who was almost 70 years old at the time.

Following American attacks into Canada, British and Canadian forces attacked the City of Washington, burning in their wake a number of American Government buildings, including the White House. In an effort to further infuriate their American enemies, the British-Canadian force recruited Black soldiers from captured plantations in the Chesapeake Bay region in Virginia, as well as Maryland and New York, swelling the ranks of the Colored Corps. In her book, *The Black Soldier,* Catherine Clinton writes:

> *Many . . . fought for the British, and some of them joined a special military unit for Blacks, called Captain Runchey's Company of Colored Men. The unit took part in many border skirmishes and several major battles including the war's most famous one, the Battle of Queenston Heights . . . After the war, about 2,000 of*

them came to Canada as refugees seeking protection from American slavery, and settled in Nova Scotia and New Brunswick.

It was during this campaign in 1814, after the British Fleet had attacked Washington and subsequently Fort McHenry at Baltimore, that Francis Scott Key, while being held captive on a British naval frigate, wrote the words to *The Star Spangled Banner*. Subsequently, this Fleet would return to Halifax where many of the Chesapeake Blacks who had joined with the British were promptly set free.

The signing of *Treaty of Ghent* on December 24, 1814 ended the war with America. Although the war ended in stalemate, it did solidify American independence and Canadian self-governance. The Colored Corps would be disbanded although Black military units would continue to play a role in Canadian border security due to the perceived threat of a future American invasion.

With war's end, runaway Blacks began streaming across the Canadian borderlands seeking protection. Three areas, the regions in and around St. Catharines, Ontario, the area around St. John's, New Brunswick, and the region in and around Halifax, Nova Scotia witnessed the greatest influx. On the 24th of February 1815, Lieutenant-Governor Sherbrooke spoke of the situation within the Nova Scotia House of Assembly:

Many families, principally people of colour, have arrived in this Province from the United States of America. They have fled from the calamities of War, and the misery, which they were suffering in their native country, to seek an asylum under the protection of the British Government, and have indulged the hope that they will be admitted as free settlers in this Province. A great proportion of these people, active, healthy, and endured to labour, have gone to the interior of the Province, affording, I trust, a large accession of useful labour to the agriculture of the country.

While housing was sought for them, the runaway slaves at Halifax were fed, clothed, and housed temporarily at the British military prison on Melville Island in the middle of Halifax Harbour.

Following the Treaty of Ghent, the Americans again demanded the return of all personal property by the British and Canadians. The British and Canadians understood very well the term "personal property" but refused to recognize American claims, declaring that no man could claim another as his personal property, thus allowing the former slaves to stay in Canada. In time, these former slaves would settle in the regions in and around the Black communities of Hammond Plains and Preston, working small farms or scraping an existence as laborers or tradesman in the regions fishing and ship building industries. Fiercely independent - and anti-American - their descendants would be among the early groups to aid escaped Southern slaves fleeing north into Canada along the Underground Railroad.

Despite many hardships and few comforts, Canada did offer limited hope. And for many slaves fleeing the United States, hope, regardless of its limits, was better than their current plight. In some States, the life expectancy of a slave was no more than seven years. Plantation owners often assumed it was more profitable to *"kill off"* their Black workforce early and to restock their working ranks than to maintain older, less, efficient slaves. Males often worked eighteen-hour days, seven days a week. Females were expected to do the same, unless they were in later stages of pregnancy, when they could expect some limited reprieve.

Pregnant slave women were deemed to be in the financial interests of the plantation for they represented a source of replacement stock. The more slave children produced, the more cost effective the plantation, and the less likely the owner would have to expend funds for new slaves. On large plantations, if the workforce could be utilized efficiently, and enough *"replacements"* created, the cost of maintenance per slave could be realized to be as little as $30 a year ($10 for clothing, and $20 for food) or the equivalent of 5 ½ cents in food costs a day. Extremely brutal plantations practicing forced breeding and structured work schedules, could cut their slave expenses even further; to as little as $24.00 a year. But such efficiency required increased brutality and a consistent breeding schedule with little room for error. If the work force died off too quickly, or birth mortality rates increased, then the financial ambitions of the plantation owner could not be realized.

In response to the increasing flight of run-away slaves, an extensive secretive network of safe houses and farms stretched to the Canadian borderlands. In addition, fishing boats and small schooners ran their illicit human cargoes north to the Nova Scotia shores where slaves would be welcomed and helped by free Blacks and their small band of White supporters. By 1820, the Underground Railroad was in existence smuggling slaves north from the United States and into Canada.

In the controversial book *Hidden From Plain View,* Jacqueline L. Tobin and Raymond G. Dobard, Ph.D., correctly remind us that, at the time of the Underground Railroad, the most important source of information for runaway Blacks was the plantation Blacksmith. For the Blacksmith was often allowed to roam the plantation freely – as well as being frequently "loaned" to other plantations. This "freedom" allowed the man to gain knowledge of the regional geography. This knowledge made him invaluable and an important contact for escaping slaves. The Blacksmith was also a messenger. He was a man who would bring the information onto the plantation informing slaves of outside events or timelines for escapes. Therefore, it was through these types of word-of-mouth contacts that tales of freedom spread describing Canada as a *"Mecca"* for the fleeing slave with the Underground Railroad their only form of transportation.

It is estimated that the Underground Railroad, at its peak of operation, was a patchwork of individuals numbering 3,000 men and women spread out across the Eastern United States all the way into Canada. Because of its proximity to Canada, the State of New York served as the main terminus for the Underground Railroad. Through New York ran four *"main lines,"* all running north into Ontario, Quebec and Nova Scotia. To the west, through Ohio and Michigan, additional spurs ran into Ontario. Using railroad terminology to hide their true purpose, these individuals, called *"conductors,"* guided slaves north to various

Canadians communities, so-called *"terminals."* These terminals were located in Amherstburg, Sandwich, Windsor, St. Catharines, Hamilton, Toronto, Kingston, Halifax (Africville), St. John, and Yarmouth with the last stop on the Underground Railroad being Dartmouth, Nova Scotia.

With the ever-present fear of discovery and capture, the route to Canada was one of high risk. Yet for many the Underground Railroad was their only option, as the harsh reality of slavery was such that many viewed it as nothing less than a death sentence. It is estimated that 30,000 escaped slaves found freedom in Canada before the outbreak, in 1861, of the American Civil War. Unfortunately, despite having their freedom, the Black population was never fully integrated into the mainstream of Canadian life. Their communities developed alongside the White communities, but as a vastly outnumbered minority. Canadian Blacks were a virtually invisible group, adopting the same cultural traits as their White neighbors, but adding a decided Black style, based on their own individual religious and historic factors.

CHAPTER FOUR

THE BIRTH OF AFRICVILLE

Though life was difficult, and the fruits of their labor often provided sparse return for their effort, most Blacks in Nova Scotia believed that Africville, on the shores of Halifax Harbour, was truly a special place; even though many would not allow their children to venture outside after dark. It was said that *"ghosts lived here"* and there were some Blacks who even claimed to have seen strange images along the shoreline. For many, these sightings were not the only disturbing sights to be seen at the waters edge. In the winter, at the entrance of the harbor, when Herring Cove occasionally froze over, it was possible to skate to the point above the wreck of the French Frigate *Tribune* and to look down through the ice at the remains of her wooden hull. The *Tribune* had sunk in 1797 after its capture by the British. During her entry into the harbor she had foundered on the rocks and quickly sunk. Two hundred and thirty-eight men imprisoned in her hull perished, many of their bodies washing up for weeks along the shoreline.

Africville derives its name from the White label later coined for the Maroon community, an abbreviation of the words *"African Village."* The Black locals referred to it as the village of *Seaside*, though by 1890, most simply called the community of *Africville*. Officially, its population was said to be only 500. In fact, during the mid-1800's it was much larger as the area was by day the social and economic hub of Black Nova Scotian culture. A community strong in its roots and heritage, where

Blacks engaged in farming, logging, local construction, and fishing, a place where families worked to establish businesses, permanent churches, and a better life for all.

Africville's growth can be traced back to the time of the early nineteenth century when the Black communities of Dartmouth, Preston and Hammond Plains battled each other to control a share of the Halifax Green Market. This infighting between the communities resulted in the undercutting of each others' prices, detrimentally impacting on the profitability of goods, much to the benefit of the larger White population. By 1815 the Halifax Green Market had become a battle zone as groups of Black men, wearing former military uniforms in order to distinguish which side of the dispute they represented, roamed the area demanding "protection payments" from vendors. These thug militias were the remnants of proud Black military units which had, only years earlier, been among the finest troops battling the Americans during the War of 1812. In Clara Dennis' book, *More about Nova Scotia*, she writes:

When British forces seized Castini, Maine, a large quantity of blue and yellow uniforms were taken, and now these were issued to the coloured men located at Preston. The York Rangers were being disbanded, and their green and red uniforms were distributed among coloured males who had settled at Hammond Plains. On market days these folks came to Halifax selling berries and wildflowers. Soon there was trouble between those who wore different colours, and there were several pitched battles before the uniforms were worn past identification, the "Rangers" having small love for those wearing the blue and yellow.

This infighting might have resulted from various natural hardships the new Nova Scotia immigrants experienced. Beginning in 1815 millions of mice overran the province, a year still known to many as the *"Year-of-the-Mice."* According to one account:

Hordes of mice ate all the crops in the fields, then entered the barns to devour what little was found there. The hay was gnawed so short it had to be shoveled from the mows instead of being removed with a fork.

As a result, the number of cats increased expediently creating a large number that eventually became wild. The plague of mice left almost as fast as it had arrived, except in Stewiacke where the mice population continuing to devastate the area crops for years afterwards.

The following year was just as difficult. It was known as the *"Year-Without-Summer."* In 1816 the Northern Hemisphere experienced lowered temperatures due to the 1815 eruption of the volcano Tambora, on the Island of Sumbawa, Indonesia. This event was probably the largest eruption ever to occur in recorded history. According to the 1935 travel book *Historic Nova Scotia:*

From May though September, an unprecedented series of cold spells chilled the northeastern United States and adjoining Canadian provinces, causing a backward spring, a cold summer, and an early fall . . . In early June, a cold front was approaching that would bring disaster. Following the passage of the front, temperatures tumbled dramatically under the onslaught of Arctic air.

When the resulting atmospheric debris reached Eastern North America on June 5, 1816 the temperature dropped from thirty degrees centigrade to five degrees within a few hours. The next day, snow fell and the ground was frozen in the middle of June. In September an early frost killed what little crops were able to grow and as a result flour sold in Halifax for five pounds a barrel, ten times its previous price.

Timed with the migration of refugees from the War of 1812, these natural hardships would leave the Black refugees destitute. Over the years, many Whites would forget about the calamities surrounding this period and, instead, recount only negative images of Blacks. From the start, an undercurrent of resentment was visible in the actions and attitudes of some of the regions White citizenry. A case in point, the 1893 previously mentioned work of Mrs. William Lawson. She wrote of the Black refugees of 1815:

> *They were a wretched class of settlers. On the plantations of their owners in Virginia and other of the Southern States, all their wants had been provided for, and consequently they were unacquainted with the thrift or the reward of labour. Freedom made them idle and miserable. The government was obliged to allow them rations during the winter and otherwise to provide for their existence. For many years they experienced the wretchedness incidental to idleness, and were a constant drain upon the benevolence of their White neighbours.*

By 1837, there was a movement underfoot among the White elite of Halifax to rid their province of Blacks. An attempt to convince Blacks at Hammond Plains to return back to the West Indies was initiated. However, the efforts quickly fell through after the Blacks refused to leave their lands. One of the reasons given for the Blacks' refusal was that the Whites had expected them to abandon their farms without compensation, effectively turning their lands over to the Whites at no cost. When the Blacks refused to go along with the offer, one of the White promoters of the relocation effort sent a letter to the Nova Scotia Legislature in which he wrote:

> *There are several of their number who have great influence among them, and being able to earn their own subsistence, do not wish to leave the province.*

Though the land around Africville was Maroon held, non-Maroon Blacks did move into the area and purchase land. In 1848, land records show the first property to be purchased in Africville by a non-Maroon was by William Brown Sr., son of Perry Brown. Perry Brown, a runaway slave from Chesapeake Bay during the War of 1812, was an activist in Hammond Plains Church protesting against economic and social conditions of the refugee Blacks. Perry Brown had emerged as a leader in Hammond Plains and had risen to prominence during Halifax Green Market riots of 1815. According 1835 census records, William Brown Sr. had initially sublet land at Hammond Plains. By 1837 Brown was no longer listed as an area resident as he had moved closer to the Halifax, Bedford Basin area, becoming a Green Market middleman and collecting goods at his home in Africville from Black farmers located at Hammond Plains. In January 1848, Brown and another former Hammond Plains resident, William Arnold, were each able buy six acres of land adjacent to Africville from White merchants. It is unclear what motivated the White merchants to sell to Brown and Arnold but it is probable that factors such as the region's ominous history along with some type of concessions, either monopoly rights or favored status for goods such as eggs, water, flowers, and berries at the Wednesday or Saturday market, played a role in the sale.

Meanwhile the Baptist church began to play a pivotal role in Black Nova Scotian society. In Lawrence Hill's book, *Trials and Triumphs: The Story of African-Canadians*, he explains the importance of the church:

> The first and foremost institution in any Black community was the Church. Religion lay at the heart of the pioneer experience because the church had been the only social organization in which American slave owners had allowed Blacks to participate freely. Furthermore, the Christian doctrine of salvation offered the slaves the prospects of an ultimate escape from their earthly bondage.

It would be the efforts of Reverend Richard Preston of the Cornwallis Street Baptist Church who would be largely responsible for the establishment of Black Baptist churches throughout Nova Scotia.

Preston was an educated and articulate man. A former runaway slave, he would travel throughout the province preaching and lecturing in order to raise funds and interest in the Baptist movement. Ultimately he founded eleven Baptist churches in Dartmouth, Preston, Beech Hill, Hammond Plains,

Campbell Road (Africville), Bear River, Digby Joggins, Moose River, Granville Mountain, Weymouth Falls, and Yarmouth. The establishment of these churches helped ensure the permanency of Black settlements and by the 1830's these settlements began to become documented on official census and colonial maps and surveys. On September 1, 1854, these churches would form the African Baptist Association with the Cornwallis Street Baptist Church recognized as the *"Mother Church"* and Preston the *"First Black Father."*

Preston was a master orator. A testimonial to his incredible speaking skills would be demonstrated shortly after the founding of the African Baptist Church in Dartmouth in 1844. Located on Crichton Avenue, the church had become known as the Dartmouth Lake Church due to its proximity to Lake Banook. Although not the primary pastor of the church, Preston would draw large crowds every time he would visit or preach at the location. It was here on one occasion, a large crowd of Whites assembled in an attempt to stop him from giving his sermon. For fear of violence and repercussions from the large mob of predominately White men, the deacons of the congregation had pleaded with Preston to delay or postpone his sermon. Instead, Preston moved the sermon outside allegedly stating: *"We will go outside, as the grace of God gives me sufficient power over men and Devils; hence I fear neither."*

At first the crowd had drowned out Preston, stopping him from being heard by the congregation assembled outside. Unmoved by the hostility, he continued speaking, eventually silencing his detractors. Hardened pioneering men who had first assembled to stop the service were now crying and asking for forgiveness for the acts of what they had attempted to do. Many came forward at the end acknowledging their guilt, asking personally for forgiveness and prayers. Some were eventually baptized, becoming members of the church itself. This would be the first and last known demonstration of its kind in Dartmouth. It would also mark one of the first incidents where a Black preacher had converted a White mob into his own parishioners.

Preston had also helped raise funds to build the first permanent Black Church in the Africville community with the Campbell Road Church (Africville Baptist Church) in 1849.

As the Black presence grew in and around the western part of the Halifax City fringes, it was not without controversy. In response to the fear that the settlement would continue to expand, the Halifax City Council authorized the building of the notorious Rockhead Prison on the eastern slope of the Halifax-Campbell Road boundary. The City followed this move by establishing the local garbage pits and Infectious Disease Hospital on the northern and western boundaries of the Black community effectively *'caging-in'* the Blacks and preventing future Black expansion or spill-over in the direction of the more affluent White regions of Halifax.

Already the area in and around Gottingen Street was a major Black section, City officials feared that eventually the narrow strip that separated Gottingen from Campbell Road would become a wall of Blacks, effectively dividing the community in half along racial lines. In time, the boundary between Halifax proper and the Campbell Road-Africville developments would become even more pronounced as the City encouraged the establishment of heavy industry, squatters, and illegal businesses within the proverbial *'no-man's land'* that separated the two areas. It was this consistent undertone of perceived racial superiority and fear that would prove to be the motivating forces behind this policy of repressive economic development; a policy that would become a hallmark of Halifax City Government for one hundred years.

The Perry Brown family would eventually move en masse to Africville. Trusted by area Blacks, Perry and William Brown Sr., as well as the Arnolds, would become kingpins, mediators, and unofficial Black managers of the Halifax Green Market. Centrally located, Africville is the closest crossing point from Dartmouth and Preston. It is also located along the direct route from Hammond Plains to Halifax. Africville was becoming the center of Black business for northern communities of Nova Scotia and a hub attracting ambitious Black men, who wished to control Black produced goods. As a result, a new Black merchant class began to emerge. It would be their children who would later become the first Black storeowners. Their grandchildren would become the first Blacks to attend schools of higher education; becoming lawyers and white-collar businessmen.

Black community leaders placed a high value on education as the primary tool for overcoming discrimination and achieving racial equality. In 1869, the Committee on Education, in a report to the House of Assembly, advised against the separation of the races believing that it was both detrimental to both Blacks and Whites. They argued:

> *The committee have had before them a large number of petitions in favour of the present law and against separate schools, and are of the opinion that so serious a change in our present educational system as the introduction of separate schools would be injurious.*

All races would attend schools together. Years later, in 1884, the question of segregated schools reared its head again, this time within the City of Halifax, as a group of local Whites attempted to promote the concept of school separation. At the height of the controversy, a principal at the Halifax National School, in a letter to an official at the Provincial Assembly, wrote:

> *I have been teaching about seven years, and for the past two years as principal of the National School. A short time after taking charge of the school, I was asked to allow some of the colored boys to attend. I consented and since that day six have attended the different departments of the school. They have all behaved well and no disagreeable results have followed their attending the school. Before they came I told the (White) boys they were coming, that they wanted an education, and as their parents paid taxes like other people they had the same right there as White children. They sit, play and recite with the other boys, and I have never heard anybody object. The attendance has not fallen off, and last of all one of the boys will be ready for High School next summer.*

This letter and others like it would be ignored. By 1885, the Halifax School Board would clear the way for the creation of segregated schools within the City of Halifax. Though Black children would still be allowed to attend predominantly White schools, in the areas where a large Black communal base existed making the construction of Black schools economically practical and convenient, segregation would be promoted. Even if educational opportunities existed for Black Canadians an education did not in itself guarantee a Black Canadian future success. As one Halifax Black wrote:

Our young men as soon as they receive a common education must flee away to the United States (in order to) seek employment . . . Very few ever receive a trade from the large employers, even in the factories, on account of race prejudices, which is a terrible barrier, and a direct insult to Almighty God. And still, some of these judicators of equal rights, after a fashion will call the young men worthless, lazy, and good for nothing, when every avenue of trade is closed against them.

At this time, living conditions in Halifax left little to be desired, and what problems facing Blacks in Halifax in terms of education paled in comparison to the problems they faced in receiving quality health care. Isabella L. Bishop, in her 1859 book, *The Englishwoman in America,* writes of Halifax:

The appearance of the town was very repulsive. A fall of snow had thawed, and, mixing with the dust, store-sweepings, cabbage-stalks, oyster shells, and other rubbish, had formed a soft and peculiarly penetrating mixture from three to seven inches deep.

In his book, *A Century of Care: A History of the Victoria General Hospital 1887-1987,* Colin D. Howell, writing of life in Halifax in the later half of the 1800's, states:

. . . in 1859, Halifax was a drab little town of slightly over 20,000 people. For many of the town's poorer

inhabitants, a large number of whom lived in substandard housing, winter meant the misery of cold and privation. The other seasons had their own particular charms. Spring brought with it an offensive mixture of mud and manure that clung to boots and the hems of ladies' dresses; summer brought the stench of rotting garbage and the foul exhalations of open sewers; and autumn churned up billowing clouds of "ubiquitous dust" that blew along the yet-to-be macadamized streets.

Even when seriously ill, the Black population stayed clear of the Halifax Victoria Hospital. Among the locals the hospital was called *"the warehouse of death"* due to the frightful levels of mortality rates within its walls. Most Blacks, instead, took their chances going to the Halifax Poor's Asylum for aid, even though the death rate there was said to be higher than thirty percent. At least at the Poor's Asylum a large number of staff were Black, and thus, a Black family would be assured that their deceased loved one's remains would be returned to them for burial. The same could not be said about Victoria Hospital.

In an age when doctors were distrusted, and medicine was in its infancy, many surgeons at Victoria Hospital relied on a continual supply of unclaimed bodies in order to *"practice up"* on the latest medical techniques. Medical classes at Dalhousie University, it was claimed, had developed an unsavory reputation for stealing bodies from Victoria for dissection. It was said, the only way a Black man could attend medical school at Dalhousie University was as a cadaver. On more than one occasion, families of deceased Blacks had been given sealed caskets believed to contain the remains of loved ones, only to find out, after the lid was removed, that the casket contained only rags and stones. Though the fate of loved ones at times remained in question, many Blacks assumed that among the body parts lining the walls of Dalhousie medical labs were those of family members.

In 1869 the Nova Scotia Legislature, under pressure from Dalhousie University and others, passed legislation allowing medical students and physicians to *"dissect"* the remains of those who had died at the Halifax Poor's Asylum. As Howell writes:

> *Many people objected to the thought of their relations being dismembered and refused permission for a post-mortem investigation that involved dissection. Their concerns, moreover, were sometimes heightened by the attitude of doctors such as Edward Jennings who put the claims of science before the personal sensibilities of the public. A founding member of the Hospital and longtime Halifax City Coroner, Jennings often acted in insensitive ways. In a complaint to the Lieutenant-Governor of Nova Scotia in 1862, for example, a Mrs. Eliza Corbett described an incident involving her husband John, who had committed suicide from insanity at the Poor House. After her husband's death Mrs. Corbett brought the body home to prepare it for burial. Immediately before the funeral Jennings arrived with his students in tow and held a post-mortem and a meeting of the Coroner's jury in front of the relatives. Mrs. Corbett objected to the post-mortem being held but Jennings ignored her. The scene was so disgusting that one of her relatives who was pregnant became so ill that "she was in bed ever since." In Jennings defense, this was a suicide and could have been a murder. A post-mortem was obviously required. Furthermore, because coroners at this time were not provided with separate laboratory facilities, post-mortems were often carried out in private homes.*

In 1882, the Halifax Poor Asylum would burn to a shell following a fire started in the basement bakery. As James Cornall writes in his book *Images of Canada: Halifax South End*:

> *The Poor's Asylum, located on South Street, was noted for its unusual architecture, and was at the time the second largest building in Nova Scotia. However, a fire started on November 6, 1882 . . . and due to poor*

management, no fire prevention measures, and no fire escapes, bed-ridden occupants were trapped on the fifth floor of the building where ladders could not reach. Faces appeared at the windows only to fall into the flames as the floor collapsed. According to the Acadian Recorder report of the day, the "stench of burning flesh was sickening" . . . 31 lives lost on that night.

During the facility's reconstruction, many of the residents of the Poor's Asylum would be moved to the Mount Hope Insane Asylum in Dartmouth. In 1898 the Yarmouth Steamship Company commissioned H. F. Hammond to create a tourist book promoting Nova Scotia. His work, *Beautiful Nova Scotia: The Ideal Summer Land,* was the first attempt to promote the region's tourism. Unfortunately, in his promotion of Dartmouth and Halifax, he wrote:

The windows of Mount Hope Insane Asylum are sheeted with fire, that slowly dies as the sun sinks lower; soon only the tail flag-staff on the Citadel, with its many streamers telling of the ships coming home, wreathes itself aloft in the dying sunset.

Seemingly, he was not aware of the haunting image his description painted on the minds of its residents.

CHAPTER FIVE

THE GREAT BLACK HOPE

Blacks Canadians would first experience economic advancement, national and international success, and notoriety though the sport of boxing. The first of these renowned pugilists would be George *"Old Chocolate"* Godfrey from the Charlottetown, Prince Edward Island Black neighborhood known as *"the Bog."* Many boxing historians recognize Godfrey as the first American heavyweight champion of color.

Born in 1852, Godfrey began fighting in the bare-knuckles circuit at the late age of 26, thus garnering his nickname. In 1882, America's first celebrated sports figure, John L. Sullivan, considered to be the *"first Heavyweight Champion of the World"* and one of the all-time best heavyweight boxers in the history of the sport, declared that *"I will fight and beat any man breathing."* Denied the opportunity to fight Sullivan, evidently, *"any man breathing"* did not include Godfrey. Only two possible reasons could account for this, either the Irish-American boxing champion thought Godfrey had a respiratory disorder that limited his breathing, or that Sullivan was scared to fight the "colored champion" for fear of losing to a Black man. In Murray Greig's book, *Goin' the Distance*, he writes:

> . . . *Godfrey won the first "Colored Heavyweight Championship of America" by knocking out Charles Hadley in six rounds in 1882. The referee for that bout was none other than John L. Sullivan. The previous year*

Sullivan had accepted a challenge to fight Godfrey at Bailey's Arena in South Boston, but, with the Canadian already warming up in the ring, at the last minute "The Boston Strong Boy" chose to draw the color line and the fight was canceled.

In 1990, the International Boxing Hall of Fame immortalized Sullivan as the first Heavyweight Champion of the World. Godfrey, who fought over 100 bouts, has only been officially recognized as *"the first Colored Heavyweight Champion of the World"* and is not enshrined alongside the other boxing greats.

George *"Old Chocolate"* Godfrey from the Charlottetown, Prince Edward Island Black neighborhood known as *"the Bog."*

Photo courtesy Public Archives of Nova Scotia.

It would not be until December 26, 1903, when American Jack Johnson defeated Canadian Tommy Burns, *"the Great White Hope,"* in Sydney, Australia, that the first Black man would be recognized as the World Heavyweight Champion. In Jim Hornby's book *Black Islanders,* he states:

Godfrey had eliminated all challengers to the title of American Black heavyweight champion by 1883. Although records are unclear in what was then an unorganized sport, it seems that Godfrey was not defeated until 1888 when he met one of boxing's greatest champions, Peter Jackson, "The Black Prince" of Australia. It took the younger and much larger Jackson nineteen rounds to beat the thirty-six-year-old Godfrey. The Jackson-Godfrey fight was considered to be for the world and U.S. Black heavyweight championship. George Godfrey continued to fight professionally into his forties, winning his last bout in nine rounds at Baltimore in 1895 . . . "Old Chocolate" died on August 18, 1901, after a short illness.

Godfrey would not be the only great Black boxer from the Maritimes; he wasn't even the best Black Maritime boxer of his generation. Instead that distinction would go to a small Black boxer from Africville, a man who would become one the most famous boxers in history - George *"Little Chocolate"* Dixon.

Born in Africville on July 29, 1870, the 5-foot-3 Dixon weighed only 87 pounds when he began his professional boxing career in 1886, reaching a top weight of only 122 pounds in his prime. Dixon would become the first recognized Black world champion in *any* sport and Canada's first world champion boxer, winning the world bantam title in 1888. He would go on to become the first boxer to win three world titles: paperweight, bantamweight and featherweight championships. Among author Murray Greig's extensive research was the remarkable story of Dixon fighting White boxer Jack Skelly on September 6, 1892 in New Orleans. Greig writes:

Skelly, an outstanding amateur who had never fought professionally before that day, was phenomenally popular. His match against Dixon was the first officially sanctioned Black vs. White title fight in Deep South, and it triggered some ugly reactions. Dixon won easily, knocking Skelly cold in eight rounds, but the champion barely escaped with his life. Throughout the bout Dixon was the target of racial slurs, and whenever he came close to the ropes ringside spectators burned his skin with cigars and lashed at his legs with billy clubs. He needed a police guard through a phalanx of hooded Ku Klux Klan members after the bout and was spirited out of town the next day after (Tom) O'Rourke (his manager) received dozens of death threats at his hotel.

Dixon would tour in carnival-like-style, fighting in strongest man challenges against "all-comers" for prize money. Officially, he fought 150 recognized bouts but it is believed he could have had as many as 800 fights in his career including a reported 22 in one week alone. Dixon's first professional fight had been against the Black Halifax boxer William "Young" Johnson on November 1, 1886. "Little Chocolate" KO'd Johnson in the third round.

George Dixon

At the time of the bout Johnson was in his late twenties. Married and the father of two young sons, he was employed as a shoemaker in his family's hardware store. The fight was an opportunity for William to prove himself and perhaps fight in the American professional circuit. By losing to 16 year-old Dixon, Johnson's boxing aspirations were dashed and he was forced to endure the humiliation associated with losing to someone barely out of childhood. Following the fight he changed his name, adding a "t", and making it Johnston. He also began to drink heavily.

James Robinson Johnston was born on March 12, 1876 in Halifax, Nova Scotia. His father, William Johnston, was married to Elizabeth Ann Thomas, the daughter of the Reverend James Thomas, the most influential Black minister at that time in Nova Scotia. Her marriage to William had been one of scandal for he had not agreed to marry her until she was in her eighth month of pregnancy. In fact, had she not been the daughter of such a prominent minister he likely would have refused to marry her.

Forced to work as a shoemaker in order to support his family, William blamed his wife and children for his lack of career opportunity. Elizabeth, besides tending to the needs of young James and his brother William Jr., who had been born on October 23,1880, worked part-time as a seamstress earning just enough money to clothe the children and to put some extra food on the family table.

By the 1880's, what love that had existed between the two was gone as both turned to outside sources for comfort; William to drink and Elizabeth to the Baptist Church. Not wanting her family exposed to his constant abuse and example of character, Elizabeth stressed the need for the children to study religion and to pursue music. James and his brother would learn to play the church organ before they were in their teens and it was widely known that the boys could recite complete passages from *The Bible* on a level rivaling the most dedicated churchgoer.

In 1882, young James began attending the inner city Maynard Street School for Negro Boys. In 1884 the school was amalgamated with the Lockman Street School for Negro Girls. Due to the number of students enrolled, the school was relocated to the North End Mission and female principal, Jane Bruce, was hired.

Bruce was a single, 37 year-old, White teacher from Elderbank, Nova Scotia. She had taught three years in Truro, Nova Scotia prior to her arrival in Halifax. Before teaching at Truro she had worked as a teacher in Boston. She was strong, determined, and prepared to ensure that the children, regardless of skin color, received the best education possible.

Almost from the start she had taken an interest in James Robinson Johnston. She saw in his character and intellect something unique. She also saw in the boy's behavior the shadowy effects of abuse and a troubled home-life. She was not impressed by the Taylor or Johnston families nor their religious convictions and openly questioned the family's behavior. Having gained the trust of the children, she is said to have often examined them upon entry into class looking for possible signs of physical abuse or neglect. Whenever she saw something suspicious she confronted the family in question. Before long she found herself both hated and feared by members of the local Cornwallis Street Baptist Church and the parents of a number of her pupils.

**James Robinson Johnston,
Nova Scotia's first Black lawyer.**

**Photo courtesy Black Cultural Centre for
Nova Scotia.**

Among her most vicious critics was Peter Evander McKerrow, a local Black church leader and the brother-in-law of Elizabeth Ann Johnston. Bruce was suspicious of McKerrow. She questioned his morality and hinted that he was a hypocrite and an adulterer.

By 1892, the hatred of many of the Black parents and Black church officials was so fierce that at one point Bruce was accused of abusing the children. One of the parents accused her of striking their child and McKerrow, with the help of the local White attorney, John Thomas Bulmer, launched a public harassment campaign and a legal suit against her designed to destroy her reputation and force her to resign her job.

During the court case it was revealed that she was a victim of reverse discrimination and was being victimized by McKerrow and the others simply because she had become privy to facts concerning their private lives. In order to discredit Bruce, Bulmer and others had accused her of calling her pupils *"darkies"* and of stringing her personal laundry out to dry in the classroom. The idea of Bruce's undergarments being displayed in a public fashion made for salacious gossip and added yet another level to the already public spectacle.

By the summer of 1892 Bruce, though being acquitted of all charges, resigned from her position at Maynard School. McKerrow continued to preach, though, rightly or wrongly, it was apparent his standing within the local Black community had been diminished. During the height of the scandal Elizabeth had given birth to her third son, Clarence. A year later she filed battery charges against her husband citing physical abuse. Though the date of their separation is not known, it appears that by the mid-1890's the couple had parted and were living separate lives.

In 1887, at the urging of Bruce, James Johnston had been transferred to the Halifax Academy. There, among White students, he excelled. At the height of the Bruce-McKerrow scandal in 1892 he had been accepted for university studies at Dalhousie University. He would graduate from Dalhousie in 1896 with a Bachelor of Arts in Literature; a tremendous accomplishment given the turmoil and difficulties he had to overcome.

James Johnston continued his education, applying for admission to the Dalhousie Law School in the fall of 1896. He was accepted and now found himself as the *'poster boy'* of Black Nova Scotia with many believing he was destined for great things. The faculty at the Dalhousie Law School consisted of seven professors. Studies included classes in British-Canadian Constitution and International Law, Law of Contracts, Torts, as well as Court Practices and Procedures. Classes lasted six months beginning in September and ending in February. Overall, the studies seemed quite intense and detailed.

In 1898 Johnston graduated and went to work for Thomas Bulmer. Bulmer, aside from being a legal advocate for the Blacks of Halifax, was also the Chief Librarian at Dalhousie University. He was said to have amassed a personal collection of over 6,000 books and traveled extensively across Canada seeking private collections and rare books. Described as being an eccentric, his passion for knowledge and materialism lay in the fact that he had been born the son of a poor farmer and had worked his whole life to achieve success. He had failed on many an occasion and at many an endeavor, but he had always bounced back seemingly stronger than before. He was a great influence on Johnston, yet at the same time, he created a dilemma for James who likely held some personal bonds of affection towards Jane Bruce, his former schoolteacher, and the woman who Bulmer had worked to destroy.

As for McKerrow, he appears to have continued his close ties to Elizabeth and James following the family break-up. Two years after her separation, Elizabeth gave birth to her fourth son, Albert, and in 1897 she gave birth to her fifth child, whom she named Fredrick.

CHAPTER SIX

CODES OF WINTER

While local Black boxers were making international names for themselves, during the mid-1880's, all-Black baseball clubs were establishing themselves throughout Nova Scotia as well as other parts of Eastern Canada. In many areas of the country, scheduled leagues were competing as so-called *"barn-storming"* Black teams touring the Canadian countryside. In Colin D. Howells book, *Northern Sandlots*, he describes the first Black Maritime baseball teams:

All-Black baseball teams such as the Eurekas, Victorias, Independent Stars, and North-Ends of Halifax, the Royals and Ralph Waldo Emersons of Saint John, the (Halifax) Stanley, Truro Victorias, Amherst Royals, Woodstock Wanderers, and Fredericton Celestials helped to promote racial solidarity and Black self-esteem, but testified to the continuing exclusion of Blacks from mainstream White society. Beginning in 1894, a regional championship for Black teams took place annually . . . The Eurekas were the dominant club of the decade. Maritime champions in Black baseball in seven of eight years between 1894 and 1902, their only loss in this entire period was to the Amherst Royals in the championship game of 1897. After 1905, the Royals, under the direction of coach and captain A. F. Skinner, took the Eurekas' place as the team to beat in interprovincial championship competitions.

In the winter, many of these baseball players would turn their attention to hockey. But because of the popularity of hockey in Canada versus baseball, it would be winter's golden game that would become the beacon of the Nova Scotia Black sports movement. Hockey would in turn become a game with ties to religion, social mobility, politics, and the emergence of Black Nationalism. For it would be hockey, *not baseball*, that would be the initial driving force for the ultimate liberation and equality of Black Canadians.

At the time, though Blacks were playing hockey in Halifax and the surrounding areas, their games never received newspaper coverage. This was due to a combination of factors including a lack of organization, racism, as well as the fact that the games were played outdoors on area ponds.

Henry Sylvester Williams, Father of the Pan-African movement.

Photo courtesy Stryker-Indigo New York.

In 1893, a 24 year-old Trinidad native, Henry Sylvester Williams enrolled at the Dalhousie University Law School. Williams would later become known as the person responsible for organizing the first Pan-African Conference, in 1900; an international movement designed to create a voice for people of African descent in the British Empire and promote the advancement of African peoples.

The Pan-African Conference was the forerunner of the National Association for the Advancement of Colored People (NAACP). Extremely intellectual, by the young age of seventeen Williams had become a teacher in his native Trinidad. By eighteen, he was a school principal. Although he loved his native country, he saw a larger calling for himself deciding to move to New York City at the age of twenty-two. Despite his brilliant nature, the only work the young Trinidadian could find in Manhattan was shining shoes on the streets in and around Grand Central Station. After being accepted to Dalhousie University, he would move to Halifax.

Upon arriving in Halifax, Williams aligned himself with the most powerful and intellectually based Black organization near Dalhousie University - the local Black Baptist church and its assemblies. It would be at the Cornwallis Street Baptist Church, near Williams' Gottingen Street residence, where this young, talented, aspiring, lawyer would emerge as a *"shining star"* within the Black community.

Williams understood the history of the Black struggle and he also knew of the historic role Canadians had played in the fight to give Blacks their freedom and a voice within the British Empire. It was this knowledge and appreciation of Canadians that had convinced Williams to move to Halifax and pursue his law studies at Dalhousie University. Williams had believed that Canadians, due to their unique history, were different than Americans and therefore more welcoming of an educated Black man. Therefore, it must have been a shock to Williams, upon his arrival in Halifax, to discover the blatant repression of the local Black community by the Haligonian Elite. In many ways, Halifax was more repressive than New York City. At least Williams could move through New York unnoticed. In Halifax, his presence was noticed and his every move viewed by the local Whites with a certain degree of trepidation. Halifax was not prepared to accept educated Blacks as they were seen as an economic and possible political threat to the century-old status quo. Williams' experiences in Halifax would be extremely negative resulting in his sudden forced departure and move to London, England, two years later.

A religious man, and one who was an ardent believer in the temperance movement, Williams refused to consume alcohol, believing it to be a social evil and one which often reduced Blacks to the lowest social, economic, and political level. This belief fitted well within the doctrines of the Cornwallis Street Baptist Church where young men, such as James Robinson Johnston and the remarkable 14 year-old James A. R. Kinney, often preached from the pulpit promoting similar views and lifestyles.

Highly intelligent, well-read, and motivated, Williams and Johnston must have been quite a remarkable duo on the Dalhousie campus, as they represented the highest pinnacles of educated Black success. In fact, they must have been quite intimidating for many Whites, who would have seen these men as years ahead of their time. What we know today speaks volumes of these men and their existence. Despite Williams being a few years older than Johnston, and several years the elder of the teenager Kinney, all three shared many things in common. They were more than educated Blacks, in fact they were the first generation of Black men who refused to answer the ageless question: *"Whose Negro Are You?"* The first of their race to demand what was rightfully theirs; the generation to refuse to stand at the back of a line.

A lover of music as well as a skilled pianist, Williams' passion mirrored that of James Robinson Johnston. Since both men were attending Dalhousie at the same time, it appears logical to assume that Johnston had been among the first to be introduced to Williams upon his arrival in Halifax. It also appears likely that it had been Johnston who had been tasked with the responsibility of ensuring that Williams was shown the community and resettled into suitable lodging. Johnston, in all likelihood, had served as the go-between introducing Williams to the Cornwallis Street Baptist Church and James A. R. Kinney. We know that both Johnston and Willams loved to sing and play the piano during church services and again it appears likely that both participated together during weekend services.

Williams was not a wealthy man. During his years as a teacher and principal at the Canaan School he had earned only 83 pounds 12 shillings a year. His years shining shoes on 42nd

Street, in front of Grand Central Station (a place which to this day is home to Black shoe-shiners) would have given him very little in terms of extra cash. He would have found it difficult to sustain himself in New York City, implying that he would have barely had enough funds to last one-year at Dalhousie University without seeking some form of outside employment. Because of his association with Johnston, and Johnston's ties to McKerrow and others, it is likely that Williams was employed part-time in one of the Black-owned and operated hardware stores on Gottingen Street or as a music teacher (or both).

It isn't clear who was the driving force behind the baseball championships of 1894, but the economic collapse of Taylor's Hardware during that year may have been the catalyst for Williams and Johnston, to begin looking for creative ways to raise funds for the ensuing years of legal studies. The first Black Nova Scotian hockey games played within an organized league would occur in the spring of 1895, and it appears that Williams was an initial mastermind behind its emergence. It would be during Henry Sylvester Williams' short stay in Halifax that interest in Black hockey would suddenly reach a zenith only to subsequently decline upon his departure.

With the help of a young Black Baptist leadership, Williams would play a major roll in the promotion of two hockey teams, the Halifax Eurekas and the Halifax Stanley, drawn from players of the Black tenements on Gottingen Street. These teams, the first *"organized"* Black clubs of their kind in Halifax, would eventually become part of an emerging Black presence in hockey throughout the region, becoming true hallmarks of Black Pride. The fact that the Colored Hockey League was subsequently organized as a way of generating gate receipts indicates the endeavor was a way to create employment opportunities and income. Subsequently, following the creation of these two club teams, Black community leaders in Halifax and Dartmouth would work to form and promote their own segregated hockey league. Williams' genius was a key element in the efforts to create Black awareness and to promote Black Pride. In doing so, he would work to preserve and promote Black consciousness, Black respect for the past, and a burning memory of the struggle that was the language and experience of the Black race on North

American shores. *The Code of the Underground Railroad* would become the language of the Colored Hockey League.

For decades it had been the practice of Black ministers and leaders to codify their language. To speak of something that, on the outside, appeared to mean one thing but to those who understood the language of the Black struggle, would have a different understanding. This practice had become an art during the years of the Underground Railroad. The Code of the Underground Railroad was found in the songs of the plantation slave. In order to ensure the success of runaways fleeing northward to Canada, Blacks communicated by way of coded messages often put to verse. These songs were sung during religious services or in the field, with each song having a specific meaning or message to those for whom it was intended. It was as Longfellow once said, *"For the soul is dead that slumbers, and things are not what they seem."*

The idea of dual-meaning words played well on the mind of Williams. He was after all, a teacher and a principal at the Canaan School south of the City of Port of Spain. *"Canaan"* was the name that Blacks had used when referring to the country of Canada during the heyday of the Underground Railroad and it was also a symbolic name given the school in honor of White Canadian Missionaries who had fought within the political system of Trinidad, decades earlier, ensuring that all children of color obtained public education. If it had not been for the Canadian efforts, Williams would have never achieved the educational success that allowed him to excel. Surely, it must have appeared ironic to Williams to realize that he, as an education Black Trinidadian, was a product of Canadian liberalism, whereas, such successes had been few and far between in Nova Scotia itself. Nowhere is this Williams dualistic-trait more evident than in examples seen in terms of colored team names. A case-in-point being the word *Jubilee.*

In 1888, following the year of the Queen Victoria Jubilee celebrations, a movement had emerged in Trinidad to create an August 1st annual holiday that would not only recognize the Queen's Jubilee but also the Black *"Jubilee of Emancipation"* the date when slavery was outlawed throughout the British Empire. Edgar Maresse-Smith, a Black Trinidad reformer, and a personal acquaintance of Henry Sylvester Williams, had been the main proponent of the movement. Though the movement gained a large amount of support within the Black communities the local Whites viewed it as an insult to the British monarchy. The idea that Blacks would consider *their Jubilee* to be as important as the *"Great Queen Mother's"* was an idea that was simply ridiculous in the eyes of many. The sensitivity of the arguments was not lost on Williams. Nor were the political ramifications of such a concept and movement.

To the White community of Nova Scotia, the Dartmouth *"Jubilees"* hockey team was named in honor of Queen Victoria and her Diamond Jubilee celebrations. To the Blacks, Jubilee referred to *"the year of Emancipation"* a *"time of future happiness"* when all Blacks would be free. Other team names would hold religious meaning: *Eureka,* a term associated with the discovery of gold was later thought to be in reference to the Klondike Gold Rush. In fact, *"Eureka"* meant, *"I have found"* a reference to those who had found God.

Later, Hammond Plains, a community with the largest contingent of people who could trace their origins to the Underground Railroad, would name their team the *"Moss Backs"*. Associated with the Underground Railroad, the *"Moss Backs"* referred to the side of a dead tree on which moss grows. At night, guided only by the stars, black slaves fleeing north to Canada often traveled by touch through dense woodlands. In the pitch darkness the practice of placing one's hand in front of the body, feeling the sides of trees and determining where the moss grew, allowed those fleeing to remain on course; for, as all slaves knew well, moss grows on the north side of a tree. And as anyone who has walked through the woods at night also knows, the ability to see at night without light is nearly impossible, forcing the person to walk constantly with their hands extended, feeling the air in front of them.

It is in the naming of the Halifax *"Stanley"* hockey team that Williams' impact is most visible. In 1890, a year prior to Williams' departure to New York City, the local Trinidad newspapers had reported on a movement within the upper echelons of British society to promote the idea of educated Black men returning to Western Africa in an attempt to *"uplift"* the primitive masses and to ensure British Empire control over the region. Arguing that environmental factors made it more feasible for Blacks, rather than Whites, to follow in the footsteps of Lord Stanley - the great explorer who had ventured deep into the Congo - these elitists believed that an army of *"Black Stanleys"* could stabilize the region and achieve the greatest benefits for the British cause. In the March 18, 1890 edition of the *Port of Spain Gazette*, the newspaper reported:

> *According to information gathered at the most authentic source a novel attempt is about to be made on the Congo. As there is no serious hope of ever rearing a real colony of White men in such a climate the idea has been mooted of drafting into the Congo dominion a number of young and well-educated negroes from the United States, to serve as educators of their backward and uncivilized brethren.*

Williams understood the implications of the concept. For generations there had been a movement within Western Societies to send the Blacks back to Africa and to rid the Western European peoples of the so-called *"unsightly spectacle of an educated Black man."* If Blacks could not be slaves, many Whites argued, there was little use for them. After all, with the influx of Irish and Central Europeans into the United States, and the British Dominions, there was now ample manpower to fill jobs traditionally held by Blacks.

By naming the team *"the Stanley"* Williams had spoken volumes, making both a political, as well as a mocking statement of the current political theories. This bold *in your face* manner did not sit well within the halls of White Haligonian Society.

CHAPTER SEVEN

THE LAST PASSENGER

Though the Colored Hockey League appeared on the outside to be simply an avenue of recreation for young Black men, in fact, it was something much more. Never before had Canadian hockey witnessed such a phenomena. Never before had a hockey league been organized using religious leadership as the guiding organizational force. Never before, or since, has the message been so clear. The league's rulebook would be *The Bible*. Their Game Book, the words, oral history and lessons derived from the Black Canadian experience and the legacy of the Underground Railroad. Their strategy, to uplift the Black man to a level that would make him equal to their White brethren, all-the-while installing a sense of leadership, organization, community, purpose, determination, teamwork, and duty in to the hearts and minds of young Black men. The Colored Hockey League was more than just a sports organization; it was in fact, the first Black Pride sports movement in history – truly a magnificent undertaking considering nothing like it had ever been attempted, either before or since.

Aside from its political aspirations, the league's religious mandate was intended to attract young men to the Baptist Church. Prior to the formation of the league, the Dartmouth Lake Baptist Church near Lake Banook had been steadily plagued with attendance problems. On account of the distance the church was from the town itself, travel in the winter for many would be too difficult, making for a sparse congregation many months out of the year. In addition, the transient nature of the Black Canadian population also created a challenge for the church as it struggled to increase its already small congregational base. If it were not for a dedicated core, of mostly women, the doors of the church would have closed years earlier.

Father James Thomas had been the Lake Church pastor until his death in 1879. Father Benson Smithers would replace him until his own death in 1885. Reverend F. R. Langford temporarily succeeded Smithers until 1893. In the same year that Henry Sylvester Williams arrived in Nova Scotia, becoming active across the harbor at the Cornwallis Church, a new and much younger pastor, Brother James Borden, would be selected to head the Dartmouth church.

Borden inherited an aging congregation with a declining membership. It was hoped, because of his age, he would not only provide long-term stability but also increase the congregational numbers by appealing to a younger audience. The future of the Lake Church depended on attracting able-bodied worshippers who were capable of attending church services during the winter months – a time of year when many of the elderly were not able to withstand the elements. This meant attracting young men like James Brown, Thomas Tynes, Jr., and others; all of whom were the children of the longtime residential families, many having been the founding families of the local church. To do this, Borden appealed to their love and passion of sport. For it was here on Lake Banook that Borden would often see these young men, including some of his own relatives, playing hockey.

Williams, a man who saw the teams as political statements, along with Borden, who wished to use the sport as a vehicle to ensure a larger number of bodies in the pews, along with others, helped organize the leagues first "official" games. Needing three teams to publicly promote and justify a league, two all-Black teams from the Cornwallis Baptist Church parish had been created to represent Halifax, the Halifax Eurekas and the Halifax Stanley, with the Stanley being made up largely of Eureka players. Half a mile across the harbor, the Dartmouth Jubilees were organized from the Lake Baptist Church. Unlike in baseball, the original competing hockey teams would only be clubs closely associated with their local Black Baptist church. The reason may have been economics combined with the fact that not everyone could skate. Therefore, only the teams with a large base of potential athletes could attract enough players to ice a full squad. It would be through these Baptist churches, acting as a sort of athletic organization, that the first hockey teams would be organized. Borden would concentrate on the Dartmouth Jubilees hockey club, a team that unlike the others in the league did not have any direct ties to baseball, and solicited the local support of the Water Street Black community. Among the players from that neighborhood included a cousin to Rev. James Borden, Charles Borden, a three-and-a-half foot tall goaltender named Henry "Braces" Franklyn, an "ice cutter" and a "waterman".

During the winter, James "Cut" Brown was an "ice cutter" who harvested ice from Lake Banook. Ice cutting was one of the few jobs a young, uneducated, Black Canadian man could do in order to make a living during the late nineteenth century, in Nova Scotia. It was hard, dangerous work for low pay and took great physical strength.

In the days before electricity, entire weekly, monthly, and yearly supplies of ice would be stored in ice warehouses to be sold door-to-door for home refrigeration, with the average price of a ten-pound block selling for three-cents. By the end of the nineteenth century the ice cutting industry had become one of Dartmouth's largest employers. The iceman was as common as the milkman.

It was near the center of a lake where most cutting would take place. Ice in the middle of lakes is harder and more pure than that near the shoreline. But before cutting, the porous and uneven elements needed to be cleared away exposing a homogeneous body of perfect ice. Sometimes as much as three inches of "rotten ice" had to be scraped away. Grooves were made into the ice using horse-drawn and hand-drawn markers creating a checkerboard design.

The cutter needed strong arms and wrists, not only to cut through the ice, but also to be able to pull cubes of ice weighing up to 300 pounds out of the water. Here, a long line of horses, each drawing a framework of heavy plank shod with steel, pulled the ice away either to specially designed boats or directly to ice cutting houses on Lake Banook.

The work, like the ice Brown cut, was colorless – it was for all who could tolerate the cold. The dangers associated with cutting through ice on a frozen lake, along with the backbreaking task of moving dozens of blocks of ice a day, seemed many. Much like Canada herself, it was work seemingly unending and unforgiving. Thirty-five years old James "Cut" Brown was not only familiar with the ice; ice had been Brown's life. He would play forward on the Borden's Jubilee team.

A laborer and "waterman" living on Water Street, Thomas "Tommy" Tynes Jr. would also play hockey for the Jubilees. The Tynes family could date their roots to Betsy Tynes, a 30 year-old runaway slave who had sailed on the *Baker and Atlee* for Nova Scotia. She had carried with her a month-old child whom she named Timothy Mahan Tynes. Betsy had been a former slave of Timothy Tynes of James River, Virginia. She had runaway three years earlier and had been a camp follower with the British Army. Timothy Mahan would eventually reside in the Dartmouth region. His son would be Tommy Tynes, his grandson Tommy Tynes, Jr.

Thomas Tynes, Sr. was a Deacon at the Dartmouth Lake Church and was contracted to work for the Dartmouth School District cleaning and shoveling, school latrines for $30 per year. Tommy, who had it marginally better than his father, worked for James Craig's Water Wagon selling buckets of water house to house as he rode the streets of Dartmouth with James Craig atop a two hundred gallon water-barrel wagon pulled by two horses.

In size and stature Tommy Tynes was not a large man. He appears to have been about 5 foot 7 inches in height and possessing a husky-muscular build. He wore a bowler hat with a suit, tie, and vest. His shoes were turned up at the front, a characteristic that develops from walking uphill on a regular basis.

A handsome man, he carried himself well and seemed younger in appearance than his actual age. In the few photos that exist of him, one senses a certain aloofness to his character – as if he was biding time awaiting a better opportunity. Tynes had worked for years as a water carrier for James Craig's Water

Wagon. Craig was one of the few water carriers with his own horse-drawn water wagon. On a good day Tynes and Craig would sell over $7.00 worth of water, allowing Craig to pocket $5.00 and Tynes the remaining $2.00. Any extra funds went for the upkeep of the horses or wagon repairs. The two men were often seen filling up their water wagon at Toddy Brook near Crichton Avenue, the source of one of the best fresh water streams flowing down from the Dartmouth Lakes. In comparison to the other Black water carriers, Tommy Tynes was fortunate. At the time, an average bucket of water would fetch two cents. Having the water wagon ensured that Tynes did not have to personally carry water buckets any great distance – a practice not uncommon during this period. Whereas an average water-carrier would earn as little 30 to 50 cents a day, Tynes was by comparison, in a league by himself.

It is clear from the quality of play noted in the first reports that Brown and Tynes had been playing hockey for many years, predating the Black hockey league by decades. Tommy Tynes, Jr. was almost thirty-nine years old and was well-known in the Dartmouth region due to his hockey skill. By virtue of his age it is possible to trace the early roots of Black hockey back to the early to mid-1870's. During the 1870's, the first Black athletes were learning to skate on lakes and ponds in ample numbers that by the mid-1880's, just as in baseball, the numbers of Black children and young men playing hockey would have been sufficient to allow for the first organized all-Black recreational games to be played. By the early 1890's, the number of quality Black hockey players would allow for the formation of an all-Black hockey league.

By the winter of 1895, the Colored Hockey League had not just formed out of air but instead it had simply tapped into, and organized, a resource that had been present for some time in the region. Many of these individuals had grown up playing the game at a time when the roots of modern hockey were only just beginning to bear fruit. 1895 was simply the first year that Black hockey was organized and had become a league with a purpose. A league that, behind the scenes, was being run by the regions best and brightest young Black men and leaders; a league with sufficient support and funds to rent arenas, and a league that was now just receiving its initial mention in the Halifax press.

Although Black hockey teams were able to play games in the local arenas, they would not receive their ice time until after White leagues had technically completed their season. As a result the Colored League would implement a challenge championship format in which teams could conceivably challenge anytime during their year dependent on factors such as the scheduling of the two best teams of the region, ice conditions, and the timing of the event for maximum attendance.

The Baptist owned *Acadian Recorder Newspaper*, one of three major newspapers in Halifax, carried the first accounts of these matches to their predominately White readers. The first game was played at the Dartmouth Curling Rink on February 27, 1895. Ironically, when the old Dartmouth Curling Rink was not being used for hockey, it served as a meeting place for evangelists. As with hockey, the meetings often evoked great passion and screams of rejoicing echoed from the ground high into the rafters. If God curled or played hockey, chances are, he did so in Dartmouth.

This was the era of *seven-man aside* rover hockey and the Colored League was no different. That night the Halifax Eurekas and Dartmouth Jubilees played to a 1-1 draw. Jubilee players, Cut Brown and Braces Franklyn, and the Eurekas Frank L. Symonds, and Agustus "Gus" Adams were noted as the game's top standouts. Although the players were Baptist church members, the style of play was extremely rough and physical. Obviously, much more physical than what was being seen in the "Senior" (i.e. Whites-only) league, as it was described that both teams engaged in *"body checking"* and *"cross counters"* (short punches) to the point of being described as *"ludicrous."*

On March 20th, the *Acadian Recorder* reported on a rematch between the Stanley and the Jubilees. Earlier that year, the Stanley had defeated Dartmouth by a score of 3-1. Playing for the Stanley that evening was Charles Allison, the son of the late John Allison of Gottingen Street. Charlie's father and two uncles had died together in what was described years later as simply a "tragic accident" in the late 1860's leaving behind three young widows and their children. His mother had struggled to raise the boy as a solid citizen within the Black community.

Now her son was a man, and with his brother Herbert, were becoming cornerstones of the Halifax Eurekas. As everyone on Gottingen Street knew from memory, few families had suffered as much, or were as emotionally strong. After a youth spent in the company of dominating, and fearless women, Charlie and his brother may have entered league play to exert their manhood and independence. If so, few could question their purpose, nor mock their determination.

This highly anticipated rematch would become the featured sports article in the *Acadian Recorder* the following day and would be described as *"one of the most exciting and amazing matches of the season."* It was noted that large contingents of supporters were on hand for each team and that several women also attended.

> *The ladies also turned out, and at times could not control their feelings. They shouted and danced and expressed their joy in many humorous ways when their favorites scored or made a good play.*

The game would take place at the Dartmouth curling rink with curling stones being used as goal posts. The use of curling stones as goal posts was not an uncommon practice as it would not be until 1900 before the Canadian Amateur Hockey Association adopted the use of goal nets. The Stanley would score the first goal over the objections of Jubilees goaltender, Franklyn, who claimed the puck had been kicked in. The *Acadian Recorder* reported:

> *They appealed it to the referee, and almost wanted to fight. Captain Braces Franklyn, who stands about 3 ft 6 inches in his stocking feet, wanted to wipe the ice up with the judge who gave the decision.*

The goal would stand, and the Stanley would add another extending their lead to 2 to 0. As the half progressed, the Jubilees began to carry the play with Dartmouth forward Charles Flint scoring and cutting the deficit to one. Flint's celebration alone was one of the highlights of the night:

Charles Flint did it amidst great cheering, and then to celebrate his good play he started around the rink at his highest rate of speed, frantically waving his stick.

The game intensified as Dartmouth's apparent tying goal was disallowed. The Jubilees argued the call until time, which ran continuously, ran out on the half. With emotions running high the play became much more physical.

The players were bunched most of the time and did not seem to worry much as to whether it was the ball or an opponent's shins that was struck. Some of the scrimmages were too ludicrous for description. Players were knocked down and left to get out of a melee as best they could.

Every goal now was followed by a feverish protest from the other team. As a result, both teams would have apparent goals disallowed. Ultimately, the Jubilees would score two additional times taking a 3-2 lead late in the match until a final, and tying, goal by the Stanley ended with an all out fight on the ice. It was reported:

The last goal awarded by the judge to Halifax ended the game; the Dartmouth men claimed "no goal"; there were cries of "goal, goal" with counter cries of "no goal"; the referee and judge (were) surrounded; the spectators were appealed to, and finally the Halifax team declined to play anymore.

After the game the Halifax Stanley claimed they had played better than the Dartmouth Jubilees but were not allowed to win. A Jubilees' player would counter the Stanley claim, stating that the Stanley stopped because they knew they were being outplayed. The score from the Stanley perspective was 4-3, as they did not recognize the official's decision disallowing their goal in the second half. Whereas, the Jubilees claimed a victory by an identical 4-3 score, as they too did not recognize the referee's decision to waving off their fourth goal. Officially the game would be declared a 3-3 draw.

The Jubilees asked for a rematch to be played the following week but the apparent bitterness from the previous two matches resulted in the Stanley declining such a challenge. Black organized hockey was now established. However, the emotion of the Dartmouth match had showed that sports rivalry transcended race and religion. Hockey was hockey regardless of skin color and moral belief.

Though covered in the newspaper, the first reports showed an underlying tone of racism. White reporters, though at times professing to have liberal views, used references to describe the games and spectators as *"dusky supporters"* and derogatory quotes of *"dey knowed we du dem, we had de bes of dem and dey stopped"*. The worst and most blatant racism and reporting would come from the pages of *The Halifax Herald* who compared the game to the fight from slavery and the plight of the Maroons. This coverage would solicit an anonymous response from an unknown Black man, in the form as a lengthy letter to the editor printed in the *Acadian Recorder,* on March 3, 1895, *six* days after the Jubilee-Stanley game.

CORRESPONDENCE

THAT "AMUSING" HOCKEY MATCH
To the Editor Daily Recorder:

The evening edition of the Herald undertook a few evenings since to give what it considers a lovely joke at the expense of a few colored youths who assembled in the Dartmouth rink to play a social game of hockey on last Tuesday evening.

It started off with some degree of truth, but really did not last long in that strain, but manufactured the greatest batch of falsehoods, trash and insults to respectable readers, and — it is to be wondered that the proprietors would allow such blatant falsehoods and rubbish to escape their notice. This article allows that such would go down to posterity, similar to the landing of the Maroons, or the abolition of slavery. Imagine its ignorance of comparing a simple game of hockey to two such memorable events. The expulsion of the Maroons from Jamaica — a race of people who held their own against tremendous odds before they were driven from their native land — brought to a climate unprepared only to suffer death from cold and hunger, but they have left behind them to commemorate their lives the erection of the fortifications at Citadel Hill. It further compares it to the abolition of slavery - a struggle which cost the nation millions of dollars and hundreds of thousands of lives — when a game of hockey that may create just as much excitement as the one in question can be seen on the common on any icy day.

Relative to the base-ball game it gets off another huge falsehood by saying that one John Kellum umpired the game, which commenced at 10 a. m. and ended at 8 p. m, when the game did not begin until 3 p. m. and ended at 5 p. m., which was umpired by one of the best known and favorites of base-ball fame in the Maritime Provinces, in no less a person than the gentle "Doc" Hann of the old Atlantas.

Now, Mr. Editor, I am not seeking newspaper fame, but merely to refute a base falsehood wherein a certain class of in-offensive citizens are made to appear as though they were arrogant savages or members of a Ku Klux Clan. Other exiting games have been played in the same place when players on both sides suffered much greater pain than on said occasion, but as a matter of course these dared not be dealt with. Such trashy articles have a very deteriorating tendency of elevating the race in no well-thinking citizen can endorse.

Thanking you for the space for this vindication of a simple game of hockey played by two colored teams. I trust in the future that the writers will be more careful in giving things as they occur and not insult his own fancy.

Signed "Stanley".

The letter sent shock waves through the Halifax community and social circles. Apparently written by an educated Black the letter had in effect referred to the *Halifax Herald* reporters as idiots. In addition, the letter had bemoaned the popular and secretive society of the local Ku Klux Klan, an organization, though outlawed in the United States and believed non-active in Canada, existed locally, made up of elitist White families and Halifax White business and government officials. It is important to note that most Canadian history books claim that the Ku Klux Klan, a violent White supremacy organization founded in Pulaski, Tennessee in 1865, did not appear in Canada until 1920. This assumption that it took the Klan 55 years to spread across North America fails to recognize the fact that many of the elitist concepts promoted by the K.K.K. were well entrenched within the upper echelons of Anglo-Saxon Nova Scotian and Canadian culture.

Even more revealing, the letter had stated that the Stanley and Jubilees were on par with the best White hockey clubs in Halifax, White clubs such as the Wanderers, Crescents and Chebuctos; teams that had often played on the commons behind the Wanderers Clubhouse at Egg Pond. Teams comprised of the regions best White players, who, only a few years later, would vie for Lord Stanley's Challenge Cup.

The White Halifax establishment pondered, who among the Black community could write such a loaded and damning letter? The words burned through the psyche of the area bigots and social and sporting elite. Who, among the Blacks, would be so clever, and well read?

By the evening of March 3, 1895, Henry Sylvester Williams was a man on the run. Forced to flee the confines of his lodgings on Gottingen Street and to seek refuge in "safe houses" of Baptist Blacks and elite Whites sympathetic to the Black cause — men such as Harry Gibson Bauld, the editor of the *Acadian Recorder*. The man who would be the future founder of the Pan African Movement was now one of the hunted. Within days Williams would take up residence in London, England and secretly register as a student at the King's College, effectively becoming the last passenger of the Underground Railroad.

After leaving Halifax, Williams would become a pioneer in the strategy of using conventional lobbying methods, including news editorials and press coverage, to influence and promote African and Black causes. The question then should be asked, was Williams, who later proved he knew the importance of the press and publicity for the advancement of the Black cause, involved behind the scenes (either directly or indirectly) in obtaining Black hockey players their first notoriety? It is clear that once he left Halifax, however, the league would not gain press coverage until 1898 when another aspiring Black, James Robinson Johnston, and Johnston's childhood friend, James A. R. Kinney, emerged on the scene.

Within months of reaching London, Williams would register at King's College. The fact that he was attending classes and yet was not "officially" or "publicly" registered as a student implies that for the first year of his stay in London he was forced to live a somewhat shadowy life. Whatever had transpired in the final days of his residence in Halifax had haunted him and he apparently believed his enemies had the will power, as well as the ability, to hunt him down. This meant that whomever Williams was attempting to avoid was well-placed in Nova Scotian social and political circles, as it was unlikely an enemy of middle class or lower class status would have the financial ability to seek Williams out in London.

During this time, Williams worked as a spokesperson for a local temperance society. He would travel the length of the British Isles and give lectures on the evils of alcohol. His audience was mostly socially well-placed women's societies and it is possible to assume that Williams felt comfortable making public speeches to these groups simply because his trips were not advertised in advance and his audience, by their very presence, afforded him a certain degree of protection.

By 1897, Williams had become comfortable enough with his new surroundings to register officially at Graybar's Inn in order to pursue his legal studies. That same year, he was introduced to Miss Agnes Powell, a 30 year-old White woman, the daughter of a career soldier. Agnes worked as a secretary within the Church of England Temperance Society. Within a year, over the objections of her family, the two would be married. At the time, mixed race relations were not uncommon in London; such arrangements had primarily existed among the lower classes. Agnes would pay a heavy price for he decision to marry Williams. She would be ostracized and disowned by her family. She would also find herself, surprisingly, hated by both Blacks and Whites alike who viewed her as either a "trophy wife" or a betrayer of her race. In the years that would follow she found little comfort in the outside world and devoted her time to Williams and the raising of their children.

For the first few years in London, Williams had been seen as a novelty to the British elite. Here was a Black man with upper-class aspirations, the Trinidadian equivalent of a Booker T. Washington. His charismatic style and intellect afforded him both public notoriety and private condemnation. For even though the elite of London liked seeing so-called *"subjugated peoples"* strive to become *"almost civilized"*, in private, many would argue that Williams was yet another example of Darwinist theory — nothing more than an ape in silk. Because Williams had married a White woman of upper class stature, he was also seen as an opportunist and a corrupting force; a man who would go to great ends in order to obtain social respectability. His children would also suffer greatly, as they were never fully accepted within either the White or the Black communities.

Williams was complex. South Africa and the Boer Crisis was heating up in the Transvaal. The Dutch Settlers and their British counterparts were in competition for the rich lands that comprised the interior regions of South Africa. In addition, South Africa was home to many prospectors in search of gold and diamonds. For the region, it was said, was so rich in wealth that one simply had only take a shovel and lift up a spade of dirt in order to find riches. Though such talk was an exaggeration, there was a degree of truth to the statement. However, for the majority of Black South Africans, the lands and wealth meant something else: a return to slavery.

In order to extract the wealth, the Dutch and their English counterparts forced thousands of Black men, women and children to work the lands and the mines. Not since the Spanish conquest of the New World had such a methodical exploitation of a people been implemented. Reports of Black suffering were front-page news in many London newspapers. Williams was shocked and angered by the accounts. So much so, that he proposed the creation of a global organization led by educated Blacks that would work to alleviate Black suffering and end the European exploitation on the African Continent. It was this concept that would move Williams to create the Pan-African Association in June 1897.

In a series of letters to British newspapers and church magazines, Williams would initiate a one-man crusade to bring to the attention of the English readership the shortcomings of European colonialism and the plight of the African Continent and her native peoples. In a letter to local Church officials he wrote:

> *Could Livingstone but see today the sad and appalling state things have assumed in that land, and amongst the people for whom he lived and for whom he spent his last drop of life's oil, what would he say? This me thinks, would be his ejaculation, 'Can Christ be here?' His surprises would be great, for the idol of greed has taken the place of right and justice in the minds of those to whom the natives have looked for light, and now they have ceased to confide in the 'so-called civilized' colonists. Moffat would weep to know that the trustworthiness of the English has lost its magnetism. The African Association appeals to the nation — which, after all, is the parent and controller of colonial proceedings — to call upon her representatives to revert to the old and beaten track, and to preserve intact her treasured traditions. The Association gladly welcomes the agencies of a high civilization (e.g. industrial schools), and a true teaching of Christ and his crucified, amongst the natives, being assured that they are always prepared to accept what is good.*

> *Yours truly,*
> *H. S. Williams.*

In a letter to Booker T. Washington in 1899, Williams outlined the movement's upcoming conference and agenda. He wrote:

Dear Mr. Washington:

So far it was decided that our conference should cover three days — morning & evening "sessions." Papers will be read by primary & secondary persons — and discussion to follow. I am instructed to get the names of representative men who are capable to deal with the following headings upon which the conference will proceed -

1. "The conditions favouring the development of high standard of African Humanity."

2. "The crudity & cruelty of civilized paganism of which our race are the victim."

3. "The industrial emancipation of our people in light of current history." This is yours of course.

4. "Africa the sphinx of history in light of its unsolved problems."

5. "Europe's atonement for her blood guiltiness to Africa" is the loud cry of current history.

6. "Organized plunder versus human progress has made our race its battlefield."

Of course there are other details which time will develop as the expected co-operation comes. This is but an outline, and from your practical and interested experience any suggestions coming from you will be gladly received.

Resolutions will of necessity follow the various items, and according to our rules, will be submitted to central governments.

Thanking you for your kindness, we shall expect from you fullest co-operation from our People across "blue pond." With the very best regards, I am,

Yours truly,

H. S. Williams

It was during the first conference that Williams began working with Dr. William Edward Burghardt DuBois. Later, W.E.B. DuBois would gain prominence as a founding member of both the Niagara Movement and the NAACP. He would also serve as editor of *The Crisis,* the NAACP literary arm. For DuBois, the Pan-African Conference in London was to have been his coming out party. Born in 1868 in Great Barrington, Massachusetts, DuBois had attended college at Fisk University in Ohio, later transferring to Harvard University and the University of Berlin. In 1896 he had written a book entitled: *The Suppression of the Slave Trade.* A year later, he had moved to Atlanta where he worked as a professor of history and economics at Atlanta University. In 1899 he published his second book, *The Philadelphia Negro.* Having been the first Black to obtain a doctoral degree from Harvard, he resented the fact that his educational and writing achievements were largely unnoticed, as he was unable to break out of the shadow of Booker T. Washington, a man he appears to have personally despised. Since Booker T. was not in attendance at the conference in London, DuBois believed that he alone would be seen as the main spokesman at the event. To his shock, he was again overshadowed, this time by Henry Sylvester Williams. In fact, DuBois had apparently been so upstaged in London that few even were aware of his presence.

Years later, following the death of Williams, subsequent gatherings were described as *Congresses* not *Conferences.* In J. R. Hooker's book *Henry Sylvester Williams: Imperial Pan-*

Africanist, he explains why such a distinction is made. Hooker states:

> *Thus, though Williams convened the first Pan-African meeting, he did not organize the first congress. This distinction would be unnecessary, but for DuBois' tendency to eliminate Williams and inflate his own role in history of the Pan-Africanism.*

As a result DuBois would claim that he had been the *"founder of the Pan-African Congress"* and therefore the *founder* of the Pan-African movement. A claim that would go unchallenged in the American press - a press unaware of the true history of the organization. The fact that DuBois was so driven by his own need for recognition that he would take credit for someone else's work spoke volumes of the man.

Afterwards, the London *Westminster Gazette* would write that William's conference *"marks the initiation of a remarkable movement on history; the Negro is at last awake to the potentialities of his future."* The same could be said about the Colored Hockey League.

CHAPTER EIGHT

KINNEY & THE COLORED HOCKEY LEAGUE

It would be James A. R. Kinney, a 19 year-old Baptist Layman, who would now become the chief organizer and a driving force behind the league. Born in Yarmouth, Nova Scotia in 1879, Kinney was the first Black graduate of the Maritime Business College, an accomplishment he achieved in 1897 at the age of only eighteen. His mother, Charlotte Kinney, had been a longtime member of Cornwallis Street Baptist Church. Later, he would become a student of the American Black leader and scholar Booker T. Washington, a man who promoted the concept of "separate but equal" in terms of White and Black society and their social development. Kinney used his oratory skills to attack those who were non-religious and inactive within the Black community. Well disciplined and mentally tough, Kinney had little patience for Blacks who blamed others for their plight or chose to live a life without religious principles and structured discipline. Preaching from the pulpit of the Cornwallis Church, Kinney advocated Black Pride, dignity and leadership.

During the weekdays, Kinney worked as the advertising manager for William Stairs, Son and Morrow Company in Halifax, a position he would hold for thirty years. The Stairs' were a prominent Halifax family having made their money in merchant trade and banking. The fact that they employed Kinney as a "company spokesperson" said a lot about the family and their social views. Believing that the eyes of the Black and White communities of Nova Scotia were upon him, Kinney approached his work with the same four disciplines and concepts that he tried to perpetuate within the Colored Hockey League – the ideals of self-discipline, professionalism, skill and teamwork.

Kinney was no fool. He had proven himself savvy enough to become a manager within a successful White-owned business, and wise enough, given his advertising knowledge and skills, to possess an incredible understanding and command of the English language; a deftness that enabled him to communicate with and approach the social elite throughout Nova Scotia. Yet, even with all this achievement and success, young Kinney had detractors. Certainly he was hated by both Blacks and Whites alike who saw him as an *"Uncle Tom"*, one who accepted White repression, or as an *"uppity-Black man"*, outside of his proper social place.

Within the William Stair Company workplace, even the most liberal of White workers would have, at times, found difficulty in taking orders from a Black man, especially given the prevalent Anglo-Empirical arrogance that was pervasive during this period. The fact that Kinney preached separation and Black determinism, and played on the idea that Blacks had to learn from Whites, probably kept him from being lynched on many a Halifax night. A truly remarkable man, Kinney, nonetheless, walked a tight rope between the White and Black communities - aware of his tenuous footing - never knowing which side would be the first to initiate his social downfall.

Kinney is one of the greatest Canadian leaders, **never** known. No more dramatic and gifted figure has ever emerged in the annals of Black history. He epitomized the Colored Hockey League and distinguished himself as a true leader. With Kinney and others at the helm, the Black community of Africville was emerging as a potential powerful middle-level social class within the confines of Halifax County. Even in the face of racist actions and the economic obstacles of local White government officials, the fact remained, by the mid-1890's the community Africville was poised to surpass many of their White counterparts.

In addition to Kinney, it would be the Ministers and Deacons of the area Baptist churches who would, by their very presence, give the Black community and the Colored Hockey League upstanding role models and organizational talent, never before seen in Black sport. By examining the concepts to achieve success as taught by Booker T. Washington and adding a mix of religious theory, these leaders strove to create a Black athlete and man that would be strong in mind, body and soul. As Booker T. Washington would write in his book, *A Negro For A New Century*, and the Black leadership of Halifax would emphasize:

> *The thing to be done (is) clear: To train selected Negro youth who should go out at once and teach and lead their people, just by example, by getting land and homes; to give them not a dollar that they could not earn for themselves; to teach respect for labor; to replace stupid drudgery with skilled hands; and, to these ends, to build up an industrial system, for the sake not only of self-support and intelligent labor, but also for the sake of character.*

Given the respect and interest that hockey elicited, it is no wonder that many within the lower Canadian social classes would use the sport to advance themselves socially. It is also not surprising that aspiring Black Canadians would also see hockey as an acceptable tool for social upward mobility. Through association with the hockey league, the Black leadership was able to serve as an example of Black Nova Scotian success. Even more amazing, given the period, evidence exists that Kinney and the religious leaders were also respected among many *lower class* Whites who recognized their leadership qualities. It had been said of Kinney, that had he been White, he would have been the Mayor of Halifax. Few disputed this assessment. Research into this period of Halifax history shows that the socio-economic as well as political and religious interaction between Black and White lower classes was rather progressive and tolerant. Only within the upper classes of Halifax society, the so-called old money, was there a dominant anti-Black sentiment. It seemed that this White elite was weary of the social rise of Blacks as they represented a competitive threat to the status quo. In many ways, the elite of Halifax lacked the social intellect portrayed by this new emerging Black leadership. If it were not for social privilege and racial barriers, the Black leadership would have already surpassed the White elite on many fronts.

To ensure that the league was on solid moral footing, the teams would recruit successful Black men to serve as team spokesmen and officers. As the eyes of the White community would be upon them, it was important that no leverage be given that would allow White bigots and critics an opportunity to use the league as an example of Black inferiority. For though this was not the United States, the Black community that existed across Nova Scotia was well aware of the limitations imposed upon. Sustained violence, though impossible to eradicate given the nature of the game, would not be advocated - pride, teamwork, and skill was instead promoted.

Because of the letter to the Editor printed in the *Acadian Recorder,* the teams now had nowhere to play. Williams' letter not only had sent shockwaves throughout the community but also had the detrimental effect of keeping the teams out of the local arenas. Halifax was still a small enough city that it could only take one or two influential people to shut the doors and keep the players and their teams from access to ice-time. Although Willams' intentions may have been noble, the result was such that not a single newspaper article or reference to Black hockey would appear in any of the numerous local newspapers. It would not be until after Kinney graduated in 1897, and James Johnston concluded his studies in February 1898, that the league would have leadership, with the ability, to move the teams back into the local arenas and onto the pages of the local newspapers.

Though the Black teams had continued to play during this two year period, their games would have taken place on the frozen inland ponds and shallow ocean inlets that dotted the region along the Bedford Basin. Evidence of this fact is found in the oral history of individuals of the modern day Halifax Black population who vehemently state that the Sea-Sides hockey team held outdoor matches on the frozen ocean-fed ponds surrounding Africville. They go on to add that the difference between skating on ocean ice and arena ice is that the ocean version is a slower surface to skate over, creating a slower moving hockey game. There were two locations where hockey could be played outdoors in Africville. The first was Tibby's Pond, a small guarded cove on the northeastern side of the community running adjacent to Campbell Road. The second was Southwestern Field near the heart of the community in an area adjacent to the Kilburn family home and near the railroad tracks. In the summer, the "Southwestern" was the site of the local baseball games. In winter the barren patch of land would freeze over allowing for pick-up hockey matches. We may never know the full extent of Black hockey development during this two-year period, since no records appear to exist. What we do know, however, is that the Eurekas never lost a game.

Johnston's business and law connections, along with his employment at John Thomas Bulmer Law Firm, not only added credibility to the league but also opened doors that had been previously shut. Kinney would use his education and his connections to promote the league, providing it with advertisements and press coverage. All the while, both men would walk a fine-line in an attempt to strike a balance between business interests, Black Nationalism, and religious doctrine.

With the arrival of Kinney and Johnston, the Colored Hockey League would begin to transform. No longer would it simply be a loosely held organization of local Black parishes and players, but instead it would begin to expand outwards throughout Nova Scotia, and eventually across the Maritimes. Baptist churches continued to be the impetus behind the organizing of teams in all the regions where a substantive population of Blacks could be found. Under the management and direction of Kinney and Johnston, the Eurekas became the league's flagship team. Based out of the Cornwallis Street Baptist Church, Nova Scotia's Black Baptist *"Mother Church,"* the Eurekas hockey club logically became the central organizing and controlling point for all of Black hockey. Kinney and Johnston, along with team members, were responsible for organizing anything from league ice-time, advertisement and promotion to finances. Because of this, the Eurekas controlled who could, and therefore could not, challenge and play for the title of *Champion* – effectively giving the team, and its management, authoritative control of the league.

It was the Colored League, the hallmark of Black athletic excellence, which allowed Kinney to achieve part of his goal of bringing Blacks into the mainstream of Canadian society. Kinney believed that only through hard work, discipline and self-imposed segregation, could Blacks achieve their true potential, and eventually compete as equals alongside White Canadians. By promoting and developing an all-Black hockey league, as disciplined and skilled as those of any regional White leagues, the concept of equality would finally be achieved. Geographically concentrated in its representative and recruitment practices, the players and officials who comprised the largest block of Colored League members presented a socio-economic cross section that epitomized Black Canadians in and around Halifax and Dartmouth.

For the most part, three main areas served as the recruiting hot beds and hubs for the league. The first was the Black enclave that stretched westward from Halifax Centre, beyond Barrington Street, down Campbell Road, outwards to Africville and the surrounding fringe corners of a suburb of Richmond. The second was the region northwest of the Citadel, the area known as Gottingen Street and home to hundreds of Black City workers and their families. The third region was the area directly across the Basin over in Dartmouth, the section of the city known as Water Street. Home to dozens of Dartmouth Blacks whose families largely derived their existence from having their husbands and son's employed as dock laborers, or so-called stevedores (men paid to unload ships manually) in the dockyards.

In the area known as the Campbell Road Section players representing four teams could be found, with the most members affiliated with Africville Sea-Sides. To the locals, the players were a source of Black community pride, for many were the sons of area families whose roots dated back to the Black Loyalists, the Maroons and the War of 1812; families who, for generations, had lived adjacent to the Bedford Basin and whose forefathers had labored a lifetime in efforts to achieve a secure future for themselves and their offspring. Among the first of these players was Eurekas' forward Frank L. Symonds, the son of Samuel Symonds, the Campbell Road Blacksmith. Later, one of the original Africville Sea-Sides players would be John "Junior" Brown, whose father, John Brown, Sr., had worked for 40 years as an express driver within the Richmond area.

1904 Colored Hockey League Champion Halifax Eurekas.

Team Members: George Adams, Charles Allison, Herbert Allison, George Taylor, Adophus Francis Skinner, and George "Charlie" Tolliver.

Team Managers: James Kinney (middle) and James Robinson Johnston (right of Kinney).

Photo courtesy Public Archives of Nova Scotia.

Up on Gottingen Street and its surrounding cross-blocks, would be the area the Halifax Eurekas called home. Henry Adams, a barrel maker residing on Gottingen Street, had both his two sons, Agustus, better known as "Gus", and his brother George, each playing for the Eurekas. James Johnson, a laborer living at #144 Gottingen, had his son Stanley in the league wearing the Eurekas uniform. James A. Mansfield, a local sodawater maker living nearby at #9 Blowers Street, had his son John also playing for the Eurekas. Even the son of Reverend Edward Saunders, a Baptist Minister from South Street, was a player in the League.

The Colored Hockey League would now begin competing with the newly formed all-White Halifax Senior League, a league comprised of the Dartmouth Chebuctos, Halifax Crescents, and the Halifax Wanderers. The shortage of available artificial ice arenas meant that playing time was at a premium, and Blacks would be the last on the list. Compounding matters were rink operators who attempted to benefit financially from the growing interest in hockey. In a letter to the editor of the local *Gazette Newspaper*, one of the owners of the local Victoria rink proclaimed:

> *The game of hockey has increased in favor to such an extent, that the directors of the Victoria rink may be justified in charging seventy-five cents for a seat.*

The average attendance fee was twenty-five cents. Few arenas outside of New York City charged beyond fifty cents to view a hockey match. In New York, the St. Nicholas Rink, owned by the Vanderbilt's, charged one dollar for admission to their St. Nicholas Team hockey matches. The dollar was a social barrier designed to keep *"common riff-raff"* out of the arenas. The problem with Halifax and Dartmouth was that, by definition, most of the paying customers who attended local hockey games fell economically under the *"common riff-raff"* label. In the end, the arena operators would realize that New York was New York and Halifax was Nova Scotia. The price of admission would either stay the same, or rise only slightly, ensuring that individuals, regardless of social standing or race, would continue to attend hockey matches at affordable prices.

In an attempt to bring attention to the company and to promote the newly formed all-White Senior League, the Dartmouth-based Starr Skate Manufacturing Company agreed to donate a spectacular silver chalice trophy, to be awarded annually to the Nova Scotia champions. At the time, a large proportion of Starr's work force was local Blacks. Master tradesmen, they were some of the most skilled talent behind the company's skate manufacturing operations - men who ensured that a quality product was produced. Such a gesture made by the company to the Senior League could not have gone unnoticed within the local Black community, given the fact that no similar gesture was made towards the Blacks. The message was clear, Blacks could make the skates, but they would not be promoted when it came to wearing them.

The players covered the initial cost of their equipment. A new pair of Starr skates cost 40 cents – a days pay for many of the players. By modern standards team equipment was primitive. Most players wore little protection. Helmets were non-existent. Shin pads, the kind often associated with soccer, were common, though unsuited for hockey, with the result being that the player's knees were unprotected and subject to injury from sticks or falls to the ice. Single blade skates screwed to boots were the norm, as most players could not afford the more expensive tube skates. Few players wore gloves, with most playing either barehanded or with cotton work gloves. Though the goalie wore pads, they were those most commonly associated with the English game of cricket and were thin-lined and limited in their protection and coverage. The goalie stick was the same as a regular player's stick and the goalie wore no helmet, mask, nor protective gloves.

With no player substitution, it was not uncommon, should a player become injured, or a skate blade break, that the game would be delayed until the player could resume play. However, to ensure the games were played in a manner that promoted both individual skill and goodwill, should a player be sidelined due to injury, the opposition was expected to pull a player to ensure all teams were equal in on-ice numbers. Injuries were common. By 1902 teams began to have substitutes on hand.

For many players, the most common and preferred hockey stick was a Mi'kmaq hockey stick, the legendary stick hand crafted by the island's native Indians. At the time Blacks and Mi'kmaq Indians from the Preston area co-sold handmade Mi'kmaq hockey sticks for 25 and 50 cents a-piece at the Halifax Green City Market. Halifax fruit vendor Tommy Sweet would later comment, *"no two sticks were exactly alike. You just picked out the one that suited you."* During this period, in 1898, players wore a variety of different skates *"all sorts of skates were worn - acmes, straps, perforated blades, and even reachers."* [6] Initially the teams' lack of uniforms made it difficult to identify and differentiate between teams and team members. According to one account:

> . . . *while all the players seemed to look alike; some had their coats on, some had them off, and one or two wore White sweaters, and it was almost impossible to distinguish, one from the other.*

Eventually, as revenue increased team uniforms and better equipment would be supplied. It would be this lack of uniformity that would impact on the abilities of the teams to initially compete at a higher level than their true potential. However, as the league obtained some success through ticket sales and equipment, uniformity and skill improved.

With all the games on an invitational basis, Kinney would arrange a match between his Eurekas and Jubilees for a "Colored Championship" to be held on March 5th 1898 at the Dartmouth Rink. Kinney and the others knew it would be important for the league to win over paying fans in order to generate money for equipment, travel, and the pursuit of his and the Baptist church leadership's goals. With the league having received no press in three years, Kinney arranged to have World Speed Skating Champion Jack McCulloch do a pre-game exhibition in an attempt to draw fans and press to the match. McCulloch was the

---

[6] *REACHER SKATES: Invented by James A. Whelpley at the age of 18. The "Long Reach" skate is credited for helping popularize skating in Canada. Named after a stretch of the St. John River near his New Brunswick home, "reachers" were unlikely to cramp ones ankles making 100-mile journeys by skate common. Their design consisted of a long steel blade that was fitted onto a wooden top. A pair of leather straps fastened the skates to the boots. A screw in the skate fitted into the heel of the boot to keep the skate from slipping. Whelpley and his brothers began manufacturing the Long Reach ice skates in 1859 and he was eventually granted a United States patent on April 8, 1884.*

first Manitoban athlete to win a world skating title, becoming the Canadian Speed Skating Championship in 1893, winning the U.S. Nationals in St. Paul, Minnesota in 1896, and the World Championship in 1897. He was an excellent hockey player, figure skater, cyclist, and oarsman, and upon turning professional McCulloch began performing skating exhibitions throughout North America. McCulloch was the night's top bill, entertaining the audience and setting the stage for the league's first championship. The *Acadian Recorder* wrote of the event:

> *McCulloch again delighted the crowd with his wonderful work; the manner in which he turned the sharp corners, particularly on the stilts, was marvelous. He also gave an exhibition of speed, skating a half mile in 1.42 (minutes).*

During the game players performed a theatrical style of hockey, which was described as lively, funny and full of high-speed spills and collisions. The *Acadian Recorder* again remarked:

> *The hockey match was productive of great laughter, and the crowd urged the respective teams, with shouts of victory . . . when they went beyond their speed and came together, there was a tumble. In one instance the puck was near the Dartmouth goal; two players went to lift it, but both missed and went down, carrying the goal post with them, and falling against the goal keeper, all going down in a heap.*

During the match, the Eurekas dominated the first half leading 4-0. It was reported had it not been for the play of Jubilees star goaltender "Little-Braces" Franklyn, the score could have easily been much worse.

According to Dr. Garth Vaughan's groundbreaking book, *The Puck Starts Here,* Franklyn's play was revolutionary, as he was the first recorded goaltender to go down onto the ice to stop a shot. At the time other leagues adopted a *"stand-up only"* position for their net minder, occasionally even issuing fines to goaltenders if they fell to the ice while playing the puck. It would not be until almost twenty years later that Franklyn's style of play would become the standard throughout all of amateur and professional hockey. Today, hockey's Hall-of-Fame brothers Lynn and Frank Patrick and their Pacific Coast Hockey League are recognized as the first individuals and league to allow goaltenders to play in this manner. This is a false. The first league to allow the goalie to go down on ice was the Colored League; the first goalie to do so being Henry "Braces" Franklyn.

Going down onto the ice was not Franklyn's only innovation, as the pint-sized goaltender would also regularly wander out of his goal to play the puck, a style that would not be seen until the emergence of legendary National Hockey League Hall-of-Fame goaltender Jacques Plante in the mid-1950's. Braces, was a half-century ahead of his time, displaying a style all his own. As one account records:

Little Franklyn of the Dartmouth team, made great efforts to stem the tide in this half, he was playing goal and if he saw the puck come near him he would dance on his skates, and if the puck came up anywhere within a dozen feet of the goal he went out after it while the point and cover stood in amazement, and before long he was out among the forwards.

During the championship game, Franklyn kept his team in play. His bold leadership and aggressive style created an atmosphere that added a degree of electricity to the match. With each goal scored, a flurry of objections was made to the goal judges and official. At times, the arguments were so heated that it appeared the game might become a slugfest as both teams jockeyed for an edge and exchanged verbal insults on the ice. The newspaper accounts record:

In the second half the Dartmouth team claimed a goal, but the young Haligonian who officiated said it was not so; he was surrounded and had to give in and the game proceeded. They got a second goal, and then a third was claimed, the judge, however, said no, but was quickly surrounded and a heated argument ensued for about 5 minutes, when he decided it was not safe for him to stay and Mr. McKerrow[7] took his place.

On this night the Jubilees would fall short, as the Eurekas would score the last two goals, winning by the final score of 6-3 and allowing the Eurekas to claim the Colored Hockey Championship of 1898. Following the game, the Dartmouth team roster would undergo a radical change. Three team players, Charles Borden, Oscar Johnson, and the team's star goaltender, Braces Franklyn, would no longer be listed on the squad or in the league.

Apparently Franklyn died in 1899. The cause of his death is unknown. However, it was dramatic enough to cause his wife, Emeline, to be institutionalized at the Mount Hope Insane Asylum. In addition, his father, who was 68 years of age at the time, would be placed into a boarding home as he was unable to look after himself. It also appears that Franklyn left behind a small family, including a young daughter of thirteen. The girl and her three younger sisters were adopted into the home of Franklyn's 28 year-old sister. At the time of Braces and Emeline's marriage, Emeline was only 13 and Braces 19. The couple was married on June 15, 1879 in General's Bridge, Nova Scotia. The fate of their family is not known.

---

[7] It is of interest to note that the replacement was not Rev. Peter McKerrow but rather a relation of his, B. McKerrow.

CHAPTER NINE

A NEW BRAND OF PROFESSIONAL

While the Jubilees would begin the year with wholesale roster changes, the Eurekas line-up would virtually stay intact, with the only notable change being the loss of James E. Dixon, the cousin of the boxer George Dixon. James would captain a new team, the Africville Sea-Sides, which would include his brothers Wallace, Allen and Richard, as well as James and William Carvery, along with James Paris and John Cassidy (a boarder living with Joseph Carvery).

The Africville Sea-Sides team name had a double meaning. To the White population, the double "S" insignia on Africville's jersey signified the "Sea-Sides" – a geographical reference to Africville and the inner harbor that it borders. The White media would print the team name as "Seasides" giving it a grammatically correct but misrepresentative spelling. The Sea-Sides uniforms were not fashioned in honor of Africville; the double "S" held a more important meaning. In the days of the Underground Railroad, it had been the mark of a *"Slave Stealer,"* individuals who helped slaves escape north into Canada. Those who were caught helping slaves were often beaten, murdered, or imprisoned. As a way of identifying captured slave stealers, slave owners often branded their victims with a double "S" on their bodies - most often on their right hands or their face - as a way to "mark" them for life. In the eyes of the slaves however, the double "S" was a sign of heroism, one of pride – *"Slave Salvation."* Anyone bearing the mark was to be trusted, respected and admired. It is in John Greenleaf Whittier's famous 1841 poem, *The Branded Hand,* about the American Jonathan Walker, a sea captain who was captured by Southerners while he was attempting to smuggle slaves at the height of the Underground Railroad, that the concept of the slave stealer is forever immortalized:

> *Then lift that manly right hand,*
> *Bold plowman of the wave,*
> *Its branded palm shall prophesy*
> *Salvation to the Slave;*
> *Hold up its fire-wrought language,*
> *That whoso reads may feel*
> *His heart swell strong within him,*
> *His sinews change to steal.*
> *Hold it up before our sunshine,*
> *Up against our Northern air.*
> *Ho! Men of Massachusetts, for the*
> *Love of God look there!*
> *Take it henceforth for your standard,*
> *Like Bruce's heart of yore;*
> *In the dark strife closing round*
> *Ye, let that hand be seen before.*

In terms of historic significance, the Sea-Sides uniform is perhaps the most important hockey uniform ever.

On February 17, 1899, the Africville Sea-Sides would make their debut against the Eurekas. In only one year Kinney, along with Johnston and the church leadership, had turned the league from one of relative obscurity into a top sports draw in Nova Scotia. In an era when the top White teams, the Crescents, the Chebuctos and the Wanderers, were commonly averaging 300-400 spectators per game, the Sea-Sides-Eurekas game would draw over 500.

Led by Eurekas' Team Captain, A. E. "Eddie" Martin's three goals, the defending champions would expose the weak Sea-Sides' goaltending of William Carvery, easily defeating the upstart Africville team by a score of 10-0. Despite the lopsided score, James Carvery, Wallace Dixon and James Dixon were noted as having strong performances for the Sea-Sides. As for the Eurekas, their overall skill level had noticeably improved from the previous year. *"Excellent teamwork"* and adjectives like *"brilliant"* were now being found in written game accounts. No longer was there loosely veiled racist comments inserted in the game reports, as only positive descriptions of high quality of play were mentioned. The *Acadian Recorder* would note, *"the Eurekas are very fast skaters and if properly trained would make a very formidable team."*

Following the game, Kinney and the others would arrange for the Eurekas team to travel to Truro, a town approximately 75 miles north of Halifax, to play the Victorias, a team consisting of members of the local First Baptist Church. The name *"Victorias,"* rather than representing Queen Victoria, simply meant what it implied verbally, *"the victorious,"* those who *"had succeeded"; "had overcome"; "had achieved"*; and most importantly, *"had won!"* Captain George Clyke, who appears on the roster of the Stanley team in 1895, would now be the star and cornerstone of the Victorias. On March 4th another large crowd would be on hand to witness the Victorias-Eurekas match. There was almost a carnival-like atmosphere in the arena, which included a *"Feu de joi"* [8] style celebration with *"a monster firecracker"* exploding amongst the contending players. In the end it would be a losing affair for the Victorias, as forward George Adams would score all four goals leading the visiting Eurekas' to a 4 to 3 victory. *The Truro Daily News* described the game as excellent:

> *No game of hockey in the Curling Rink has ever excited as much enthusiasm, as the one played on Saturday night between the Eurekas, of Halifax, all colored boys, and the Victoria's, colored players, of this town.*

It is clear from the result the Victorias were an experienced team who had been an organized team for sometime. After this

---

[8] *Note: Feu de joi is the tradition of kindling a fire in a public place as a token of joy. Traditionally either a bonfire or the firing of guns but in a hockey arena, one would have to settle for only a monster firecracker.*

year, six of the seven players would not record another game in the league. Only George Clyke remained. Surprisingly for the Eurekas, their Captain, Eddie Martin, did not make the trip to Truro, deciding instead to play that same night for the Sea-Sides in Dartmouth. With over 300 spectators in attendance, the Dartmouth match would produce a surprising result as the upstart Sea-Sides would upset the Jubilees, marking a turning point in the Colored Hockey League. Over the next few years it would be Africville Sea-Sides and not the Dartmouth Jubilees who would now challenge the Halifax Eurekas for top honors. The *Acadian Recorder* wrote that:

> *. . . nearly every one present was of the opinion that the Jubilees would prove the victor judging by the showing both teams made against the champion Eureka team.*

The Jubilees would have a series of new players in their lineup. This included Walter Saunders, a man who played for the Stanley in 1895 and who appeared to be the league's unofficial emergency replacement. It was noted that James "Cut" Brown and Tommy Tynes *"both played well and displayed their old form."* With the death of Franklyn, Freddie Borden, another relative of Rev. Borden, would now become the team goaltender. Possibly playing his first game at that position, he was noted to be *"a little nervous and seemed to lose (his) heart after the first goal was scored."* After a scoreless first half, Sea-Sides forward James Carvery would almost single-handedly lead his team to a 3-0 victory.

> *In a good second half the Seasides began to rush matters and made the game very fast and furious which resulted in three goals, all shot by James Carvery, the star player of his team and the fastest man on the ice.*

Five nights later, the Eurekas and Jubilees would be scheduled to play. Their match would be called off at the last minute, as the Jubilees could not ice a full squad. Not wanting to let the fans go home disappointed, H. Young of the Chebuctos, along with several of the Chebuctos players who were in attendance, quickly formed a team playing an impromptu game against the Eurekas. This would be a historic event, as it would mark the first recorded game between professional level White and Black hockey players. The final score was a 9-7 Eurekas' victory. In a short period of time it was clear that these Black players had honed their game to the point where they could not only compete with the powerhouse White teams of Nova Scotia, but also defeat them.

The Eurekas and the Jubilees would schedule an April 2nd makeup game to be played in the Dartmouth Arena. But even with Sea-Sides regulars Wallace and Allen Dixon added to the Eureka's lineup, there would be a shortage of available bodies. As a result each team would be forced to play one man short, icing only three forwards per-side, instead of the regular four. Eddie Martin would score two goals in leading the Eurekas to a 7-0 victory over Dartmouth.[9] George Tolliver and Charlie Allison would also score twice, but the star of the game would be Eddie Martin. As reported:

> *On several occasions the puck was carried down the rink by the Jubilees, but "stone wall" Martin at cover was generally in the way and barred the entrance to his territory. A few minutes later Martin seizing the rubber with all his might-and-main, shot down the rink with lighting-like rapidity and scored the seventh and last goal.*

It is apparent that Martin was clearly a star in the League. His presence on a team could single-handedly change an outcome of a game and swing the balance of power in favor of the team he played on. With paying customers in the stands, players would not go without reward. One just has to look at

---

[9] *The Eurekas 4-3 victory over the Truro Victorias did not count towards the championship totals.*
The 1899 Colored Hockey League final standings, according the Acadian Recorder, were:
Eurekas 4 wins 0 losses, 26 goals - 1 against, Seasides 1 win 2 losses, 4 goals - 15 against, Jubilees 1 win 4 losses, 5 goals - 20 against.

prize money in "barn-storming" baseball games of the time to realize that there was a financial incentive for winning. With the recent passing of Eddie's father, John Martin, a dock laborer employed over thirty years as a Stevedore on the Halifax waterfront, the 23 year-old hockey player would now become the patriarch of the family, helping to support his 57 year-old mother Adeline and 25 year-old sister Rebecca. This would be the last recorded game Martin would play with the Eurekas. He had established himself as one of the early stars in Nova Scotia hockey and, by switching teams, he would now become a thorn in his former team's side. The following year Eddie Martin would begin playing full-time for the Sea-Sides. Not only would his jersey change, but also the *fortunes* of his former teammates. By 1900, professionalism had entered into the League.

At the end of the 1899 season the Sea-Sides organized themselves officially as an amateur athletic club with James Parris as President. Interestingly, the team would feel the need for a Treasurer - T. G. MacDonald. This indicates that the clubs and players involved were acting as semi-professional rather than recreational teams. The professionalism of the Nova Scotia Senior League was being paralleled in the Colored League, with rising local interests; hockey, regardless of color, was now becoming big business.

CHAPTER TEN

MARITIME CONTENDERS

As early as 1848, the Black settlement of Loch Lomond near Saint John, New Brunswick, had emerged as thriving Black community with sufficient numbers of school-age Black children necessary to organize all-Black sports teams. By the 1870's, the Black Baptist churches of the Maritimes had effectively linked the Black communities of Nova Scotia to their Prince Edward Island and New Brunswick counterparts with an on-going exchange of communication taking place. And as early as the 1880's, barn-storming Black baseball teams from New Brunswick had begun traveling the region.

New Brunswick was home to at least three well-traveled and well-known Black teams, the Fredericton *Celestials*, the *Royals* and the *Ralph Waldo Emersons* Baseball Clubs of Saint John. As in Nova Scotia, the names of these teams would also be symbolic. The Celestials were named in honor of the North Star - the constellation that guided Blacks along the Underground Railroad as they traveled at night through the dense woods along the American borderlands and into New Brunswick. The Royals named in honor of God, Jesus and the Holy Ghost; powerful symbols of the Baptist belief and a message to all that *"God was on their side."* The Ralph Waldo Emersons named in honor of the American Philosopher who had based his life on the concepts of optimism and morality. Perhaps the greatest philosopher of his time, Emerson was an abolitionist and a man who took great issue with the symbolism and hypocrisy of modern society and religion. He believed in the simplicity of life and earned a reputation for urging followers to remember the past and to learn from life's experiences. The fact that the Black athletes of Saint John named their team in honor of him held political, social and religious significance. An indication of the political and moral undertone Black sports clubs in Canada represented and presented whenever they took to the field. Although there is no record of these teams participating in the Colored Hockey League of the Maritimes, it appears that these three clubs were a driving force behind Black sports in New Brunswick and the source of the first pools of Black hockey talent in the province. Evidence of the game's growth throughout the Maritimes is found in Charlottetown, Prince Edward Island. In the winter of 1899, the West End Rangers Sports Club would be formed with Thomas Mills as Team President. The Rangers would be based out of an interracial neighborhood on the western edge of Charlottetown called "the Bog", an area whose history parallels that of Africville.

Court battles between the local residents and the City had united the races and created a sense of community among the Black and White groups. Also, this small neighborhood had a strong sports tradition that had further united the area and had already produced two of the greatest boxers of the day, George "Old Chocolate" Godfrey and George "Budge" Byers.

Again the Baptist church would play a key part as reflected in their name, the Rangers. The Whites believe the name to refer to *"the keeper of the British Royal Park,"* while to the Blacks it meant something different. To them, Ranger, referred to a *"pew in a church."* (It was also a name in honor of the Black Loyalists who fought under the banner of Butler's Rangers during the height of the American Revolution).

The Rangers hockey uniform incorporated the use of a bright yellow sash that was worn loosely over the team sweater. The sash had the initials W.E.R., and was similar to the one worn by Dunmore's Ethiopian Regiment, with the words *"Liberty for Slaves."* Aside from the Sea-Sides uniform, the West End Rangers jersey was one of the most symbolic uniforms ever created.

The Rangers played their first "official" game on New Year's Day, 1900, on Government Pond. The match would be an intra-squad game involving the single men versus the married men from around the Black community. In total, forty players participated in a hard-hitting affair with many players being hit on the shins, noses, and the mouth with sticks. During the match an estimated twenty-three hockey sticks were broken, seventeen shins reported bruised, five noses had their *"claret"* cleared of them, six teeth knocked out, and one man had his skates broken. The single men would defeat their married opponents, and in honor of the occasion, a goose dinner was held that evening at the club's room in which the defeated side had to foot the bill.

The West End Rangers hockey team c.1900.
Team Members in photo: Edmond Byers, A. "Harry" McNeill,
George "Hurley" Mills, John T. Mills, Albert Mills and
Team President Thomas Mills.
Photo courtesy Island Studies Institute Prince Edward Island.

The West End Rangers would play most of their games in an intramural league format, consisting of several teams within the Rangers' organization. Whenever the team played outside their own club it would be the Mills' five sons, John (Jack), Albert (Bert), Lemuel (Lewis), Oliver, and George, who would anchor the team. Former champion speed skater and cyclist, Jack Mills, would be the star and captain. Before playing for the Rangers, Jack Mills had set a provincial long-distance speed skating record, skating 18 miles in 50 minutes, an average speed of 21.6 miles per hour.[10] Because of his brother's stick making ability, George Mills would also be referred to as "Hurley" Mills (a reference to the Hurley-on-the-ice, an alternative early name for ice hockey). Jim Hornby's excellent book, *Black Islanders*, describes what made the Bog different from Africville, and other Maritime regions, was its level of integration.

In Nova Scotia the Black population was racially segregated by law into separate schools; in New Brunswick, the schools were segregated in practice. In Charlottetown, Black and racially mixed children all fell into the underclass, and they went to schools for the poor. The Bog School was integrated simply because the Bog was integrated.

This integration had also been reflected in sports such as boxing and baseball and now, with the creation of the West End Rangers, in hockey. The first "officially" recorded game between an all-Black and all-White hockey team would take

---

[10] *It would not be until the late 1940's, early 1950's that improved skates would enable the fastest hockey players in the National Hockey League (Max Bentley, Norm Dussault and Milt Schmidt) to reach rates of speeds between 22.5 and 23 MPH over a short sprinting distance. As late as the 1950's, the average Canadian professional hockey player averaged speeds of only eighteen miles per hour.*

place later that year, in 1900, as the Rangers played a game against the top Senior League team in Prince Edward Island - the *Abegweits*.

The Abegweits, it was said, made *"the mightiest of Nova Scotia's warriors to tremble"*. Surprisingly the Rangers, in their first non-intra squad match, narrowly lost by a score of 5-4 (actual reference records a 5-3 1/2 goal game, possibly a disputed goal due to height of puck when entering into the goal or a goal scored by one's own team on themselves). Later, the Rangers requested a rematch, but after their embarrassing near loss, the Abegweits never responded. There is no evidence that a rematch ever occurred.

On February 21 of that year, the Eurekas and Sea-Sides would play for the Colored Championship at Dartmouth rink. The talented 26 year-old Walter "Jack" Thomas would replace Eddie Martin on the Eurekas' squad. At the time Thomas was employed as a domestic. He lived in the home of 70 and 68 year-old William and Elizabeth Brown. As for Martin, he would face his old team for the first time. It would be a closely fought match in which the Sea-Sides played a physical game in an attempt to slow down the faster and more talented Eurekas. Although much improved, the Sea-Sides lost 3-0. Overall, the quality of play of both teams was noted by the *Acadian Recorder* as some of the finest, regardless of league:

> It was nip and tuck from start to finish, and kept the spectators in an ecstasy of excitement. Such rushes, such dashing and passing has not been seen within the confines of the rink for sometime, and it was a pity the hockey enthusiasts were not out in larger numbers, as such a game may not occur again. The Seasides were by far the heaviest team, and there was a great deal of unnecessary rough play on the part of both sides, especially the Seasides.

One week later, on February 28th, the Sea-Sides traveled to Truro to play the Victorias as part of the towns Winter Carnival. Prior to the game it was advertised that both teams would participate in a parade-like procession through the streets of

Truro before arriving at the arena for the night's game. Admission would be 20 cents and the *Truro Daily News* reported that, unlike the 1898 game, *"firecrackers were prohibited."* Strangely enough, with all the prior attention the game received, no game summary would appear in any newspaper in Truro or in Halifax. Truro would defeat the Sea-Sides 3-1 and in the return match held at the South End Rink in Halifax two weeks later, the Sea-Sides would return the favor defeating the Victorias by the same 3-1 score. This marked the first organized games in major Halifax area rink without the Eurekas involvement.

The final game of the season for the Colored League involved the Sea-Sides and Eurekas in a non-championship, benefit match to raise the needed money for the Crescents to travel to Montreal to challenge for the Stanley Cup. Held March 19th at the North End Rink in Halifax, the Crescents and the Chebuctos (the team the Eurekas defeated the year prior) played first, followed by the exhibition match between the Eurekas and Sea-Sides. Over 700 people would be on hand to would witness an emotion filled game, as the Eurekas would suffer their first ever loss by a score of 5-1.

> *The Seasides scored first, and made the Eurekas play with great vigor. The game then became fast and furious, and to all appearances the Eurekas had the better of the first part of the first half, but they could not score, the Seasides' goalkeeper being always in the way. There were several disputes over goals, and at one time the teams threatened to leave the ice but the referee induced them to continue.*

Much of the underlying friction was over Eddie Martin's inclusion on the Sea-Sides roster. As long as the Eurekas had continued to win, Martin's change of team may have only caused some ill-will between his former teammates and himself, but now that with the loss, his presence on the Africville roster would start to become of issue. Although the Eurekas still retained the title of league champion, the future of Martin as a Sea-Sides player would continue to be a source of animosity between the two teams.

As for the Halifax Crescents, they would not fair well in their challenge for the Cup against the Montreal Shamrocks. Led by future Hockey Hall-Of-Fame player, Lieutenant-Colonel Harry Judah Trihey, the defending Stanley Cup Champion Shamrocks would successfully defend two challenges for the Cup that year, one from Winnipeg in midseason and from the Crescents at the end of the regular season. The series against Winnipeg was close, exciting, and well attended, but the contests against the Crescents went almost unnoticed as the Shamrocks retained their championship status by defeating the Crescents by the scores of 10-2 and 11-0.

It was not uncommon for teams that challenged for the Stanley Cup, hockey's most coveted prize, to bolster their rosters before they went to play. The question begs to be asked, "Just how good were these Black hockey teams?" Although, the Crescents were soundly defeated, it is apparent that the Eurekas, possibly bolstered with other top players and the latest equipment, could have been considered a serious challenge to the Cup. At worst, these all-Black teams were on par with many other top senior top-level teams throughout Canada. As the league now entered its highest, most competitive stage of development, one point was clear: the players of the Colored Hockey League of the Maritimes possessed some of Canada's finest players.

CHAPTER ELEVEN

SEA-SIDES EDDIE IN HOT WATER

There would be no mention of game accounts in the Halifax media in 1901. Various reasons may have contributed for this absence of press coverage, of which, could have included a potential backlash due to Johnston's and Kinney's political involvement.

John Thomas Bulmer died on February 9, 1901. In accordance with his wishes the law firm, for which he had worked decades to build, was left to James Johnston. It is unknown why Bulmer left Johnston the law firm. Bulmer left behind a wife and three children. Perhaps some arrangements had been made to liquidate some of the firm's assets and to afford the family a "cash-out" option? The turnover is unclear. A year later, Johnston married Janie May Allen of Windsor Junction, Nova Scotia.

It was also during this period that the local Conservative Party was actively recruiting Johnston and Kinney in an attempt to ensure that they would organize and guarantee the Black vote. The idea of Blacks voting in a solid block worried many non-Conservative members who feared the prospect of a Black man being elected to public office. Johnston and Kinney would have been seen as potential political candidates of the future as they were not only astute politically but also carried a solid base of respect and support among both Black as well as lower class Whites. Years later, in 1908, when it appeared that Johnston might run for political office, rumors were rampant that he would be targeted for murder if he did so. He never did run and the rumors disappeared.

Finally, the two men attempt to promote the idea of an annual Black Jubilee Celebration across Nova Scotia. Modeled after the efforts of the Blacks of Trinidad, a decade earlier, this undertaking was one of the few examples of the influence and possible contact which had continued to exist between Henry Sylvester Williams, Johnston and Kinney. The efforts to establish a Black Jubilee fell short and were soon abandoned. By now the Colored Hockey League was well established and the demands associated with it, along with the other factors, made it almost impossible to dedicate the necessary time required to organize a Black emancipation event.

Based on later reports about the league, Eddie Martin, now full-time with the Sea-Sides, would lead Africville to its first Colored Championship in 1901. The Eurekas and the Sea-Sides had scheduled a best of three series, with each winning once with the third game finishing in a 3-3 draw, following 20 minutes of overtime. As a result, a fourth game would be needed to decide the championship, in it the Sea-Sides would defeating the Eurekas by a score of 4-2.

That year, the West End Rangers sent Captain John Mills to Truro to arrange for a game between the Rangers and Victorias. It was agreed the two teams would meet at an arena midway between their communities at Pictou, Nova Scotia. The result would be an astounding 20-0 trouncing of the Victorias by the Rangers. Although the Rangers and Sea-Sides did not face each other, the Rangers would claim a share of the Maritime Championship largely based on the margin of victory over a team who had defeated the Sea-Sides in a game the prior year. The Rangers quality of play would inspire a poem to be written about the team:

> *It's all very well — to talk about the Abbies;*
> *And it's all very well - to talk about the Vics;*
> *But for tough old hockey fightin—*
> *The kind we take delight in.*
> *Yer orter see the Rangers use their sticks.*

The following year on January 22, 1902, the West End Rangers issued a challenge in the *Halifax Herald Newspaper* to play for the Colored Hockey Championship of the Maritimes. The Sea-Sides and Eurekas accepted the challenge with the two matches scheduled to be played in Halifax with an agreed future visit to Charlottetown by the 1901 Champion Sea-Sides.

Sea-Sides Captain Eddie Martin arranged for the first game to take place in the Empire Rink on February 18th. As a result of non-media attention of the previous year, Africville would place large advertisements in local newspapers to promote their game. Subsequently, one of the largest crowds to ever attend a hockey game in Nova Scotia would be on hand to witness the first, Inter-Provincial Maritime Championship hockey game. With over 1,200 people in the stands, not only was the Colored League beginning to out-draw the Senior League, but Martin, and the Sea-Side management, had showed that they could successfully organize their own games. This set the stage for control of the league between Africville, the traditional home of the most powerful entrepreneurial Black families in Nova Scotia, and the Eurekas, managed by a generation of formally educated, ideological, Black Nova Scotians.

The West End Rangers appearance and play would not disappoint. The *Acadian Recorder* reported:

> *[The Rangers] . . . made a fine appearance on the ice, in handsome and gorgeous costumes of yellow and Black, their Black jerseys and knickerbockers being trimmed with yellow, with a band of the same color around the waist, a sash with the letters W.E.R. and on their breast crossed hockey sticks.*

According to accounts, the Rangers dominated early, with the Sea-Sides unable to move the puck up ice and into their opponents end. Only twice in the first 16 minutes of play did the Sea-Sides reach their opponent's side of the ice. It would be Africville's exceptional goaltending and defensive play that would keep the Rangers from dominating the score.

The work of William Carvery in goal for the Haligonians in the first half, however, stood out with great prominence; he stopped shot after shot, and even in the senior league (White league) better work would not be seen. In Cassidy he had an able assistant; he was scheduled for point, but he really was a second goal keeper; he had pads like the goal defender, and at times both men were in the nets and they stopped score after score.

The game would remain scoreless until the 24th minute when John Mills tallied the first goal of the game for the Rangers. After the Sea-Sides tied the score at one, the play became much more physical, resulting in two first half injuries to both Sea-Sides' Wallace Dixon and Rangers star player, John Mills. Mills would be helped from the ice, unable to continue. With Eddie Martin replacing Dixon at forward, the complexion of the game would change.

Martin is a particularly strong player . . . in the absence of one of the Mills brothers, with the result there was more end to end play than before; it was not only lively, but there as an abundance of hard boy checking and the captain of the Rangers afterwards declared never before had they been in a game with such heavy use of the body.

With each team exchanging goals, the game would be tied 2-2 at the half. The second half would be a closely fought affair. In dramatic fashion Richard "Dick" Carvery, skating the length of the ice, would score the game-winning goal as the bell rang to end the game. The resulting goal ignited a heated argument as the Rangers official timekeeper said he showed another minute remaining in the game. The Rangers pleaded but to no avail, as the Sea-Sides would be declared the winner by the final of 3-2. Fans poured from the stands to congratulate the Sea-Sides' players in their conquest. Captain Mills would state that the Rangers had been squarely beaten, but did comment that they would have liked to play the extra minute. Afterwards, game accounts were favorable towards both teams praising the quality of play displayed:

> *The damp ice prevented the puck from traveling too fast but it was good hockey, both teams showing much skill, and with such a hard fought game, and at times abounding in heavy body checking, tripping and rough play, the spectators were kept in high pitch excitement . . . The Seasides . . . showed themselves possessed of plenty of pluck in doing their best . . . The Island team showed they possessed much knowledge of the game, they are fast skaters, check in good style, are full on offside, but their weakest point was their shooting.*

What is notable about this statement is the comment referring to the Rangers' poor shooting. In a later letter from John Mills, it is clear that the Ranger team played a different style when it came to what was considered a *legal* shot.

The next night the visiting West End Rangers would play the Eurekas at the North End Rink. Although similar advertisements had been placed, there would be approximately 500 fewer fans in attendance than the previous night's match-up, with roughly 700 on hand to witness the game. Again the ice quality was poor and the speed of play would be of benefit to the Eurekas. John Mills, who had been injured the previous evening, would not play. In this game, unlike the game against the Sea-Sides, the Rangers would play more physically resulting in a number of injuries for each side. Once more the Rangers would outplay their opponents in the first half, but again they would have nothing to show for their efforts, as the game remained scoreless well into the second half. Eventually, the Rangers would score two goals. Later, the Eurekas would attempt a dramatic comeback. According to the *Acadian Recorder*:

> *[In the] Second half the Eurekas carried the play but the visitors body-checked heavily ... The Eurekas went to work with great vim and soon Skinner shot his goal. They were delighted with their success some of them jumped on their skates; others hurled their sticks though*

106

without any series consequences. ... It was a lively finish; body-checking, tripping and slashing prevailed; some of the players indulged in going at each other with their sticks, though without any series consequences, there were may hard checks against the boards when scores seemed imminent.

But it would be too-little-too-late, as the Rangers would win by a score of 2-1. Later it was noted,

The Eurekas made a splendid fight, and though defeated they have no need to feel ashamed of being beaten by such a crack organization of colored players.

After the game, both teams held an after game party at the Eurekas' unofficial clubhouse on Creighton Street.

Two days later, the Sea-Sides and Eurekas agreed to play three games to determine the Colored Hockey Championship. Originally scheduled to be played after the Sea-Sides returned from their March 4th match in Charlottetown, Africville decided at the last minute to cancel their road trip and instead stage their series with the Eurekas early. This decision to cancel prompted sharp criticism in the *Charlottetown Herald* newspaper, whose editors accused the Sea-Sides of being afraid to play the Rangers on their home ice. The newspaper concluded that the Sea-Sides had *"a case of showing the White feather."*

On the night they were originally scheduled to be in Charlottetown, the Sea-Sides begin their best of three series with the Eurekas. Over 400 people would be on hand to witness the game. However, moments before the game began, the Eurekas refused to play if their former captain, Eddie Martin, was allowed to dress for the Sea-Sides. A year earlier, after a game in which Martin had played an exceptionally rough and physical game against his former team, it was the Eurekas understanding that Martin would *never* appear in a game against his former teammates again. The Sea-Sides refused to withdraw Martin and at 9:30 p.m., after an hour-and-a-half delay, the game was called off.

Rink Manager H. B. Clarke was forced to refund the crowds' money. Because of this, Clarke would later announce that neither team would be able to play at the Empire Rink while under his management. The next morning the headline read, *"DID NOT PLAY, Eurekas object to a Seaside Player"*. In response the Eurekas' Captain, A. F. Skinner, would write a letter to the sports editor of the *Acadian Recorder* explaining the teams refusal to play. He wrote:

> *While the Eurekas regret the circumstances that caused them to refuse to play their game with the Sea Sides last night, they feel that they are not to blame in the matter. In justice to the public and to themselves, I may say that the Eurekas refused to play with a certain player on the Sea Sides because there was a distinct understanding between the (acting) manager of the Sea Sides and myself whereby this certain player was to be debarred from participation in an games between the Sea Sides and Eurekas. Moreover, the Sea Sides could well have dispensed with the services of this player because they had seven other players in the rink and the Eurekas were further willing to play with six men on each side but even to this the Sea Sides would not agree. The suggestion of the referee to play the game under protest would not have sufficed, because there was no tribunal to whom such protest could have been referred.*
>
> *After the last game with the Sea Sides last March, the Eurekas decided not to play any games in which this player participated and this decision was duly reported to the manager of the Sea Sides. The Eurekas went on the ice last night expecting to play with the Sea Sides as agreed, but when the latter's manager flatly refused to withdraw his man, the former felt that their only course was to leave the ice, as one of the senior league teams [the Dartmouth Wanderers] did (in the midst of a game) not so long ago when an opposing team likewise refused to remove an objectionable player.*

The Eurekas play the game for the sake of the sport alone, and believe that their action was justified. Thanking you in advance for space,

Yours truly,
A. F. Skinner,
Captain Eurekas,
Halifax March 5th, 1902.

The following night the Eurekas were scheduled to play the Dartmouth Victorias, not to be mistaken with the Truro Victorias, at the Dartmouth Rink. Unfortunately, this would be the only account of the Dartmouth Victorias. It is clear from the accounts of the day, and Colin D. Howell's research in his book *Northern Sandlots*, that the Victorias were a known local area baseball team. The question arises, just who was this other, mysterious, team? The answer to this question was found at the northern end of the province, in a placed called Stellarton, Nova Scotia.

Stellarton, Nova Scotia was a mining community with a small, but distinct, Black population. We know from the limited historical record that Stellarton had a Black hockey team at the turn of the century. As early as 1876 the local Victoria rink had been in existence. However, in 1892 it burned down and it would not be until 1906 a replacement rink, known as the Stellar, would be built. Prior to the fire, Black hockey had been played in the form of occasional recreational games at the Victoria rink as well as having developed separately on the adjacent frozen streams and ponds. For the most part, it had been the ponds and streams of Stellarton which had served as home to this region's Black hockey players. Few realized that Black hockey existed in Stellarton. Furthermore, historians have failed to recognize the long-standing and incredibly unique hockey tradition of the Stellarton pond and stream hockey. Stellarton hockey was enhanced by its surroundings. Coal was king. It was everywhere. In fact, when the locals played hockey on the ponds they would dig holes through the snow and ice down to the exposed coal line along the surface of the ground. Holes were dug along the boundaries of the ponds at approximately two-foot intervals running the length of the frozen playing area. These coal outcroppings were subsequently ignited with matches. The coal, because of its highly unusual flammable content, would produce a small bright flame, bright enough to illuminate the immediate areas adjacent to the streams and ponds making it possible for night games to be played. As a result, decades before the invention of electricity, hockey was the first sport to be played at night.

It is clear there were two Victoria teams. This raises the question of whether this team was also associated with the Truro Victorias club. What adds credence to this is the 1898 Truro roster in which six of the seven members would never play for Truro again. Oddly, none of their surnames match the names of people living in Truro at the time. Further research indicates that a number of "unrecorded" Black teams were in existence throughout the Maritimes playing in small communities such as New Glasgow, Nova Scotia, Pictou, Nova Scotia, and Fredericton New Brunswick. These teams operated in obscurity due to the absence of arenas and newspaper coverage. Most, if not all, of their games were played outdoors. Unfortunately, the history of the Dartmouth Victorias may never be fully understood or known; on the very night they were to play the Eurekas, virtually the entire Sea-Sides team showed up. Only Sea-Sides Team Captain, Eddie Martin, was absent. Instead of notifying Martin that he was off the team, the Sea-Sides clearly orchestrated this in order to re-enter into league play. After being banned from playing at the Empire Rink, the Sea-Sides players knew the Eurekas would not walk off the ice again in Dartmouth. In the end, by showing up without Martin, it was clear the Eurekas controlled the league. This was *Kinney's League* and in order to play, teams played by the Eurekas rules or they would not play at all. For this game, Walter Saunders from the Victorias would replace Martin in the lineup. Martin, one of the greatest players of the day, never played again. The *Acadian Recorder* reported:

> *Those who waited behind to see the Eureka-Victoria game were accorded an unexpected surprise, both in the composition of the Victoria team, which included five of*

110

the Seasides in the first half, and six in the second half,
and in the fast exciting play considering the condition of
the ice.

The Eurekas would score the game-winning goal with under two minutes to play, defeating the Sea-Sides by a score of 3-2. Despite the loss, the Sea-Sides still regarded and promoted themselves as the champions of the Maritimes. This did not sit well with the West End Rangers and on March 21st the *Acadian Recorder* reprinted an editorial written in the Charlottetown two days earlier disputing the Sea-Sides claim as the "Champions of the Maritimes."

Claim championship

SPORTING EDITOR RECORDER, —-

CHARLOTTETOWN, March 19th.

Sir, — Replying to a report currently in Nova Scotia hockey circles that the Seasides, of Halifax claim to be colored champions of the Maritime Provinces, I, as captain of the W. E. Rangers, of Charlottetown, would say that the Seasides have in no way any reason to call themselves thus. Of course the Seasides beat our team in a match consisting of a mixture of baseball and hockey, which the unjust referees allow to pass. In the first half we were cheated out of 5 minutes, (Captain Martin told me this the next night, he was timekeeper) for the simple reason that the score was one all, and our men were fresh and theirs were dead from playing a rough game. In the second half the Seasides scored the winning goal (by one of our men putting the puck in for them) just one minute before time was up. Mr. A. Tabbe, one of the timekeepers, (who is manager of the Seasides) immediately sounded the gong. I, as timekeeper, protested, but he would not listen; he would not even compromise and call it half minute. The next night we beat the Eurekas in a clean game. The Seasides arranged to play the Eurekas best 3 in 5 for championship. The first game was to be played in Halifax, Tuesday, March 4th. Both teams met, at the rink; the Seasides insisted that Martin should play, they knowing that the Eurekas had resolved never to play with or against Martin. This shows plainly that the Seasides never intended to play. Next night, March 5th, the Eurekas beat the Seasides at Dartmouth by a score of 3 to 4. The Seasides played under the name of Victorias, which team was composed of 6 Seasides (barring Martin) and 1 Victoria. The Seasides then arranged a game with us (which they never intended to play), which was to be played in Charlottetown on March 11th, but, being sure of a defeat, they canceled the game at the eleventh hour. Now, I will say one word to the Seasides: be sportsmen, and honest enough to give up all claims of the (colored) championship to the W.E. Rangers, of Charlottetown.

John T. Mills,
Champion W. E. Rangers

On April 2nd A. E. Martin would reply explaining the Sea Sides position.

Reply to West Rangers.

SPORTING ED. RECORDER: —-

In reply to a letter in your issue of the 21st from the West End Rangers in regard to their game with the Seasides, I must say on behalf of the Seasides that I think the Seasides are the only colored team that has any claim to the championship and I think the public will agree with me as there was over a thousand people seen how we won it. Mr. Mills claims that I told him that we beat them out of five minutes time in the first half, which is false; for I was not a timekeeper. Mr. Tabb was our timekeeper, and says he rang the bell on the time he got from the Ranger Time-keeper; they also spoke about us besting them in a mixture of hockey and baseball. I can't see where the baseball part comes in at, unless it was the lifting of the puck, and as far as the grievance between the Seasides and Eurekas I don't think it was any of Mr. Mills business, and it showed how much of a gentleman Mr. Mills was to take such an interest in matters that didn't concern him whatsoever. In regard to our intended trip to the Island, if we had of had our tickets forwarded to us as the Rangers had – and as they promised to do – we would have made the trip, but the tickets never came so therefore we could not to. The Rangers are like another team I know of, if they do not win every game they play, they say someone cheated or the referee was against them, but I don't blame the Rangers so much for I can understand where they got their cue from. They know more about the private business of the three colored clubs in Halifax than I or a great many others do. I wonder if the Rangers had of lost the last night game when some of the Rangers were playing with their heads tied up, if they would of considered it such a clean game. Mr. George Mills told Mr. Tabb and myself and others that he would sooner play with the Sea-Sides he would not have waited for over a month before doing so. Mr. Mills asks the Sea-Sides to be sportsmen and give up the championship to the W.E. Rangers, of Charlottetown, but the Sea-Sides have arranged different; when they are done with it they will present it to the Victorias of Dartmouth or the Eurekas.

Thanking you for so much space and assuring you I will not bother you again,

I remain,
Yours truly,
A. E. Martin.

On behalf of the Sea-Side Hockey Club.

The Rangers complaint was a valid one since the White hockey leagues prohibited a stick from coming above one's waist. The majority of the Nova Scotia Black players were also baseball players, this high sticking style of play may not have been considered unusual; instead it would most likely be viewed as natural. Martin was said to have had an incredibly hard and accurate shot. Descriptions of his play indicate that he may have been a pioneer of the slap-shot.[11]

---

[11] *This is twenty-five years before future hockey hall-of-fame player Frank "Bun" Cook introduced the slap-shot to the National Hockey League and half a century before Bernie "Boom Boom" Geoffrion and Andy Bathgate perfected it as an effective way to shooting the puck in the 1950's.*

CHAPTER TWELVE

CAKEWALK OVER THE ICE

The bitterness from the previous year would carry over to the following season. On the 20th January 1903, the Eurekas issued a challenge in the *Acadian Recorder* to the Sea-Sides to play for the championship, but this time the Sea-Sides did not respond. Their oversight to send any response to the newspaper opened the door for the Eurekas send notice to the *Acadian Recorder* a week later laying claim to the Colored Hockey League Championship by virtue of default. The Eurekas' notice read:

Failing to receive a reply to the challenge issued to the Seasides on the 20th inst., the Eurekas, of Halifax, now claim the colored amateur hockey championship of Nova Scotia, and are prepared to defend the title against any colored team in the province.

A. F. Skinner
Capt. Eurekas
Jan. 28th, 1903

Three teams came forward to challenge the Eurekas: the Truro Victorias, the West End Rangers and a newly organized team from Amherst, Nova Scotia, called the Royals, a name which, in addition to referring to monarchy, also refers to the Father, Son, and Holy Ghost (House of God).

A series of matches involving all four teams were scheduled so that a Maritime Champion could be declared and thus avoid the confusion and arguing of the previous year. The 1903 season kicked off with the Royals who would begin the season's play with the Eurekas on February 14th. Like the other hockey teams from Nova Scotia, it would be members of the Royals baseball team who primarily comprised the newly formed hockey club. In their first game they would lose 5-0 against the powerful Eureka team.

Storms delayed the West End Rangers arrival onto Nova Scotia shores by eleven days forcing the rescheduling of games. The next game would see the Eurekas playing to a tie versus the Truro Victoria's on February 24th – the final score was not reported. The day before the Rangers were to play the Eurekas, the Sea-Sides hockey team, having been shut out to the four team league due to the Martin episode of the season before, would finally issue a challenge of their own.

Seasides again challenge.

The Seaside hockey team do hereby challenge the winners of the Eurekas vs. West End Rangers game to play for the colored championship of Nova Scotia.

Albert R. Tabb, Mgr.

Despite the challenge, there would not be an official response from any team. By including the West End Rangers in the challenge, clearly a message was being sent by the Eurekas and Kinney. The Sea-Sides would not organize matches and again they would not play. On February 27th, one week after it was originally scheduled, over 400 people would attend the first game of a best-of-three series between the Eurekas and the West End Rangers. The first two games to be held in the New Exhibition Rink in Halifax with a third, if necessary, to take place in Charlottetown.

To travel between Prince Edward Island and Nova Scotia, people would take the CGS Stanley Steamer between Charlottetown and Pictou. The CGS would make daily trips unless the ice became impenetrable, forcing her to work out of Georgetown on the eastern side of the Province. Sometimes, during harsh winter weather periods when the ocean froze, the service would be stopped altogether. Iceboats became the only way to get off Prince Edward Island.

WILLS'S CIGARETTES.

Fitted with a sail and resting on three sharp steel runners, iceboats are designed to create a near frictionless contact with the surface of the ice, thus making it capable of speeds several times greater than the prevailing wind speed. Lightly built, iceboats are equipped with leather straps and iron runners on each side of the hull to allow them to be easily pulled across the ice flows and snow. These straps served a dual purpose as they are also attached to the crew, acting as a safety harness should someone fall through the ice while pushing the boat.

Iceboats did not move well over packed ice. During

particularly bad winters, numerous ice flows would clog the Northumberland Strait resulting in the boats having to be carried over several large hills of ice. The roughly fifty-one mile crossing from Charlottetown, Prince Edward Island, to Pictou, Nova Scotia, would cost four dollars per person or two dollars for those who helped the crew carry the boat.

Traveling in two iceboats, it took the Rangers seven hours to cross the strait. Once in Pictou, the team had to take a train ride of several hours to Halifax. The Rangers would lead the Eurekas 1-0 after the first half. This was truly a phenomenal feat, considering the rigors that they had to overcome just to make the game that day. According to the *Acadian Recorder*:

> *The Rangers started without [George] Mills, their regular cover, who was on a delayed train, and Stanley, their spare man, took his place during the half. It was a nip and tuck fight throughout this half, with but one score, [Albert] Mills doing the trick for the visitors after 8 minutes play.*

In the second half, George Mills finally arrived and took his place on the ice. The Eurekas replaced team Captain A. F. Skinner with George Taylor at one of the forward positions and in the second half the Eurekas began to carry the play. Thirteen minutes into the second half Gus Adams carried the puck down towards the Rangers goal, passed to his brother George who scored, tying the game at 1-1. Taylor and Tolliver would add two more goals as the Eurekas would win the first game by a score of 3-1. The next day the *Acadian Recorder* reported:

> *The Rangers are an active, fine looking crowd of men, and in their attractive uniforms presented a fine appearance on the ice. They have some fine skaters, and play a clean game, but on the whole are not as strong as the Eurekas, who have good men in every position, including some shipping lights, and who introduce some of the tactics which have made Upper Province teams formidable.*

The quality of play improved each year, a fact that did not go unnoticed by the regional press. The *Truro Daily News* wrote:

The Eurekas were jubilant over their victory, which they clearly won, proving themselves the superior team. George Adams was the star of the game; his stick handling and his speedy skating would have done credit to much more pretentious players, and he had able assistance form his brother Gus, who played in excellent form. Tolliver's high jumping acrobatic body checking was a feature, and Taylor and Skinner in both their positions played a fine game. Flint and Allison did not have much to do on the defense, but they were equal to emergencies.

The *Acadian Recorder* also recognized the quality of play:

There were four brothers on the Rangers named Mills, all good players. [Albert] was particularly smart and active, and a good skater; [Lemuel] did good work on the right wing; George at cover lifted in fine style, and checked well, while John is a very clever rover. McNeill who was in goal last year, is now one of the best of the forwards; [Edmond] Byers at point is a big fellow, a cousin of George Byers, the pugilist, and Crosby made some great stops in goal, and but for him there would have been a larger score . . . The colored teams are showing much improvement over recent years, and are playing good hockey."

The following evening the Eurekas and Rangers would play the second game of their series with approximately 300 spectators attending. This game would be a much more physical affair than the previous night. The *Acadian Recorder* reported:

During the contest there were many accidents and the game had to stop frequently while some injured player was being fixed up. In the first half George Adams of the home team was struck over the eye and his vision was so much affected that he was obligated to retire the rest of the half. In the second he came on with a bandage over the optic. Byers, and the Rangers received a severe blow on the temple during a scrimmage and he retired for ten minutes. Several other players were also slightly cut, but no one else received any severe injury . . . When the puck was faced off in the start of the game it traveled into the territory of the home team, and both sides showed much persistency. The play was very fierce and hard for over 15 minutes, each side fighting with all their strength to score the first goal. This was done by the Rangers in 16 minutes. So far most of the play was in Eurekas' ground, but after the face off the home team braced up and carried the puck to the other end of the rink and kept it there for several minutes, until finally G. Adams shot it into the net. This evened the score, and the balance of the game was very swift but without any result, and the half ended with the score standing 1 to 1.

The rough play would continue into the last half resulting in a number of delays due to injured knees and ankles as well as damaged equipment. Five minutes into the last frame the Rangers would score again taking a 2-1 lead. The Eurekas disputed the goal. According to the *Acadian Recorder:*

When only ten minutes remained another goal was scored by the visitors, but the Eurekas disputed it, claiming the referee's whistle had not been blown. The Eurekas did not make any effort whatever to stop this goal and an argument on this subject occupied a quarter of an hour. At its conclusion the Eurekas decided to continue play. They made a determined effort but only succeeded in scoring once more, making the score 4 to 2 when time was sounded.

During the half-time break, Tolliver and Flint of the Eurekas performing the *"cakewalk"* dance, on skates, entertaining the crowd.

120

The Cakewalk refers to the dance originally known as the *"Chalk Line Walk"*. Originating in Florida by African-American slaves, this form of dance became popular around 1850 on slave plantations across the American South. Over time the dance evolved into a exaggerated parody of the White, upper class ballroom figures imitating the walking, bowing, waving of canes, doffing of hats, and the high kicking grand promenade mannerisms of the master's house or *"Big House."* The Idea of the Cakewalk was that of a couple promenading in a dignified manner, high stepping and kicking, mimicking high society. The name would evolve into Cakewalk from plantation owners who baked a cake on Sundays and held a dance contest for the slaves; with the winner getting the cake. Thus the origin: *"That Takes the Cake!"* The Cakewalk would become the first dance to cross over from Black to White society and would stay popular until the 1920's.

After the game, the Eurekas entertained their hockey competition. There is no indication that the Eurekas ever traveled to Charlottetown to play the final and deciding match. A week later the Eurekas would accept a challenge from the Sea-Sides for a best of three series for the championship, the first game to take place Friday evening, March 6, in a rink to be agreed upon. None of these games were ever reported.

The final game of the 1903 season would take place between the Truro Victorias and the Amherst Royals on the Aberdeen Rink on March 7th in Amherst. It was reported as the first colored hockey game to ever be played in Amherst. The play was described as *"very exciting"* and *"very fast throughout"* with the game remaining scoreless due largely in part to the quality play of the 14 year-old Truro goaltender, James A. Clyde. The second-half would see the Truro team play improve. As reported in the *Truro Daily News*:

> *The second half the Truro boys started in to rough it and found that they were up against the real thing and after a hard fight of 15 minutes scored the first goal. The Royals then tried very hard to score but did not succeed until about 6 minutes before the time was up when [George] Ross got the puck on a pass from [Joe]*

Parsons and shot it through which made the score 1 to 1.
The Truro boys then claimed that it was no goal and the
captain called his team off the ice and would not play off
so the game was called a draw. The Victorias done
some good combination work and [James] A. Clyde in
goal made some good stops but their defensemen were
poor lifters, J. Martin their cover point was struck in the
breast with the puck and was put out for a few seconds.
L. Martin put up a star game in goal for the Royals and
so did Cook as point, H. Ross played a good game as
Cover Point and brought his man down every time. The
wings, [George] Ross and Cumming played a good
clean game and also Parsons as center, L. Lee as rover
was always after the puck and although received a sever
cut on the head with a stick finished out the game.

Later, after A. F. Skinner's arrival in 1905 as the coach of
the Royals baseball team as well as the captain of the hockey
team, the Amherst Royals baseball (and possibly the hockey
team) would replace the Eurekas as the dominant club in Nova
Scotia. Both George Ross and Joe Parson would become the
cornerstones of the 1906 and 1907 Maritime Champion Amherst
Royals baseball teams.

CHAPTER THIRTEEN

A RETURN TOUR

The Sea-Sides would begin the 1904 season by issuing a challenge for the Colored League Championship. On January 28, 1904, the Eurekas responded:

Eurekas accept.

The Eurekas, of Halifax, accept the challenge of the Seasides to play any colored hockey team in Nova Scotia. Games to be best two in three for championship. Dates and rink to be agreed upon later.
A. F. Skinner
Capt. Eurekas.

P.S — Captain Carvery can see me any evening after 7 p.m. at 146 Creighton St. to arrange details.

The Eurekas Clubhouse was located at 146 Creighton Street. Apparently no details had been finalized. On February 9th, a new team emerged and issued a challenge printed in the *Acadian Recorder.*

The "Moss Backs," of Hammond Plains are willing to take chances with the Sea-sides, and will play any agreed upon, either in Halifax on Hammond Plains.

Albert Emmerson, Captain Moss Backs.

Evidently, the confusion of who was going to play whom would be left to James Kinney to straighten out. Kinney, the League Officer of the Eurekas, would issue an announcement in the press: (The only such time that he would issue a statement publicly on behalf of the league.)

We, the Eureka hockey team, confirm our acceptance of the Seasides challenge and now challenge them or any other color hockey team in Nova Scotia for a game or series of games for the championship; time and rink to be agreed upon.

Jas. A. R. Kinney

Ultimately, Kinney would have the last word - the Sea-Sides would be playing the Eurekas. There would not be any public record of the Hammond Plains Moss Backs ever playing a game, although due to the number of Blacks living in Hammond Plains and the availability of ice, it is apparent that organized Black hockey continued in the community.

Subsequently, the Eurekas would receive a challenge from the Truro Victorias with the first of two games at the New Exhibition Rink in Halifax on February 19th. Before the game, the Victorias objected to the inclusion of two of the Mills Brothers on the Eureka roster. The Mills family had recently moved from Charlottetown to New Glasgow, Nova Scotia and no Mills brother belonged to Cornwallis Street Baptist Church in Halifax – the Eurekas home parish. Truro argued the Mills brothers could only play for one parish team, that being the one in New Glasgow (a team that would not receive any known press accounts until the 1920's). The Eurekas countered stating that Jack D. McDonald (a star in the senior league) was playing for the senior league New Glasgow and North Sydney teams. With the Victorias threatening to take the 9 o'clock Intercolonial passenger train home, the Eurekas withdrew their objections and agreed to Mills inclusion. Alex Nelson, of the Halifax Crescents officiated what was to be a rough game, a style of play that had now become a hallmark of the Colored teams. The *Acadian Recorder* wrote:

> *The Eurekas upheld the reputation of the colored hockey enthusiasts of Halifax at the New Exhibition rink last evening when they defeated the Victorias of Truro, 4-0. Two goals were made in each half. The visitors made a gallant struggle, and there was more play about the center of the rink than elsewhere, but the skating of the home team, together with their body checking, proved effective in bringing about success. About 500 spectators were present, and they were greatly amused in witnessing a game out of the ordinary style, though the delays were just as numerous as in other games. Martin, of the visitors, received a bad cut on the leg, but after repairs he continued on playing . . . Both teams did some good stick handing and displayed excellent knowledge of the rules as regards offside, but tripping, slashing, body-checking and interference were included as part of the game. They used their hockeys like chopping sticks, swinging them above their heads and bringing them down with a thud, which generally landed on the ice, but at times on somebody's shins; they bumped into each other at random, they fell again and again, but they did not seem to feel the slightest effects there from . . . Tolliver's playing was the feature, his aerial flights over the sticks of his opponents when rushing with the puck caused roars of laughter; his flying body checks brought down many an opponent, who looked with surprise at the suddenness of the shock, while he bumped into the players with much force, and in one case his shoulder reached the jaw of one of his opponents and there was almost a knockout. He was penalized only in the second half, and he was shortly afterwards again sent to the boards as he thought he was*

in a boxing match and landed on the ribs of one of his opponents. The Truro men, however, say Tolliver will not have things so much his own way tonight and they are confident they will be able to divide the honors with the Haligonians.

The following night's game would be a much closer affair. The Eurekas would play a very rough game in order to counter the Victorias superior stick handling and passing ability. The *Truro Daily News* reported that the Victorias *"are among the fastest skaters in the Province".*

Leading the way for the Eurekas was Charles Tolliver, described as *"the famous battering ram of the Eurekas, who comes with such force to butt with his head, that when he goes up in the air he comes down as if he was doing the high dive."* After the initial face-off, the puck was kept mostly in the Eurekas' territory until 8 ½ minutes into the match when George Adams, against the flow of the game, passed to Skinner who scored the first goal for the Eureka's.

The match would pair George Taylor of the Victorias against his uncle Joe Taylor of the Eurekas.

George Taylor . . . checked his uncle so hard, that when they came together like two steam engines, they would stand and look at each other as if to say, "Well, I think we have met before."

Shortly after this Joe Taylor of the Eurekas was given a two minute penalty for slashing; resulting in the Victorias scoring a power play goal tying the game at one-a-piece. Truro would take a 2-1 lead on a disputed goal as the seconds counted down to the half. The Eurekas stated the puck went into the net after the first half gong had already sounded – yet the goal stood. In a fast paced second half the Eurekas would come out carrying territorial play and trying to find the equalizer:

The Eurekas made shot after shot but the stonewall defense of Williams and [George] Clyke prevented any score. Towards the end of the half Tolliver tallied

126

another for the Eurekas by a pretty shot from center. During the remaining four minutes of play neither side was able to score, and the game ended two goals each.

The two games brought a critical response from the otherwise generally positive accounts the *Truro Daily News* had previously printed about the League:

> *. . . it is not exactly scientific, being more forcible . . . Combined with the checks used in hockey, the football tackle was used quite frequently. Sometimes the player forgot themselves for a time, and imagined they were playing baseball, swinging their sticks like bats. Then to vary the monotony, they entertained the spectators by few fistic exhibitions which were loudly applauded.*

Based on the results of the two games, the Eurekas claimed victory. The Eurekas would now enter into a best of three series with the Sea-Sides. There would be a full-page advertisement taken out on February 24th in the local *Acadian Recorder* as the game was being billed as *"a great battle for the championship"*.

The two teams had not met since the four games they played in 1901, which saw the Sea-Sides win two of four games with one draw, winning the championship. Since the Eurekas had always

127

claimed to be the better team stating they never had a chance to officially regain their title from the Sea-Sides. Since 1901 the Sea-Sides had only played one official league game, that with the West End Rangers, whom they defeated by the close score of 3-2. A day later, a second half-page newspaper advertisement would follow the first promoting the game with prices listed as 25-cents for general admission and 35-cents for balcony seats. The quality of hockey had now become among the best seen in the country.

The hockey games between the colored teams, the Eurekas and Seasides, are always fraught with interest, and about 500 people went to the North-end Rink last evening to see their meeting to decide the championship. At one time people went to see those games as a burlesque, but the members of the teams have made such improvement that the games are now good exhibitions of hockey. The Eurekas, who have recently have had the Mills Brothers of the Charlottetown West End Rangers added to their numbers are stronger than ever, and they did not have great difficulty in disposing of their opponents. The Seasides made a gallant fight; their forwards at times showed too much speed for their opponents, but they were almost always met by the Eureka's excellent defence, who cleared their goal in splendid style.

With the Eurekas entering the second half leading 2-0, the Sea-Sides would step up their game scoring two unanswered goals battling back and tying the game. The Eurekas proved to be too much scoring three straight and defeating their rival by a final of 5-3. The *Acadian Recorder* reported:

The Eurekas won fairly and without dispute. [Herbert] Allison is as good as ever in goal; [Oliver] Mills gave a splendid exhibition at point while [George] Taylor is an exceptionally good lift and by his clever work scored one of the goals. [George] Adams played his usual great game and [A. F.] Skinner is the most reliable player on

*their team, and he had his share in their scoring.
[Lemuel] "Lewis" Mills is a clever player and skater,
and his goal was one of the prettiest plays of the
evening. [Charlie] Tolliver was very quiet; he
eliminated much of his usual body checking, but he was
watchful, and he got two of the goals from one-hand
shoots. The Seasides made a fight that earned them
every credit as though beaten they were not disgraced.
[James] and Allan Dixon, with [Dick] and James
Carvery, formed a splendid forward line, who again and
again carried the puck into their opponents' territory.
[Wallace] Dixon did well at cover, while [John] Cassidy
used his body with great effect, and his opponents
regarded his prowess to such an extent that they were
quite content at times to avoid him. [William] Carvery
was not up to his standard in the first half but in the
second made many of his old-time stops.*

The second game between the Eurekas and the Sea-Sides
would take place March 3rd at the Empire Rink in Halifax.
Unfortunately, no game reports were made available. It appears
the Eurekas did not lose since they were still recognized as
champions when they set out to play three games against the
Dartmouth Jubilees in North Sydney in early March, 1904.

The tour was an attempt to expand the league's exposure and
interest among the region's population. The Eurekas and the
Jubilees traveled to Cape Breton Island for a three-game
exhibition series for the benefit of the local White and Black
populations. Realizing the significance of the event, and the
entrepreneurial nature of the series, the *Acadian Recorder* sent a
reporter to cover the series by proclaiming it as the *"first games
of hockey played in Cape Breton by Colored people."* The
newspaper proclaimed to all that the series would be well worth
the entry fee as the quality of the two squads would ensure that
the public could *"expect good sport."*

The first game was played on a Monday night at the local
arena in North Sydney with subsequent matches being played at
the downtown rink in Sydney the following two evenings. By all
accounts, the games were a great success and the White response

had been incredibly positive. Although the descriptions would be tainted with racist images and stereotypical racist descriptions, overall the teams play received favorable press.

Some Features of Last Night's Game.

Cartoon in The Sydney Post "Some Features of Last Night's Game."

Caption one: "Rooters from the Coke Ovens."
Caption two: "Johnson checks the Referee."
Caption three: "Where is the Puck?"
Caption four "The Hockey Goal Keeper."

In the first game in Sydney on March 8th a large crowd would witness the Eurekas defeat the Jubilees by a score of 5 to 4. The following night the two teams would play again with the Eurekas winning 5 to 2. *The Sydney Post* newspaper reported the game with overt racist overtones and remarks, using the words *"cullud"* and *"all coons look alike."* A racist cartoon accompanied with the article. Ironically, aside from the racist remarks (intended to humor the White readership) the quality of hockey played was not criticized but instead complimented.

*During the first half of the game the Jubilees were
putting things all over their opponents, but in the second
half the Eurekas woke up, "Babe" Tolliver and his
'bredren' settled down to work, and regardless of the
many knocks bestowed upon them, even when they were
on the shins, put up such a fast and aggressive game that
they carried everything before them. Allison, goal for
the Eurekas, put up a star game, stopping the puck in
every conceivable way, standing up or sitting down;
position was nothing to him. Lattimore, at point and
Laidlaw of the Jubilees team, was strong, while Johnson,
when not giving his attention to the fair ones, was a
good fast skater and clever stick handlers. "Baby"
Tolliver is a "hot baby" and made things warm all
around. Captain Taylor of the Jubilees, is a very
dignified gentleman and when checked fell and rose
again very gracefully. [Albert] Kelly, who despite his
name, is as Black as the next one, played center for the
Jubilees and did it work. The names of the rest of the
players have escaped us, which makes it impossible to
give them individual notice, but the game and players
were good and apart from the novelty of seeing them
play they gave the spectators good value for their
money.*

Approximately 250 people had attended the third game (in
three nights) between these two teams at the Rosalyn Rink. The
Sydney Post reported:

*the game was fast and furious in both halves . . . The
players fell all over each other, and slashed and checked
to the immense delight of the onlookers, who cheered . . .
whenever a woolly head struck the ice unnecessarily
hard.*

On that night the Jubilees managed to score late in the game
defeating the Eurekas 2-1.

After three days in Sydney the Eurekas traveled south to the
middle of the Province to play in Truro. It would be their fourth

match in four nights and the *Acadian Recorder* reported the Eurekas performance as a creditable one:

> *. . . considering that the Eurekas had played a hard game every night since last Saturday night, and had just completed a long train ride from Sydney . . . The Victorias were confident of victory, but the clean, scientific work of the Eurekas was too much for them and the Vic's rough play resulted in several of their players being penalized. For nearly 20 of the first half the teams struggled for the mastery with the puck almost continually in Victoria's territory until Skinner's swift shot glided into the net amidst the wildest excitement. Seven minutes later Skinner again scored, and the Truro supporters became disheartened. No further score was made and the half ended 2 – 0 in favor of the Eurekas. The Eurekas got two more in the second half. At the commencement of the second the Victorias played with renewed energy, and after 10 minutes' play [Alexander] Paris scored their first goal, and 10 minutes later [Marty] Martin tallied another.*

A 4-2 Eureka victory finishing their tour and returning back to Halifax.

The Colored Hockey League was now one of the best known and skilled sports organizations in Eastern Canada. In less than a decade, they had risen from obscurity to a place of prominence. Hockey was allowing the Blacks to gain social mobility and acceptance in Nova Scotia and across the Maritimes. It wasn't supposed to be this way.

CHAPTER FOURTEEN

THE DESTRUCTION OF
THE LEAGUE

The Colored League was on the rise and James Kinney was rapidly becoming one of the leading voices of Black Pride and self-determination within Nova Scotian society. Small in body stature, Kinney had developed his brain over brawn. As a child he had suffered an injury that had left him with a pronounced limp. The injury had prevented him from playing sports. Therefore, it was ironic that he would be the leader of a hockey league unlike any, before or since. He was a modern-day Achilles – a hero among his men – with a limp that displayed human frailty. Undaunted by his physical limitations, Kinney had developed reason and intelligence to a level seldom seen within Nova Scotian society. His ability to mold the English language into a sword of reason, a sword that he was now prepared to wield against all enemies of Blacks, underscored the true sense of the Black struggle in Canada and the beating heart that was the Colored Hockey League and this, the Kinnean Crusade.

That same year, when the Halifax School Board attempted to authorize the establishment of a distinctly segregated school in Halifax City, it was Kinney who went on the offensive attacking those who were the main proponents of this racially influenced form of education. In a letter to the Editor of the *Halifax Evening Mail* in 1905, Kinney demanded that the School Board reverse its attempt to segregate, arguing that the legal system of Nova Scotia had determined forty years earlier that Black children would be guaranteed as equal an education as their White Canadian brethren. In a determined and prophetic tone, he wrote:

> . . . *colored pupils shall not be excluded from instruction in the public school in the section or ward in which they reside . . . Educational authorities know quite well that colored schools in districts not a stone's throw away from the city of Halifax have been without teachers for periods as long as two years, owing to lack of them...Be careful, gentlemen, how you proceed, for history records that whenever justice has been denied and duties evaded, retribution invariably follows.*

For a Black man to threaten the White establishment called for a response. However, Kinney had powerful friends and any attempt to "put him in his place" would be met by both Black as well as White opposition. Kinney would succeed in his quest to deny the Halifax Board its efforts to instill a *"separate but equal"* policy. But his threatening tone, and his seemingly enhanced position of power within the Black community carried a cost. It is ironic that Kinney, a firm believer in Booker T. Washington's concept of separate but equal would not be in favor of its implementation in the Halifax schools. Only one explanation could account for this; Kinney believed that the Blacks of Halifax were already fully integrated within the educational system and as a result, any move to separate Blacks educationally would be tantamount to a step backwards.

During the same period, the City of Halifax moved to expropriate lands in the Africville area as part of an agreement with two powerful railroad barons. The resulting political and legal fight between the local Black residents and the City would be a pivotal point for Kinney, Johnston, and the league.

By choosing to fight the City of Halifax and the railroad land expropriation, James Johnston had made enemies far beyond Halifax. The Halifax & South Western Railway Company (HSWRC) was a subsidiary of Mackenzie, Mann & Company

Limited, one of the most powerful business entities in the Western World. A private contracting company that promoted railroad expansion on a global scale was led by two men: William Mackenzie and Donald Mann. Of Mackenzie and Mann, it was said that they were two vicious railroad barons who relied on others to do their dirty work.

In the case of the HSWRC, the task of obtaining land for the Halifax leg of the railroad had been given to the Nova Scotia Legislature and the City Council of Halifax. As early as 1901, Mackenzie, Mann had lobbied the Provincial Legislature with the idea of creating a direct railroad link between Halifax and Yarmouth, the two major ports of Nova Scotia. Yarmouth was the main terminus for goods flowing from Nova Scotia to the United States; Halifax was the chief port for the goods moving into Canada. By linking the two regions, goods could be moved across rail lines, effectively creating a multimillion-dollar financial windfall for Mackenzie, Mann. At the time Mackenzie, Mann, controlled vast stretches of railroad lines across Canada and parts of the United States. By some accounts more than 2,500 miles of track were directly under their control. From Nova Scotia, through Maine, and as far west as the Canadian province of British Columbia, Mackenzie, Mann owned large tracks of *"the right of way"* and controlled the free flow of railroad goods. The HSWRC would be the final link to the Mackenzie, Mann monopoly. As was envisioned, from the time goods arrived at port in Yarmouth or Halifax until the point of their distribution, the goods would be under the control of Mackenzie, Mann & Company Limited or one of its subsidiaries.

Not wanting to burden itself with the messy task of land expropriation, Mackenzie, Mann had stipulated early on in the discussions between themselves, the Province, and City political representatives in Halifax that it would be the responsibility of the Provincial Legislature and City of Halifax officials to ensure that land was made available for the railroad. Both political groups agreed and pledged their guarantee that once construction entered the final stages of completion along the Halifax stretch of the rail line, the necessary land would be afforded to the HSWRC. The problem facing the Halifax politicians was how to get the land without having to pay for it. Most of the land needed for the HSWRC was located along the coastline running west from South Halifax through Africville and out towards Bedford.

From 1901 to 1905, Mackenzie, Mann & Company worked to buy up all the independent railroads in Nova Scotia to prevent outside railroad competition ensuring a complete railroad monopoly across Nova Scotia.

The first major acquisition for Mackenzie, Mann was the Nova Scotia Central Railroad. Purchased in the summer of 1902, the line linked the communities of Middleton and Lunenberg. The cost of this stretch of track was not cheap. The company paid $525,000 for the route – a tremendous amount of money and evidence as to the amount of funds Mackenzie, Mann were prepared to spend in order to achieve their goals. Nine months later, the company acquired the Nova Scotia Southern Railway, a company that existed only on paper but controlled a twenty-mile section of undeveloped right of way near Lunenberg. Two years later, Mackenzie, Mann would acquire both the Victoria Beach Railway Company and the Halifax & Yarmouth Railway Company, paying a combined $1 million for both. Subsequently the company would purchase the Liverpool & Milton Railroad, effectively completing their quest for regional control.

It was widely reported that William Mackenzie and Donald Mann took a special interest in their Nova Scotia acquisitions, traveling across the province in their private train coach to meet with area politicians and reviewing their vast fiefdom of iron rail and ties.

William Mackenzie was born in 1849 in Kirkfield, Ontario. Prior to his railroad career he had been a schoolteacher. In the early years of the Canadian Pacific Railroad's (C.P.R.) expansion across Canada he had worked as a railroad contractor. His leadership abilities and intelligence had ensured him success early on, allowing him access to key officials associated with the C.P.R. In 1886, along with Donald Mann, a former lumberman from Acton, Ontario, he had formed Mackenzie, Mann & Company Limited in order to secure railroad contracts for the construction of regional rail lines across Canada and the United

States. Within a decade, these two men had achieved incredible success and were household names across Canada.

Mackenzie understood the role of power and privilege and he worked hard to ensure that any controversy associated with his railroad endeavors were swept under the rug and never given public exposure. In order to secure this he purchased the *La Press Newspaper* chain then the largest newspaper chain in Canada. His company's close association with other papers guaranteed that negative press was kept to a minimum, ensuring that his opponents were never given a platform to vent their accusations. So successful were these dealings of William Mackenzie and Donald Mann that King George V knighted them both in 1911, effectively making them the Canadian equivalent of royalty.

Rather than compensate the Black residents of Halifax, the City chose to argue that the Blacks had no legal claims to the property and as such would not be awarded any compensation for lands taken. Seven properties, owned by John Brown, Walter Thomas, Alex Carvery and William Carvery, were of interest to the City and were slated to be seized. But the men, with the help of Johnston and Kinney, petitioned both the City Council as well as the Courts, seeking a halt to construction and a negotiated settlement. The City refused to halt their efforts leaving Johnston to move forward on his own through the courts. It would be a battle which lasted five years as the City and its attorneys worked to draw out the case and to undercut the will and financial strength of Johnston and the Black community. Johnston was forced to carry the financial burden almost entirely by himself as he was determined to legally prove the land claims of the men and to defeat the City and its legal cronies at their own game.

More than ever before, Johnston was carrying a larger burden of responsibility as he equated himself with Black associations and ongoing Black social and political issues. The death of Peter McKerrow from Tuberculosis on December 22, 1906 only compounded his commitments and obligations. Johnston succeeded McKerrow as Secretary of the African Baptist Association Nova Scotia, becoming a major force behind the scenes in Baptist Church Congregational dealings. At the

137

same time Johnston became a Master Mason of the local Black Freeman's Lodge. There was no middle ground for Johnston and the strain apparently began to affect his marriage.

Halifax railyard looking northward towards Africville with Dartmouth across the harbor.

As for the lawsuit against the City, what made the situation even more intriguing was that a number of the men Johnston was representing were high profile players of the Colored League – men well known in the community. Their willingness to take on City Hall caused a ripple effect and a series of subtle "paybacks" began as the City and its supporters worked to undercut the Black opposition. The first casualty from this backlash would be their league.

The teams no longer received ice time. When they finally did, it was not until conditions were so poor that the ice was virtually unplayable. With no ice-time, there was no coverage. Challenges between teams would no longer be printed, and if any games did occur, the results of matches were no longer recorded for the public record. No longer would a value be placed on the Colored Hockey League. Immediately following the peak of its success, the league would receive no press in

1905 and only one reference in 1906, the lone reference being a match between the Eurekas and the Jubilees played at the Empire Rink on March 29th of that year. Posters were made advertising Charles Tolliver and the Eurekas but the game would be poorly attended with only about 100 people in the stands. It would be reported that the game was *"not as interesting as usual between the colored teams"*. Pools of water on the ice resulted in the players becoming drenched while the spectators *"had to keep dodging to escape shower baths"* from the leaking roof. Tolliver would play as advertised making some end-to-end rushes while also performing his infamous *"flying body check"* on opponents, but the poor ice conditions slowed the game and dampened the quality of play. The Eurekas would defeat the Jubilees by a final score of 3-2.

During the same period, "The Pride of Africville," George Dixon, retired from the boxing ring after losing a 15-round decision to Monk Newsboy on October 12, 1906. Two years later, Dixon was found near death in a New York alley wearing only his boxing trunks. Apparently Dixon, in financial difficulty, had been training for a comeback. It appears that he was forcibly locked out of a downtown boxing gym during a bitterly cold evening and thrown into an exit-less alleyway. The circumstances leading up to this incident are unknown. Punching doors until his hands were bloodied, no one responded to his cries for help. Left to die in a frozen New York City alley, Dixon, when finally discovered, was non-responsive and was rushed to hospital. He was pronounced dead of exposure on January 9, 1909, at the age of thirty-eight. Ironically, he had died within blocks of where his ancestors had departed New York a century earlier during the Black Loyalist evacuation to Nova Scotia. Like Dixon, the Colored League now found itself outdoors. Its enemies also expected it to die a slow death.

Except for two brief mentions in the Truro newspaper 1910 and 1911, the league and its games would not be covered again until after World War One. Just as in the 1880's, the teams would be playing back on the ponds with little public notice.

Aside from effectively killing the league, economic repercussions also began to occur. The hiring of Blacks for City jobs was curtailed and employment preferences shifted to the hiring of foreign emigrants to work jobs traditionally earmarked for Blacks. This overt act became so evident that it caused some within the White community to speak out on behalf of displaced Black workers. In a letter dated February 26, 1906, William Roche, the manager of Roche's Wharf in Halifax wrote to City Hall:

I beg to suggest that you manifest your interest in them (the Blacks), which you often expressed, by instructing your Foreman of Works to employ the colored men when they offer to work; and to give to them a preference over those who are not citizens, and who pay no taxes in Halifax.

Roche's letter was politely ignored. The last thing the City Fathers wish to do was strengthen Black economics and resolve. At the same time, in order to weaken the resolve of the petitioning Black hockey players, the City appears to have moved in the shadows to ensure that the men and their teams would be denied ice time at the area arenas; effectively preventing the sale of tickets and a regular income and wage for the men. This move meant the league would be forced to operate on the lakes and ponds throughout Halifax County. The economic ability of Black men to provide food for their families was now in question. The City, if they could not steal the land outright, was prepared to starve the Blacks and their families into submission. The screws of the City Council were turning and the Blacks of Halifax were in its vice.

By 1907 the assault on Black economic businesses had shifted from individual merchants to an attack on the whole Black community. The Health Department, at the urging of unnamed White businessmen, announced an effort to put an end to the Halifax Green Market, a tradition that had existed for well over one hundred and twenty years. The Market, the economic life of both local Blacks and Mi'kmaq Indians, was said to be in violation of Health Department codes (codes rarely enforced) prohibiting the sale of food on sidewalks. Blacks and Mi'kmaqs would now have to buy "vendor stalls" at a new White controlled market house being built. Many of the Blacks and

Native Indians objected publicly to the closure believing that the move was a deliberate attempt to drive them out of business or steal their profits. Leading the fight for the Green Market closure were the editors and owners of the *Halifax Herald Newspaper* – a company long said to be anti-Black.

When the new market opened in 1908 a number of Black farmers refused to vacate the Green Market. They were subsequently removed by force from the street – their goods seized. The last vestige of Black enterprise was effectively crushed. From 1908 on, the economic options open to Black area farmers was limited as they were forced to sell their goods through the White controlled new market cooperative.

By 1910, it was becoming apparent that anti-Black sentiment was on the rise across Canada. In that year, Prime Minister Sir Wilfred Laurier stated: *"We see in the United States what grave problems may arise from the presence of a race unable to become full members of the same social family as ourselves."*

His sentiments were echoed a year later in the Canadian House of Commons during open debates on the question of whether or not limitations should be imposed on Black immigration into Canada. As one Member of Parliament stated: *"Would it not be preferable to preserve for the sons of Canada the lands they propose to give to Niggers?"*

In the Province of Alberta, home to a small Black settlement population, anti-Black politicians described Blacks as *"a possible menace to the supremacy of the White race."* Later, additional calls for a *"White's only"* Canada would claim: *"Eskimos don't live in the tropics so why should Negros live in Canada?"* Some Canadian writers pondered the question: *"Are we in Canada to intermarry and become a mongrel race?"*

In the face of such hatred, men such as Kinney and Johnston continued to press on in their efforts to afford change, opportunity, and acceptance for their fellow Blacks. Only now, every step was an uphill battle.

CHAPTER FIFTEEN

BETWEEN LOSS AND SUFFERING

Following the July 1900 Pan-African Conference, Henry Sylvester Williams journeyed to Jamaica and Trinidad in an effort to gain support for a Pan-African Association. His success in London had given him local celebrity status and many turned out in Jamaica and Trinidad to hear him speak. Upon his return to London, Williams continued his legal studies, establishing a monthly newsletter entitled *The Pan-African*, which existed for only six months. The pressures of laws school and family prevented him from working full-time on the newsletter.

In 1902, following graduation he moved his family to Cape Town, South Africa, becoming that nation's first Black attorney. His presence created a public scandal in Cape Town and he was the subject of scorn and White boycotts. Within three years he and his family would return to London. In 1906, he entered politics and won a seat on London's Marylebone Borough Council making him the first Black man elected to public office in England. Two years later he moved his family to Trinidad where he resumed his legal career.

At his return he was thirty-nine years of age and the father of four children. His wife continued to be the talk of the social elite who saw in her the worst qualities of White womanhood. A quiet woman, she continued to keep her sorrow hidden and remained firm in her loyalty to Williams.

In 1910, Williams represented James Wallace, a man who had been accused of impersonating a police officer. Wallace had discovered a young girl and her fiancé engaged in sexual intercourse at a local park. He told the couple that he was a police officer and proceeded to arrest the girl for indecent exposure. A short time later Wallace forced the girl to engage in sex with him telling her that he would arrest her if she did not agree to his demands. The Court had found Wallace's defense weak and sentenced him to six years imprisonment.

The writer J.R. Hooker in his book *Henry Sylvester Williams: Imperial Pan-Africanist* describes Wallace as *"unsavory, and possibly unbalanced."* It seems apparent that the case was troubling and Wallace blamed Williams for his sentence. A short time later Williams' health began to deteriorate, once even collapsing in Court. Over the months his health continued to decline. Unable to resume his legal practice, and with the family finances exhausted from expensive hospital stays, Williams was admitted to the Port of Spain Colonial Hospital on March 25, 1911. A day later he died in his sleep. He was 42. The cause of his death was undetermined.

At the time of Williams' death no one fully contemplated the impact he had on Black culture and history. In *The Bible, The Book of Psalm Versus 1 to 3* it is written: *"And he shall be like a tree planted by the rivers of water, that bring forth his fruit in his season; his leaf also shall not whither, and whatsoever he doeth shall prosper."* No greater words could sum up the life of Henry Sylvester Williams.

Given the events surrounding the Wallace trial, and the sudden decline in Williams' health, foul play should not be ruled out. Williams' declining health and symptoms were similar to those afflicting someone suffering from cyanide poisoning. Administered in a small dosage, the poison would cause a gradual shutting down of one's body. Was Williams murdered? We will never know. What is known, however, is that besides Wallace, many would have had reason to see Williams dead as he represented a symbol of Black Pride and determination in the face of White bigotry.

Williams left behind his wife, Agnes, and five children. The family was destitute. In order to survive they were forced to sell off most of Williams' personal and business belongings. Friends urged Agnes to place the children in an orphanage and return to England. She refused. In order to survive the family sold their home. In time they moved into a modest residence and took in boarders in order to pay expenses. Added income came from the canning of fruit and the sale of preservatives that the family sold to local businesses or in the public market. Agnes appears to have held on to her family until they were old enough to be on their own.

One of the most intriguing aspects of Williams' death is its timing and place of occurrence. In 1911 Trinidad was a major port of trade for vessels from Halifax. Was Williams the victim of a payback? Did someone recognize him from his time in Halifax and arrange for his murder? We do not have any evidence of correspondence between Williams and James Kinney nor with James Johnston. This lack of communication appears odd given the three men's earlier association and similar career paths. By 1911 James Johnston started to carry a gun for his own protection. When word of Williams's death reached Halifax, did Johnston fear that he was next?

It is more than a coincidence that at the same time that the Blacks, led by Johnston, were winning their legal fight in Court for reparations against the City and HSWRC, a number of businesses owned by Whites - Whites who had been the major critics or business competitors of Blacks - burned to the ground. On the evening of January 12th someone started a fire in the interior of the Halifax Herald Newspaper Building - a newspaper long known for its elitist White perspective and anti-Black sentiment. At the same time, the Cragg Building on Barrington Street, home to the Cragg Bros. Hardware store - a store opened in 1889 and had been one of the main reasons for the failure of the Thomas family hardware, was gutted. The Barnstead and the Sutherland Buildings also went up in flames. Were the Blacks sending a message to area Whites? Was this "an eye for an eye," a payback for Williams' death and other past events?

Four White-owned buildings to go up in flames almost simultaneously would require an orchestrated group effort. If it were the work of Blacks it would have been an effort organized either on Gottingen Street or out in Africville. If this was payback, then who better to accomplish this task than members of the Colored League -- men who had had their league destroyed, lands stolen, and business enterprises crushed at the hands of Whites. On January 12, 1912, someone had sent the White Elite of Halifax a message. The message: *"Burn Us - We Burn You!"*

Though Johnston and the Black families at Africville had won their court battle for land compensation, the resulting settlement had been such that it failed to cover the legal expenses incurred. Johnston had defeated the most talented attorneys that the City could muster. Yet the victory, though emotionally satisfying, rang hollow.

In the five years that Johnston had battled the City and HSWRC he had been forced to sink everything he had financially into the fight. At the same time, he had continued to act as the local moneyman for Black relatives and in-laws in need. People who had constantly tugged at his purse-strings expecting something for nothing, assuming that he could afford to give it, failed to recognize that the candle could only burn from both ends for so long. By 1912, having been the savior of the Blacks, Johnston was now being criticized and defaced by these same people who accused him of being nothing more than a slumlord on account of his failure to maintain the properties left him by his aunt; properties that he rented to local Blacks at levels far below rates charged by Whites. Nobody seemed to associate Johnston's generosity with his inability to maintain the properties. How many Black families could claim that Johnston had evicted them from his buildings, even when they failed to pay their rent? None! How many times had those who had been given funds by Johnston promising to pay him back kept their word? Few!

Ironically, following Johnston's legal and moral victory over the City he was approached to work on behalf of the Intercontinental Railroad to represent them. It was a major development in Johnston's career but it was also a burden that created an unexpected circumstance. The Intercontinental Railroad accused some of its employees of theft and wanted to set an example. The majority of those accused happened to be Black laborers and Johnston was placed in an unenviable situation of leading the Intercontinental legal assault against the men. Was he set up? Was this an attempt by Mackenzie, Mann and others to discredit Johnston? Johnston's selection was not by chance. By prosecuting Black railroad employees Johnston was suddenly suspected by certain groups within the Black community. The pressure affected him and he began to drink heavily. By early 1915 his marriage was suffering and in an attempt to save it he took his wife on a vacation to the United States. During his absence, his wife's' brother, Harry Allen, was asked to watch the home. Allen had been boarding with James and his wife so the request did not appear to be unusual. When the Johnston's returned they discovered Harry had been entertaining his girlfriend in their home and the woman had spent a number of nights sleeping over. Angered by the actions of her brother, Janie began to argue with him.

For the next month tensions between Harry Allen and the Johnstons continued to build. Arguments between Janie and Harry were frequent and James often came home to a house in turmoil. On the evening of March 3, 1915 the verbal insults reached a crescendo following a vicious argument during dinner. Harry Allen stormed out of the kitchen and went upstairs. James Johnston remained at the dinner table playing solitaire while his wife washed the dishes. When Harry returned he had James' revolver in his hand. Among the last words spoken by James Johnston were *"My God, Harry, don't shoot me!"* Seconds later bullets shattered Johnston's skull.

In his book *Bluenose Justice,* Dean Jobb describes what happened next:

> *Three bullets hit Johnston in the head; powder burns around the wounds suggest the gun was fired at point blank range. Bleeding from his wounds, Johnston was still able to chase Allen outside. They scuffled on the lawn of the house next door before Allen fired a fourth bullet into Johnston's head, killing him. A neighbour finally tackled Allen, who was in such a fit of rage that he was strangling the corpse . . . Allen fled the scene before the police and coroner arrived but was back within the hour. "I am the man you are looking for," he*

146

announced to Detective Frank Hanrahan. Later, on the
way to the police station, Allen was told Johnston was
dead. "My God," he said. "What have I done? What
has come over me?"

The most successful Black man in Nova Scotian history was dead. He was thirty-nine.

During James Johnston's funeral an estimated 10,000 Haligonians, White and Black, lined the streets to watch his coffin pass, and to pay final respect. At Allen's trial the defense attempted to spare the young man from a death sentence by arguing that his actions had been in self-defense. The surprise witness for Harry would be Johnston's wife, Janie. In order to save her brother from the gallows she helped concocted a story claiming that James had been an abusive husband, and had threatened Allen on numerous occasions. Though Janie and her statements subsequently saved her brother from death, they also painted such a vile picture of Johnston that his reputation would be destroyed for decades. Not until the late 1980's, after historians took the time to carefully re-examine the life of Johnston did a more truthful and positive assessment of the man emerge. Allen was subsequently sentenced to life in prison; he would serve fourteen years before being paroled. He would live out his final years in Toronto where he died in 1935. Today at Dalhousie University there is an endowment in memory of Johnston.

CHAPTER SIXTEEN

KINNEY'S CRUSADE

With the death of Johnston, Kinney was left to move forward on his own. With few allies in Halifax he turned his attention out of the province, attempting to gain the support of Black leaders interested in the establishment of a home for Black orphans—an institution which would serve as a legacy to Johnston. Again, we do not have all the facts pertaining to Kinney's efforts during this period. However, one startling discovery is a partial record of correspondence which exists between James Kinney and Booker T. Washington, dating from the fall of 1915. It is apparent from the surviving correspondence that Kinney had traveled at one point to Boston, Massachusetts where he had met with Washington. Subsequently, Booker T. "unofficially" traveled to Halifax, Nova Scotia, where Kinney and his wife entertained the couple.

Dr. Booker T. Washington
c/o The PARKER House
Boston, Mass.

September 16th 1915

Dear Mr. Washington:

I enclose the six programmes as you asked me, I have had so many calls for them as Souvenirs that the supply is now exhausted.
I am sending you also six newspapers which contain a pleasing report. Trusting you and party had a pleasant return trip homeward, or perhaps I should say to Boston. I remain

Respectfully yours.

Jas. A.R. Kinney (signature)

PS. I did not get a chance to ask you for the pamphlets, etc. I handed you for your inspection during the address. I Prize these very highly, please send them to me.

Dr. Washington:
Do you know where these pamphlets are?

From James A. R. Kinney
Halifax, N.S. Sep. 24, 1915

Dear Dr. Washington: I thank you for your letter of the 18th inst., and much appreciate your kindness in returning my pamphlets, and your recent publications which will be read with intense interest.

I do not wish to bore you with details of my life, but let me say this much: My father died when I was 2 ½ years old, and at my most impressionistic age, between 15 and 18, I began to read of you, and I treasure these pamphlets because they taught me the rules of the game of success in life —

1st That it made no difference what color you were, if you could deliver the goods when opportunity arrived.

2nd Dip down your bucket among the White men you know, and who know you.

Now Dr. I am striving to live by these rules, never allowing, if possible, a White man to surpass me in knowledge of my business, and while I have not achieved greatness, I am travelling on the upward way.

I am anxious that you should full realize how you have touched by life, and while I have not been Tuskegee trained, I feel I am one of her products. Yours very respectfully,

Jas. A.R. Kinney

October 11, 1915

Mr. James A.R. Kinney
42 Kings Place
Halifax, N.S.
My dear Mr. Kinney:

    By this mail, I am taking the liberty of sending you a copy of one of my books. "Up From Slavery" which I hope you will find time to read.

    I am deeply interested in the details contained in your letter of September 24th of your life, which I have read with interest. It is a great satisfaction to know that perhaps my own words and actions have had some influence in helping you to become a success in life.

    Let me thank you and all of your friends there again and again for your great and unexpected kindness to Ms. Washington, the party that was with me, and myself during our brief visit to Halifax. It was entirely a surprise to us.

    I very much hope that you will be able to connect yourself in the future with our Negro Business League and cooperate with us in every way possible.

    I am writing our good friend the Secretary today.

Yours very truly,
Booker T. Washington
(Signature)

In 1916, Kinney would put his beliefs to practice when he again battled the City of Halifax, this time protesting the placement of a racist sign in the window of a City Government building in full view of the Citizen's Public Market. The sign read: *"For Colored People Only – Free Lunch Today."* Kinney had seen this as a slight to the Black farmers who had brought their wares to the market for sale. He also saw this as an attempt to separate the Blacks from the Whites, implying, in a time of War and forced rationing, that the Blacks were receiving preferential treatment over other Canadians. In a rare move, the Mayor of Halifax personally ordered the sign taken down, later apologizing publicly to Kinney assuring him that the sign *"was placed without his orders, and . . . (such as display) . . . would never happen again."*

Such was the public power of Kinney and the respect that he generated.   Within the White community Kinney was seen as the "kingpin" of the Black cause. Within the Black community he was seen as a "perfectionist," determined to force all those around him to live by and be accountable to his same high standards.

On October 26, 1917, ten days before the tragic Halifax Explosion, the Home for Colored Children opened near Campbell Road.   An anonymous editorial had appeared in the *Acadian Recorder*. Though the editorial had not been signed, it bore all of the hallmarks of a Kinney letter. It read:

> *The wealth of a nation is its child life, so that the conservatism of its youth becomes a prime matter of great importance and especially so at this present world upheaval when so much of its real manhood is being sacrificed in the cause of human freedom. It is our duty to see that all the children, who are to be the men and women of the future, be given a fair start in life. A thrifty, intelligent and law-abiding neighbor is a greater asset to the community than a worthless dependent, regardless of his race or creed. With this as the guiding motive, this Home is*

*established and on these principles its founders
and friends appeal for active sympathy and kind
consideration on the part of a generous public.*

Determined that the Nova Scotia School for Colored
Children would establish itself as a permanent institution, carved
from beaded sweat and the callused hands of Black Canadians
and their non-Black allies, Kinney moved to take his crusade
national, arranging for a series of public notices to be placed in a
number of Canadian newspapers. The Kinnean Crusade had
come too far to stop now. He was within reach of the "Promised
Land", a land that he alone would shape. No longer would
Kinney allow another Black child to experience the pain that he
had endured as a fatherless child. No longer would he allow a
Black child's tears to go unanswered. No longer would he allow
anyone to ignore the plight of the underprivileged. He would be
the voice in the Canadian wilderness. He would be the leader of
the forgotten. And most importantly, for all the children, he
would be the father that he had never known; the man that his
father would have wanted him to be.

**Kinney and the
Child Care staff
out front of the
Home for Coloured
Children.**

**Photo courtesy
Black Cultural
Centre for Nova
Scotia.**

That year, Kinney made a written appeal to the citizenry of
Nova Scotia and the Canadian Dominion. He wrote:

153

I ask you to help support the Home for Colored Orphans and Neglected Children because responsible citizenship entails duties and obligations as well as rights and privileges. When my race or any other group of the community demands equality of citizenship they must be prepared to render the same service that other citizens render. We must make our contribution toward the public good in some form or other just as the other members of the community do.

Years later, with the successful relocation and reopening of the Home, Kinney subsequently quit his job at William Stairs, Son and Morrow Ltd. to concentrate full-time on the needs of the orphaned children. It soon became a family affair as Kinney's wife, daughter and later his son took over parts of the daily operations, allowing James the opportunity to act more in a supervisory role in than that of a staff member.

By the late 1920's The Stairs Company begun phase out of the hardware business and to concentrate on the sale of heavy machinery used in construction. By the late 1950's the company had moved from its location on Lower Water Street, a building it had occupied for 149 years, to a new facility up on Kempt Road, one more suitable for the housing of large tractors and other heavy machinery. The company would also change its name to that of the Nova Scotia Tractor & Equipment Ltd., effectively eliminating any visible reference to its past. Today, few realize the proud legacy of Nova Scotia Tractors; the company is seen as a major construction enterprise in the province and nothing more. Gone are the days when it was seen as a radical business beacon of social progress, a "safe house" for Kinney; a business run by a powerful family who refused to bend to outside pressures or deny the Black man a prominent position and voice. Time has a tendency to hide the past, to cover up records of events from long ago. Nova Scotia Tractor is a case in point.

During the time of Johnston's death and Kinney's correspondence with Booker T. Washington, war had begun to be waged in Europe. With thousands of Black Canadians fighting overseas, Kinney used the conflict as a backdrop in the a struggle for equality, along with lecturing on responsibilities that all men, regardless of race, have to bestow upon themselves in society. In 1918, while addressing the 65th Meeting of the African United Baptist Association, Kinney, by now a seasoned warrior in the struggle for Black equality, wielded his sword again exclaiming both his, and perhaps also the Colored Hockey League's, motto:

I will in all these ways aim to uplift my race, so that to everyone bound to it by ties of blood, it shall become a bond of ennoblement, and not a byword of reproach.

He continued reading to the assembled delegation a copy of a speech from the Dean of the College of Liberal Arts at Harvard University:

I will never bring disgrace upon my race by any unworthy deed or dishonorable act. I will live a clean, decent, manly life, and will ever respect and defend the virtue and the honor of womanhood. I will uphold and obey the just laws of my country and of the community in which I live, and will encourage others to do likewise. I will not allow prejudice, injustice, insult or outrage to cover my spirit or sour my soul, but will ever preserve the inner freedom of honor and conscience. I will not allow myself to be overcome of evil, but will strive to overcome evil by good. I will endeavor to develop and exert the best powers within me for my personal improvement, and will strive increasingly to quicken the sense of racial duty and responsibility. I will in all these ways aim to uplift my race, so that to everyone bound to it by ties of blood, it shall become a bond of ennoblement, and not a byword of reproach.

Later, on the question of Black Canadians and their increasing numbers within the ranks of the Canadian Army Overseas, Kinney said:

White, Black, and Red, are now going "over the top" in a splendid union of patriotism and loyalty which

155

inculcates its own lesson. There is also a degree of generosity mingled with its devotion, for the red man looks back to the wrongs unredressed, and the Black man cannot yet be said to have entered fully into the heritage of the square deal which the nations are pledged to give to all their citizens. Yet the men of both races have flung aside their grievances to share whole-heartedly in a struggle, which is to remake the world for all races. If this be a pledge, as it certainly is, that we may count on the unflattering allegiance of Black men and Red Men for all time to come, it should ensure to both a rightful place in that wider democracy and ample justice which are to be ushered in after the war – an acknowledgment of Heaven's Eternal Law, the Fatherhood of God, and the Brotherhood of Mens.

CHAPTER SEVENTEEN

A BATTALION OF FORGOTTEN SOLDIERS

For all their ties to the empire, Canadians for the most part paid little attention to the political and military developments taking place in Europe. The Old Continent was an ocean away, and though Canadian foreign policy was inextricably bound to and mandated by the British government, few in Canada grasped of the consequences of such a political reality. Europe was in political ferment by 1914. Germany continued to flex its political muscle, looking for an opportunity to increase its influence and power. Britain watched the German actions with increasing alarm and her concern was made manifest when on Sunday, June 28, 1914, Archduke Franz Ferdinand, the heir to the Austrian throne, and his wife, were assassinated by a Serbian nationalist during a visit to Sarajevo.

Convinced that the Serbian government was behind the assassination, Germany seized upon the opportunity to urged the Austrians to take an aggressive stance, promising them full military support should the Serbs fail to acquiesce to Austrian demands and make reparations for the murders. The Austrian demands were harsh, and the Austrian Government secretly believed the Serbs would never accept them. Both Austria and Germany knew war was inevitable as both countries had an agenda beyond recompense for the assassinations. Austria needed a military victory to bolster its aging empire, which was on the verge of collapse. Germany had eyes upon the territories it could gain by force of arms. With Russia and France promising to aid Serbia should a military conflict occur, the stage was set for what was to become the bloodiest and most devastating war in history. On August 4, the German Army moved against Serbia's allie France by invading via neutral Belgium. Britain and her Empire, as treaty guarantors to Belgium neutrality, were drawn into the escalating conflict following Germany's refusal to withdraw.

The war, many said, would be over in six months. For its part, the British War Office in London had asked the Canadian Government to supply them with 10,000 troops -- ample men to meet the expected needs. Eager to impress, Canada instead promised 25,000, an impressive commitment given the fact Canada's full-time army numbered only 3,110 men.

Recruitment began immediately. Within a month, following a very successful recruiting drive, one hundred troop trains were on the move across the country loaded with high- spirited young volunteers in search of travel and adventure. Their destination was Valcartier, Quebec, a new military camp specifically organized to house the anticipated 25,000 troops. Upon arrival, and to the pleasure of the Canadian commanders overseeing the task, 32,655 men were counted. Within two months, the first contingent of the Canadian Expeditionary Force (C.E.F.) was sailing to England in the largest convoy of men ever to cross the Atlantic. In total, 30,617 men, 7,697 horses, 127 field guns and other equipment had been loaded onto 30 ships.

December saw the first Canadian troops crossing the English Channel and landing in France. By February 1915 the complete First Canadian Division had landed and given brief trench warfare training, then assigned to a four-mile line of trenches in the Armentieres Sector. By now the war had ground to a halt with a horrendous number of casualties claimed on both sides. Defensive zones dominated a six hundred-mile front of trenchworks, barbed wire and gun emplacements -- a seemingly impregnable killing ground of destruction, mud, and death.

In mid-April, Belgian sources in Ghent informed the French that the Germans had placed a rush order for *"20,000 mouth protectors to protect men against the effects of asphyxiating gas.*" The Belgians feared that the Germans were preparing for an all-out gas attack and assault along the trenches opposite the German 26th Reserve Corps -- an area held by Algerian troops of the French African Light Infantry and the Canadian First Division. The French had concluded, without further investigation, that the idea of gas warfare was absurd and that the Germans, fearful of the consequences of such actions would never dare use gas. The French inaction was one of the greatest blunders of the war, leading to one of the most crucial battles in history.

On April 22, following an intense artillery bombardment, the German 26th Corps released 60 tons of chlorine gas into a light northeast wind blowing south over the Allied trenches near the Armentieres Sector. The thick clouds of yellow-green chlorine - fifteen feet high - drifted over the trenches blocking out the sun, and killing every man in its path. In the panic, two entire French colonial divisions dissolved as the Algerian and French defenses crumbled, and troops fled in horror. In their wake they left behind a gaping 4-mile-wide hole in the Allied lines exposing the Allied flank and leaving the road to Paris virtually undefended. As the German advance moved forward, it threatened to sweep behind the Canadian trenches and encircle fifty thousand British and Canadian troops. Canadian field commanders, in desperation, ordered their men to close the gap and initiated a series of counterattacks against the enemy advance. What happened next was one of the most dramatic moments ever recorded in the annals of war. Canadian troops, outnumbered ten to one, walked unprotected towards the mountain of gas clouds and the hidden German enemy, effectively becoming the first army in modern history to bear the brunt of a chemical warfare attack.

With no protection from the deadly gas, the Canadian troops used whatever they could to cover their mouths and faces, the most common solution being handkerchiefs soaked in water or human urine. Already dire, there appeared no conceivable way the situation could get worse - yet it did. The Ross rifles that the Canadians were issued continuously jammed when engaged in rapid fire. With a useless weapon, the Canadians were forced to face the German advance with little more than bare hands and bayonets. Eleven thousand Canadians advanced into the gas clouds -- six thousand died. Of the five thousand who were to survive the first round, it is estimated that one-third had been forced to abandon their rifles during the heat of the battle.

The Germans had not expected the Canadian action. Because of the fierce Canadian resolve the German advance was temporarily halted as the German commanders, unable to gauge the battle, assumed that they were facing a greater force than was the case. Regrouping two days later, they tried again. Once more the gas came, once more the Canadians held. The Germans were dumbfounded. Their commanders could not explain the actions of the enemy. Who were these men?

On May 7, 1915, three weeks after the infamous Battle of Ypres, word of the German sinking of the passenger ship RMS Lusitania with a loss of 1,195 lives reached the Canadian troops. Among the victims were one hundred Canadian women and children en route to England to be with their husbands and fathers who were serving in the Canadian Expeditionary Force. Though the world's attention had been concentrated on the loss of American lives and the impact the sinking had on U.S. and German relations, the slaughter of the Canadian civilians only hardened the Canadian troops' resolve, in the end ensuring that for the duration of the war, the German soldier's greatest and most feared enemy would be the Canadian soldier. Later in his War Memoirs, British Prime Minister David Lloyd George summed up the hatred between the Canadian and German troops by stating: *"Whenever the Germans found the Canadian Corps coming into line they prepared for the worst."*

Not all of the volunteers rushing to the Canadian Expeditionary Force recruitment centers were White. Thousands of Native Canadian Indians as well as thousands of Black men were among the throngs of recruits. In the case of Native Indians most were accepted with little fanfare. As for the Blacks, however, acceptance into a regiment would depend on the attitude of the recruitment offices. Some regiments in the provinces of New Brunswick, Alberta, and British Columbia accepted Blacks with no questions asked. Others registered the men as Indians in order to avoid a White backlash. In the case of Blacks in Nova Scotia, however, those in rural communities had a greater chance of being accepted than in major centers such as Halifax, as the rural units had a smaller base of recruits to draw from. Regardless, in the early stages of the war White Canadians were not the only Canadians fighting in Europe.

On Prince Edward Island and in and around Charlottetown, where Whites had lived side-by-side with Blacks, and where interracial marriages existed, Black recruits were accepted into the Canadian military ranks. In Halifax, doors were closed and area Blacks were forced to sit out the first wave of recruitment.

On November 6, 1914 Arthur Alexander, a Black attorney, originally from the United States and living in North Buxton, Ontario, wrote Sir Sam Hughes, the Minister of Militia and Defense, in Ottawa:

Dear Sir:

The colored people of Canada want to know why they are not allowed to enlist in the Canadian militia. I am informed that several who have applied for enlistment in the Canadian expeditionary forces have been refused for no other apparent reason than their color, as they were physically and mentally fit.

Thanking you in advance for any information that you can and will give me in regards to this matter I remain yours respectfully, for King & Country.

Arthur Alexander,
North Buxton, Ont.

Two weeks later, he received a reply.

Sir,-

The Honorable Minister of Militia and Defense has duly received your letter of 6th instant enquiring about coloured people not being allowed to enlist in the Canadian Militia for Overseas Expeditionary Force.

Under instructions already issued, the selection of Officers and men for the second contingent is entirely in the hands of Commanding Officers, and their selections or rejections are not interfered with from Headquarters.

I have the honor to be,
Sir,
Your obedient servant,
[Signature illegible]
Lt.-Col.
Military Secretary.

For the next year Black recruitment continued on a piece-meal basis across Canada. It is estimated that by war's end 5,000 Black men would serve in the CEF, men who would receive absolutely no mention in the "*official*" texts of the Canadian Army histories; men who would fight and die for the British Empire and European freedom all-the-while experiencing only token personal freedom at home. Patriotism is a strange creature. The Black man, since the earliest days of Canadian history had been one of the greatest defenders of Canada. Yet, his accomplishments have never been fully told nor recorded. It is as if the Black man had never existed. In truth, if it had not been for the Black man carrying a rifle, Canada herself would have never existed.

From the earliest days of British North America and the landing of the Black Loyalist forces in Nova Scotia, to the War of 1812 and beyond, Black regiments served with distinction along the borderlands separating the British and their Canadian counterparts from the Americans. During the American attack on Canada in 1775 and the subsequent siege of Quebec City, it was a Black Canadian regiment, who comprised part of the "undaunted fifty," who defeated the Americans beneath the Citadel of Quebec. The American General Richard Montgomery had invaded Quebec in an effort to make the territory the 14th State of the Union. He was defeated and killed along the slope rising up to the Citadel. The American failure to invade Canada repeated itself during the War of 1812 when, in the early days of the conflict Black Canadian regiments and soldiers led the charge against the American invaders from New Brunswick to the gates of Fort Detroit. In the 1830's, a Black regiment defeated the Mackenzie - Papineau forces ensuring that British North America remained as one. Additionally, Black soldiers were the first to be mobilized in the British Colony on Vancouver Island in 1856 in order to prevent an American annexation of the region following the discovery of gold in the Interior of British Columbia. Historically, when the Americans had moved north, either militarily or years later as simple gold rush prospectors, the first forces they often encountered were Black men dressed in British military scarlet-red uniforms.

"D" Company, A Black "Guard" postcard is an example of Canadian humor c.1906 denigrating Black Canadian military contributions.

On November 21, 1915 Sam Hughes' office received another letter concerning Black enlistment. It read:

Hon Sir:

On behalf of St. John's Coloured residents I desire to return thanks to you for remarks made in regards to Coloured Men enlisting in Canada's fighting lines. I received a letter from you along the same lines, dated October 6/15. I showed the letter to the Coloured Boys shortly after it reached me. Some of them tried to enlist but were turned down. I sent them back again with the threat that I would call for a showdown if they did not get a chance, after a while 20 were accepted, sworn in, etc., ordered to be ready to join the 104th at Sussex, 15 Nov. They reported, went forward at noon with about 50 Whites.

On arrival they met the 2nd Commanding Officer who told them he knew nothing of their coming, and to get right away from there as he would not have them at all, in fact insulted them. He told them that a Coloured Battalion was being formed in Ontario and to go there. They arrived back in the city at 9:30, the same night Nov.15/15. Reported to the recruiting office Mill St., They were told there to come around in the morning. They went from there to other Recruiting Officers, but nothing has been done for them.

They have been told that they are not on the payroll, not entitled to subsistence money, and that in fact they are only Militia men. These men are all poor men, some with families. On an average each was making at least $12.00 per week when they threw up their jobs to enlist and fight for their Empire and King.

Nothing has been done for these people by the Military here, it is a downright shame and an insult to the Race, the way our people have been used in regards to wanting to enlist, etc.

England and some of her allies are using many Coloured troops, and the Coloured people are talking of appealing to the embassies at Washington whose countries are using Coloured Men to be allowed to enter the Foreign services.

I have counseled against this as I believe you will right the wrong.

I wish you would have this matter cleared up at your earliest moment of leisure and issue a general order that Coloured, where fit, shall not be discriminated against by the Military Recruiting Offices in Canada.

I am quite against a Battalion myself as I am directly opposed to segregation.

Yours "for a square deal for each and for all"

John T. Richards
274 Prince William St.
(St. John, N.B.)

On one occasion in an effort to drum up support for the idea of Blacks serving in the Canadian Military, and to promote Black business success in Canada, Black leaders in Toronto invited the President of the Canadian Imperial Bank of Commerce, Sir Edmund Walker, speaking at their luncheon. Walker was an expert on Black history and was a well-respected voice when it came to espousing the righteous qualities of the Black man.

As Professor Robin Winks recounts in his book, *The Blacks in Canada: A History,* Walker's view on history and the Black struggle were a bit more than what his audience had expected. Winks writes:

He also chose to "speak frankly," as he said, and he told his audience that Negroes should not hope "to jump to the front in one or two or three generations," since they were the closest of all people to aboriginal man. "The White man's scale is immeasurably greater than the Black man's. That is a thing that the colored race should remember with pride," he concluded somewhat obscurely.

His audience did not know how to take his statements and attempted to mask their displeasure by promoting the positive aspects of some of his earlier comments. However, try as they may, it was difficult to overlook some of Sir Edmund's theories. As Winks points out:

Walker made no reference to social equality, and his entire exposition, based on environmental theories then fashionable, suggested that, while he found no inherent inferiority in the Negro other than his proximity to primitive man, he nonetheless found Blacks seriously retarded.

What the Black leadership failed to realize was that though they were making political inroads in their fight to have Blacks accepted en masse into the Canadian military, it would likely be a much longer wait before Blacks would be seen working in the front teller windows and inner offices at the Canadian Imperial Bank of Commerce.

By the Spring of 1916, as the recruiting drives picked up and the first signs of a drop in volunteers' began to be realized at recruitment centers the question of allowing for the large scale mobilization of Black volunteers reached the Canadian House of Parliament. During a question period the Honorable William Pugsley addressed the chamber, asking:

Have any effective steps been taken to enable coloured citizens of Canada who are desirous of enlisting for service abroad to enlist, or for the formation of a regiment of coloured citizens? I have brought this question before the House on at least two previous occasions, in consequence of representations, which were made to me by some coloured citizens of New Brunswick, as well as some from Ontario.

The Minister of Militia made the statement that the matter was under consideration. There is a good deal of complaint and very considerable amount of feeling among our coloured citizens that they have not been treated fairly. They have been told that their services would be accepted, and when they have gone to the recruiting office where they were told to go, they have been sent away without receiving any satisfaction.

The Minister of Militia, I think, has in mind the idea that a coloured regiment might be raised in Canada. I should like to know what steps, if any, have been taken towards this end.

In response, the acting Minister of Militia and Defense, the Honourable A. E. Kemp, replied:

I understand there are a number of coloured people in the various units throughout the country; but I am not aware that any effort has so far been made to organize a unit composed wholly of coloured citizens. Some steps may have been taken, But I have no information to that effect at present. I shall make inquiries.

Within a month voices had grown louder on the question. In response, the Canadian Army Chief of General Staff, Major General W. Gwatkin wrote:

1. Nothing is to be gained by blinking facts. The civilized negro is vain and imitative; in Canada he is not being impelled to enlist by a high sense of duty; in the trenches he is not likely to make a good fighter; and the average White man will not associate with him on terms of equality. Not a single commanding officer in Military

167

District No. 2 is willing to accept a coloured platoon as part of his battalion (H.Q. 297-1-29); and it would be humiliating to the coloured men themselves to serve in a battalion where they were not wanted.

2. In France, in the firing line, there is no place for a Black battalion, C.E.F. It would be eyed askance; it would crowd out a White battalion; and it would be difficult to reinforce.

3. Nor could it be left in England and used as a draft-giving depot; for there would be trouble if negroes were sent to the front for the purpose of reinforcing White battalions; and, if they are any good at all, they would resent being kept in Canada for the purpose of finding guards, etc.

4. It seems, therefore, that three courses are practicable:

(a) As at present, to allow Negroes to enlist, individually, into White battalions at the discretion of commanding officers.

(b) To allow them to form one or more labour battalions. Negroes from Nova Scotia, for example, would not be unsuitable for the purpose.

(c) To ask the British Government if it can make use of a Black battalion, C.E.F., on special duty overseas (e.g. in Egypt): but the battalion will not be ready before the fall, and, if only on account of its relatively extravagant rates of pay, it will not mix well with other troops.

5. I recommend courses (a) and (b).

W. Gwatkin
Major-General
Chief of the General Staff

As the furor over Gwatkin's remarks began to grow, it would be Gwatkin himself who would join a list of Canadian officers who would propose the creation of a labor battalion comprised of Blacks. Gwatkin and the others understood the need for men to work behind the lines supplying logistical support to the frontline troops. What they failed to understand was that the battle lines between the front and the rear, as the 1918 Battle of Cambrai would demonstrate, were often blurred.

At the Battle of Cambrai, units comprised of logistical troops, were called into battle in order to stave off a German counterattack. Accounts of Black cooks and dishwashers being issued rifles and ammunition and hastily being sent to the front appear in Canadian military reports - some of these men having never fired a rifle before.

On November 25, 1915 Sam Hughes, in response to a letter written by John T. Richards, Esq. in St. John, New Brunswick, wrote:

Dear Sir, -

I am in receipt of your letter of the 21st instant, in behalf of St. John's coloured residents, who are desirous of enlisting for Oversees service.

I have given instructions that coloured men are to be permitted to enlist in any battalion, and I shall be pleased to hand your letter over to my Adjutant General for immediate report in connection with the circumstances mentioned by you. As soon as I get a report I will write again.

Faithfully,
Sam Hughes

Within days of issuing a standing order allowing for universal recruitment of Black Canadians, to Hughes began to receive correspondence from regimental leaders in various parts of the country. Not many objected to the inclusion of large number of Blacks within the ranks; however enough concern was raised as to the loss of White recruits who would refuse to fight alongside Blacks that Hughes and the Canadian Government were forced to seriously consider adding a separate all-Black regiment to the Canadian military.

On July 5, 1916, the C.E.F. authorized the creation of the No. 2 Construction Battalion to be headquartered in Pictou, Nova Scotia. D. H. Sutherland, a White railroad subcontractor from River John, Nova Scotia was promoted to a rank of Lieutenant Colonel and moved from his previous duties with the 193rd Overseas Battalion, a unit that was composed of men from the farthest six eastern counties of Nova Scotia, including Pictou. The 193rd was 300 men over strength and unit commanders were advised to release men to other units in Nova Scotia in need of recruits. Sutherland apparently had angered someone in the 193rd and his reward was to be the leader of the first and only all-Black Canadian battalion in World War One. Of the nineteen officers who commanded the No. 2, only one was Black. His rank was that of Honorary Captain. The man, William A. White, would serve as the unit Chaplain and would rise to the rank of Colonel by the war's end, making him the highest-ranking Black military man in the British Empire. Ironically, his position had been intended to be only a "token" gesture. But White, due to intellectual capacity and respect from both the White officers and regular troops soon became the unofficial poster boy of the battalion epitomizing the highest standards of Black military service. Years later, one of his daughters, Portia White, would become the most famous Black Canadian female vocalist in history. During the 1940's, she sang to packed auditoriums across North America and Europe. A woman who never recorded a record yet her voice was legendary and a symbol to all Canadians who struggled to succeed in the face of adversity. Portia White would die in 1968 at the age of 57.

In his book *The Black Battalion 1916-1920: Canada's Best Kept Military Secret,* the writer Calvin W. Ruck reminds us that the term *"the promised land"* was first voiced by Black militia men who had fought on the side of the British during the Revolutionary War; men evacuated from American seaports, following the British surrender, going north into Canada where they could be granted their military land allotments based on service. The fact that the slave runaway often referred to Canada as "the promised land" showed how well defined the term had been and how great an impact military service had been on the psyche of Blacks.

Recruitment for the "Black Battalion" began almost immediately. Recruitment posters were sent across Canada and even in the northern regions of the United States, wherever large Black populations resided posters appeared. The American government did not object to the concept of Black men departing the United States for Canada. The idea appealed to them and they openly supported the recruitment of Blacks for the C.E.F., even though the U.S. was not officially at war.

When the recruiting drive had finished, the battalion numbered 1,049 men of all ranks. The geographic demographics were amazing. Black Canadians and Americans from seven provinces (British Columbia, Alberta, Manitoba, New Brunswick, Ontario, Quebec, and Nova Scotia) and thirty American States plus Washington D.C. (Alabama, Colorado, Montana, Georgia, Pennsylvania, Louisiana, Michigan, Virginia, Ohio, Arkansas, West Virginia, Florida, Missouri, Massachusetts, Oklahoma, North Dakota, Kentucky, Kansas, Rhode Island, South Carolina, North Carolina, Vermont and Texas) had responded to the call. The largest groups were from Nova Scotia and New Brunswick.

Black hockey players would be among the many who would volunteer to serve their country. In Dean Jobbs book, *Blue Nose Justice, True Tales of Mischief, Mayhem and Murder,* he describes a story of the former Dartmouth Jubilee star player, Gilbert Richard Lattimore, and his *"dynamite love affair"* that may have been the catalyst for Lattimore's decision to volunteer for service.

Early one morning in 1914, Thomas Riley came looking for Lattimore at Myrtle Robinson's house. Robinson, a White woman, had been dating both Riley and Lattimore and as a result, the former hockey player found himself at the center of a potentially dangerous love triangle. That morning Riley began to repeatedly call for Robinson and Lattimore to come outside or else he *"would blow up the place,"* Because of their failure to step out and talk to the furious Irishman, Riley, being a man of

171

his word, tossed a stick of dynamite onto the sidewalk in front of the house. The blast shattered hundreds of panes of glass in the surrounding area. Fortunately, no one was injured but the Halifax police did arrest Riley for attempted murder. Oddly, instead of trying to have Riley convicted, Lattimore resisted testifying against the man who had tried to blow him to pieces. Also, at the preliminary hearing, Lattimore would not admit to being involved in any love-triangle, stating instead that he was at Robinson's to attend to business with a man named Miller, who also lived there.

The former hockey player even went so far as to disregard a subpoena to testify, and only after he was arrested, and locked in jail, did Lattimore actually appear in court. His refusal to tell the truth about the incident resulted in Riley, who had defended himself, being acquitted.

Maybe Lattimore was apprehensive because he felt no matter what he said the White judge and jury would not convict Riley? Maybe Lattimore was being threatened and was scared of the consequences if Riley was convicted? Either way, the ordeal must have influenced Lattimore's decision to enlist in the Canadian Army. Lattimore would serve in the all-Black No. 2 Construction Battalion.

On March 27, 1917, the first wave of No. 2 troops embarked from Halifax for Europe. At the dockside, crowds of White and Black citizens waved at the men as the troopship *Southland* carrying a contingent of 3,500 troops (including 605 Blacks and nineteen officers 18 White, 1 Black) sailed out of Halifax Harbour east towards England.

Prior to sailing Major-General W. Gwatkin again attempted to intervene in the Black unit's fate. In a letter to the Canadian Naval Secretary he wrote:

H.Q. 600-10-35f.d.25

We want to send overseas a labour battalion, composed of Negroes, with whom White troops object to travel.

We should like to embark this battalion, by Itself, in the NORTHLAND due to the leave Halifax, N.S., on the 10th or 11th proximo.

Do you object to that vessel sailing without an escort? I suppose she would (be) looked after as she approached home waters. The shipping Company concerned is prepared to take the risk.

W. Gwatkin
Major-General
For Military Secretary
Interdepartmental Committee

To which he received a questioning reply:

With reference to your memorandum H.Q. 600-10-35f.d.25 of 21st instant regarding the sailing of the "NORTHLAND", I regret the ship cannot possibly proceed without an escort. Cannot she be hastened to sail with other troopships from Halifax on 9th March?

[Signature illegible]
Commander
Naval Secretary
Interdepartmental Committee

The individual feared a backlash and scribbled their name in such a manner as to make it illegible. It is worthy to note that General Gwatkin had either misidentified the ship that the Black unit was sailing on or someone had transferred the men to the *Southland,* fearing Gwatkin's actions. As the *Southland* sailed towards England she joined up with other Canadian troop ships and proceeded by convoy to Liverpool where the men disembarked on April 8th. In his book, *Nova Scotia's Part in The Great War,* M. Stuart Hunt writes:

During the passage great precautions were taken to guard against enemy submarines. No lights were shown,

173

no bugles blown and a constant watch was kept day and night for floating mines and submarines. This period was the worst in the history of submarine warfare, as more ships were sunk during the week April 1 to April 8, 1917, than anytime during the War.

That afternoon the men boarded trains at Liverpool Station and were transported to the military encampment at Seaford. For the next 10 days they would be isolated in quarantine as the British Military insisted that all troops remain in isolation in order to prevent the spread of any contagious diseases which may have been carried over from Canada. Because the No. 2 battalion was below required military strength it was redeployed as a company with only 506 men and 10 officers. The remaining men were reassigned to other units and duties on base.

While at Seaford, the No. 2 participated in a Sports Day competition which included soccer matches and a baseball tournament. They would win the competition and be awarded the Silver Trophy by the British YMCA. The fate of the trophy remains unknown.

On May 17th the men crossed the Channel to France. Arriving at Boulogne, they boarded trains and were moved across the French countryside on a 3-½ day trip that ended at La Joux, in the Jour Mountains. It was at La Joux that the men were assigned to units of the No. 5 District Canadian Forestry Corps. For the next five months the men worked as loggers and sawmill workers cutting trees and making railroad ties for the transport to the front lines. Though the official records imply that the unit remained at La Joux for the duration of the war, almost half the men were actually sent to other regions of France to aid in logistical support. It would be these men, estimated to be 230, as well as the 99 soldiers and 9 officers reassigned at Seaford who would be involved in some of the heaviest fighting on the Western Front.

In the early dawn of November 20, 1917, Canadian and British forces massed opposite the German lines at Cambrai launched one of the greatest offensive assaults of the war. Armed with 476 tanks (the first time tanks would be used in battle) the British-Canadian force moved against the shocked

German defenders in a lighting strike offensive. In the air more than a dozen squadrons of British and Canadian Royal Flying Corps fighters swarmed down on the retreating Germans hammering the luckless enemy from the air. The tanks moved forward and with the support of tens of thousands of British and Canadian infantry, broke through the frontline German defenses advancing six miles within a few hours. In the midst of this bloodletting, two British and Canadian cavalry divisions swarmed down on the Germans cutting them to pieces. It appeared that the Germans had been routed, but just as the allied forces began to celebrate their victory the Germans counterattacked. Twenty German divisions smashed into the edge formations of the British-Canadian drive. In pincer-like fashion, Germans swept through the allied defenses into the rear support columns. Taken by complete surprise by the German counter measures, the Canadian Corps rushed logistical units to the front to prevent a German encirclement or breakout. Among the soldiers sent into battle were scores of Black Canadian servicemen - men who had never fired a shot in anger.

So savage and all-encompassing was the battle that Canadian records to this day can only speculate as to how many rear echelon units were actually involved. Confusion was the order as units were rushed to the front with little fanfare or announcement. Men who were officially thought to be resting behind the lines were in fact battling for their lives against a relentless enemy assault. Units that officially were never present at the battle, such as elements of the No. 2, were in fact well represented. We do not know how many Black Canadians died, though we do know that six of the nine baseball players who made up the No. 2 Construction Battalion's All-Star team were killed in action. We can only assume that that some of these players were, in fact, also Colored Hockey League players.

So horrific was the Battle of Cambrai that before it would end the Germans would record approximately 50,000 casualties, while the British and Canadians would register 45,000.

Though records are incomplete, we know that former Colored League players Gilbert Richard Lattimore, Adophus Francis Skinner, Wallace Dixon, Alexander Joseph Paris and John Mansfield had all served with the No. 2. All but Mansfield

had returned.   On January 14, 1918, Mansfield, the former
Halifax Eurekas' player, had been killed in France at the age of
48.   The cause of death was not recorded, however, his death
would have a chilling effect on Captain White who wrote in his
diary:

> *It is nice to be dead and out-of-it –*
> *I use to think that I did not want to die but when work*
> *and worry get hold of you death is sweet.*

It is apparent from White's statement that the unit had seen
action at the front.   Such dire statements are not usually muttered
during extended stays at lumber camps.

Former player George "Charlie" Tolliver's two sons and
former Sea-Sides manager Albert R. Tabbe's son served in the
No. 2 along with future Black hockey players George Brown
(Halifax Eurekas), James Paris Jr. (Africville Sea-Sides) and
Joseph Palmer Clyke (Truro Victorias).   After the War, these
sons of former players would return, becoming the next
generation of Black hockey players.

By the summer of 1918, with the entry of the United States
into the war, and the first arrival of American troops to Europe,
the Allies were once again on the offensive.   The Canadian
Army along with their Australian counterparts would play a
disproportionate role.   On August 8, Australian and Canadian
troops attacked Amiens.   They smashed the German lines and
create a breakout leading to the largest Allied territorial gains of
the war.   Within three days the Australian-Canadian attack had
penetrated 12 miles causing panic among the retreating
Germans.   Over the next two months, the Canadians alone would
advance eighty miles capturing 32,000 German prisoners, 623
field guns, 3,000 machine guns and 350 mortars.   Canadian
casualties exceeded 50,000.

In the weeks which followed the arrival of the No. 2
Construction Battalion in France the Nova Scotian based 85th
Highlander Battalion allowed sixty-six Blacks to join their unit.
The 85th would become one of the most famous and bloodied
units in Canadian history taking part in the Battle of Vimy Ridge
in April 1917.   They would fight through Passchendaele,

Amiens, Arras and the Hornelle River Campaigns. When the battalion was finally permitted leave from France, following the Armistice of 1918, they were given the honor of taking part in the Great March of Triumph through the City of London on May 3, 1919. When the men arrived back in Halifax on June 8th an estimated 60,000 Haligonians and Nova Scotians lined the piers to welcome them home. M. Stuart Hunt wrote of the men:

It will suffice to remark, however, that this magnificent body of fighting men - the very flower of Nova Scotia's manhood (were) noted by the military leaders and authorities in England as the finest body of troops sent over from Canada.

For much of the war, approximately half of the No. 2 Battalion remained in the lumber camps near La Joux. Following the Armistice, the unit was transferred to Etaples and was given orders to prepare for transport back to England via Boulogne. On December 14, 1918 the battalion set sail from France to Liverpool. Housed at Seaford the men would remain in barracks for six months awaiting transport back to Canada. In June, 1919, while on parade participating in a military review, a race riot erupted between the Black Canadians and their White counterparts after the Black unit was refused a military salute by the White Canadian officers. As the men passed by the viewing stands a group of White soldiers blocked their route forcing the contingent to stop. Within minutes a bloody brawl had taken place with dozens injured on both sides. When news of the incident reached Canada, there were calls in the Houses of Parliament for the Government to make an example of the Black *"undesirables"* and to *"put them in their place."* Rather than press the matter, the Canadian Government quickly transported the men back to Nova Scotia. When the No. 2 arrived home an advance party of men were sent to the outskirts of Truro and ordered to set up a camp for the others expected to follow. Local Whites, not happy with the prospect of Black soldiers near their community, attacked the men with clubs and other weapons, beating some to near death. Later, as word spread of the assaults, outraged Black servicemen attempted to march on the town and extract payback for the assault. They were prevented from entering the community by armed White soldiers ordered to shoot the men if they tried to pass. For a brief period a dangerous standoff existed. It was only defused following the attempts of the No. 2 White officers to separate the two parties.

During the war, Black and White Canadians had fought and died together in the trenches along the Western Front. Equality, comradery, and shared sacrifice had been the hallmarks of the struggle. Now, with the troops returning, and no "Hun" to threaten the world order, Nova Scotians could return to the old ways. Once again, local hatred and stereotypes had re-emerged. Once again, it was open season on the Black man.

By the end of the war, Canada, with a population of only eight million, had succeeded in raising an Army of 620,000 men in addition to the tens of thousands of others who had served in other military branches. Boys as young as ten and men as old as eighty had served in the Canadian Expeditionary Force. The entire country had been impacted by the war. In total, 425,000 Canadian troops had fought in the trenches. Of these, 66,000 had been killed and over 200,000 wounded. Of the dead, 25,000 had no known grave. Uncounted for were the tens of thousands of men who had suffered severe psychological injuries.

The War had cost Canadians dearly; a generation had been destroyed or changed forever. Among the social elite of Halifax, no family suffered more than the Stairs. Long time supporters of Kinney and the Black cause, their sons were among the first to volunteer for service. From three Stairs families a total of six brothers and cousins would be killed. Two sons of Edward Stairs, Lieutenant Kenneth Stairs and Lieutenant Philip R. Stairs would die. One would be killed at Cambrai while the other would die from influenza. The George Stairs family would lose two sons as well. Captain George W. Stairs was killed at St. Julien in 1915. His brother, Captain John C. Stairs would be killed 16 months later at Courcellette. Gauvin Stairs would lose both of his sons: Captain Gauvin L. Stairs would be killed at Moquet Farm near Courcellette; Private Graham Stairs would die of pneumonia on December 10, 1915, at Halifax prior to being shipped overseas with the 85th Battalion.

With the death of these six Stairs men the family clan was emotionally devastated, and a second generation of tolerant Whites who would have carried on the Stairs legacy of social and political support for the Black Haligonian cause ceased to exist.

Following the Armistice, the No. 2 Construction Battalion was quickly decommissioned and its surviving members returned to Canada. No official battalion history was written. No complete battalion roster was issued. All references to the contribution of Black Canadian soldiers was ignored or simply forgotten.

The acceptance of non-Whites in the Canadian Expeditionary Force had its detractors. The idea of Black men saving White Western Civilization made White supremacists uneasy. Officially the Canadian military, as late as the 1990's, claimed that Blacks never served on the Western Front as a fighting force. Unofficially, this was simply because many were serving individually in non-segregated units, evidence exists in the wartime photographs of the period. In the end, however, no complete records of the number of dead, missing, or wounded Blacks were maintained, as they simply were not considered important enough to warrant documentation.

To this day, some historians contend that Black Canadians never fought on the Western Front. They cannot explain the many Black families who received notices of sons and fathers killed in action. Nor do they attempt to set the record straight by reexamining their own records for the purpose of determining once and for all the full historic picture of Black Canadians and their wartime service. Nor can they explain one of the more infamous incidents of the war, when the only known Canadian soldier to return home in a basket (having had both his arms and legs severed in battle) was identified as a Black man. According to one Canadian account, it was not the practice of the Canadian Army to forewarn families of the true nature of a loved one's injuries. It is also claimed that on one occasion, a family member, upon receiving their loved one "in a basket" committed suicide by throwing herself in front of an arriving troop train. One can assume that this incident and account are linked.

Institutional racism has denied Blacks their heroic place in Canadian military history. Cultural ineptness and a lack of moral willingness continue this shameful legacy to this day.

CHAPTER EIGHTEEN

BLACK RAIN

For many returning Black soldiers the world would be, figuratively and literally, a different place. While serving their country, some of the hell that had raged in Europe was brought home to Halifax. On December 6, 1917, at 8:45 am, the Belgian Relief vessel, *Imo* collided with the French munitions ship, *Mont Blanc* in Halifax Harbour.

The collision created a fire, which ignited benzene onboard the *Mont Blanc*. The burning liquid subsequently ignited 3,000 tons of picric acid, dynamite and gunpowder. Within twenty minutes of the collision, the ship blew up, creating a blast which carried the ship over one mile into the air and setting off the world's greatest man-made explosion before Hiroshima. Over four square miles of Halifax was destroyed. Homes, offices, churches, factories, vessels, the railway station and freight yards were obliterated. The blast created a tidal wave in the harbor and shattered windows sixty miles away. Buildings collapsed trapping hundreds under the debris.

With a population of less than 49,000, at least 2,000 people died and 9,000 more were injured, including many who were blinded by flying glass. Among the dead were 500 children. Two thousand buildings were destroyed and another 1,500 damaged. Twenty thousand people were made homeless and total damage exceeded $40 million. In an *Horizon History* article entitled *The Big Bang,* Janet F. Kitz writes of the explosion:

*Survivors recall a peculiar silence immediately before
the explosion, followed by sound and a blast of wind
which stripped off clothing and blasted windows inwards
in piercing shards. The oil and explosives fell in a
"Black rain" and the force of the explosion created a
tidal wave that pounded the harbour area, adding to the
death and damage.*

Survivors walked around in a daze, many with pieces of metal,
wood or shards of glass embedded in their bodies. Some were in
such shock that they did not even realize the extent of their
injuries. Accounts of survivors without limbs and sitting up,
staring silently out across the harbor are common. The shock
from the explosion had created a buffer to the pain and allowed
many to focus on the immediate scenes around them rather than
grasp the magnitude of the disaster. In the first moments
following the explosion people moved about in silence -- too
numb to scream - too numb to cry.

A young boy was seen carrying his younger sister on his
back. Her face sliced from the flying glass, with one of her
eyeballs hanging like a Christmas ornament. They passed by
survivors in silence, the little girl's hands and arms wrapped
tightly around the neck of her brother symbolic of an
unbreakable bond. Among the stillness of the dead, young
children were heard crying out to their fathers and mothers,
"Daddy! Where are you Daddy?"

A letter from a survivor dated the following day described
the horrors of the explosion:

Halifax Nova Scotia, 7 December 1917

Dear Dad,

*I presume that by the time you receive this you will have
read in the papers of the terrible disaster here, but
possibly an account of the affair, as I have been able to
gather it, will be of interest to you...I had just reached
the office yesterday morning, and was taking off my belt,
when I heard an awful explosion which shook*

everything. Then came another one and I knew nothing more until I found myself on my hands and knees trying to get out from under the building, which had collapsed on top of us. I was cut on the head in a number of places but, beyond that, was not hurt. We crawled through the windows and everything was Black, every window in the barracks had been broken and men were beginning to appear from all quarters, terribly cut about the head and hands and some with broken legs and arms. The conditions were appalling . . . I can't begin to tell you of the awful sights. Dead bodies laid out in row . . . and the whole North End nothing but charred embers. The hospitals are full. Five hundred were sent to Windsor last night to be looked after. Every available place is being used to house the homeless. Families are separated and they have no idea yet who has been killed, though the estimate is more than 2,000. The place looks like a deserted city with its boarded windows and, to make things worse, a fearful snow storm is raging now . . . As I am writing this last sentence, word came in of six of our men who had been killed.

Love to all,

Cuthbert

The destruction of Halifax also sounded a death knell for the Black community. The explosion ripped the heart out of Gottingen Street, the North End, and parts of the community of Africville. Records of the number of Black residents killed in the Halifax Explosion apparently were not kept. Among the dead was a first Colored Hockey League players, Edward Johnson, formerly of the Dartmouth Jubilees.

Within hours of the efforts to gather the dead for burial, centuries of discrimination had reemerged to remind all that even in death, equality was a fleeting concept for most Blacks. Though no official records of Black casualties were gathered, a clue to the actual numbers of Black dead could be seen in one simple incident that took place following the explosion. For decades, it had been illegal to permit Blacks to be buried in Halifax's Anglican cemeteries. On this occasion, a cemetery near Gottingen Street refused to allow the burial of two hundred bodies. No explanation was given, though in all likelihood, the only possible explanation could have been that the victims in question were not White. Subsequently, as the victims lay unburied and the threat of disease grew, efforts were made to prepare a mass grave to dispose of the bodies. Even in death, race mattered. However, this type of behavior among the people of Halifax had not been without precedent, as even the needs of deceased social elite had superseded the needs of living Black families.

Five years earlier, on April 30, 1912, the Halifax based rescue ship, the *Mackay-Bennett*, had returned to Halifax with 192 bodies from the *Titanic* disaster. To prevent the White public from witnessing the ghastly task of unloading the bodies, the ship was docking on the outskirts of the city down by the Campbell Road/Africville area. In Shirley Hill's article, *"Embalmers from Across Maritimes Called in for Titanic,"* she states that the ship had run out of coffins and a tarp covered a pile of bodies on the deck. The victims were taken off and given last respects in conjunction with their social class - the wealthy in covered coffins, the second-class passengers in gunnysacks, the third class in tarps and sheets, and the crew on stretchers. One can only imagine what kind of impact this had on the Black population witnessing the procession of bodies coming off the ship.

During the 19th Century there was a popular song that epitomized the Black struggle. The words are haunting when read in the context of the attempts to bury the Blacks killed from the Halifax Explosion. The song goes as such:

> *I walk through the churchyard*
> *To lay this body down;*
> *I know moon-rise,*
> *I know star-rise;*
> *I walk in the moon-rise,*

I walk in the starlight;
I'll be in the grave and stretch out my arms,
I'll go to judgment in the evening of the day,
And my soul and thy soul shall meet one day,
When I lay this body down.

Given the difficulty of burying Blacks at Anglican cemeteries, the haunting melody seems almost prophetic.

Halifax City was not the only location devastated by the explosion. The community of Dartmouth also paid a heavy price. Hundreds were injured or killed. The Mi'kmaq Indian Settlement at Tuft's Cove was devastated. For the survivors, the trauma of the explosion was so much that the community never resettled.

The ice arena on Wyse Road was flattened, only a bell tower remained. Scores of buildings along the dockside were either destroyed or had been washed away.

The explosion rattled windows and caused items to fall from shelves in Truro sixty miles away.   At the Protestant Run Children's Orphanage on Campbell Road an estimated 200 children had been killed. Hundreds of others would be maimed for life or severely injured. On the Halifax docks, over 100 workers had been killed and scores of others could be seen lying in pools of blood awaiting rescue.

Many of the residential homes borne the brunt of the explosion and had imploded on their occupants. In many homes women and children had been seated at the kitchen table in front of the kitchen stove enjoying a morning pre-school breakfast. These same individuals were now trapped under tons of rubble screaming for rescue as their overturned stoves turned the household wreckage into modern day bonfires. Screams of the innocents being burned alive could be heard across the charred landscape. Rescuers, half-dazed and injured, clawed until their hands were bloodied in a desperate race to free the victims ahead of fire.

In the area in and around Richmond, the first hours following the explosion were comparable in sound to a hellish symphony as screams echoed over the landscape carried over the currents of the warm ghoulish air.   Screams of the helpless trapped in flames and the moans of the survivors lying helpless along the cold surface mingled in an orchestrated cry of desperation. Within hours the sounds of death would be replaced by a deadened silence, a final calm, carried along the waves of warm winds blowing across the landscape of burned homes and charred bodies.

Photo titled View of Halifax, N.S., after explosion, looking towards Pier 8 from Willis Foundry.

Photo Courtesy by Library and Archives Canada.

Though Halifax would be rebuilt, Gottingen Street and the North End never recovered, becoming mere shells of their former selves. The neighboring community of Africville would continue its slide into oblivion. The explosion had destroyed the Richmond train station near Africville. Instead of rebuilding the structure, it was replaced by a new railway station in Halifax. The new station would be built on the east side of Hollis Street at South Street, and is still in operation. This relocation of the former station from the Africville region of Halifax would not only have an economic impact to business, communities around the former station, but directly impacted Africville residents' jobs.

By 1919, Halifax was well on its way to recovery from the explosion. New buildings were being built at record pace and much of the downtown core and the Richmond region showed scant signs of the destruction.

With the war in Europe coming to an end, the residents of Africville petitioned the City in an effort to obtain an expanded police presence and an end to the existence of houses of prostitution located near their community. The City's response was quick and to the point:

> *That the residents of Africville district form their own Police Department and anyone they appoint to act as a policeman the Mayor would swear in as a Special Constable, as the City Department have no spare men to send such a distance. In the event of any serious trouble being reported the Chief is always in a position to send a squad to the district.*

It is important to note that Halifax police records for the latter half of the nineteenth century indicate that 40 percent of all the arrests made for the crime of prostitution involved Black women. Given the fact that Black females made up less than 1.5 percent of the region's population, this figure is stunning. For many Black females the options available to them economically were limited and many were forced into prostitution simply to feed themselves or to supply food for their families. This "whoring" of Black women had a sinister undertone. The women were traditionally the most dedicated and stable elements within the family unit. It was the women who tended to the needs of the children. It was the women who were most active in the local churches and community. By denigrating them to the level of prostitutes the whole social fabric of the Black community was placed in jeopardy and a social stigma was attributed to them. When this fact is placed into context the City's deliberate efforts to undercut the social and economic advancement of Black men, an even more disturbing picture arises. In a society where most families relied on the male to supply the economic income for the household, the efforts to deny Black men the ability to earn a wage raised questions as to their effectiveness as fathers and husbands. The fact that a Black child could not walk down a city street in Halifax for fear that his mother or sister would be solicited for sex by White males created an environment where the family and children lived in shame and inner anger – anger often directed towards the father due to his inability to support his family or prevent the child's mother or to sister from being shamed.

Every time the Blacks attempted to better themselves they were met with organized White opposition. By 1920, with the first wave of Black soldiers returning from Europe, many Black families simply had enough of the lack of opportunity and moved to the Boston, Massachusetts, area in search of better economic and social conditions. It is ironic that by 1920, Canada, a country having long prided itself as a *"bastion for the downtrodden Black"* would see an exodus of Blacks to a system many considered *"less hospitable."* In truth, Nova Scotia, economically speaking, was even more repressive to Blacks than some American southern states.

Even seemingly innocent decisions caused economic hardship on the Nova Scotian Black community. An example of this occurring was when the Provincial highway laws changed. On April 15, 1923, all vehicles were to be driven on the right-hand side of the road, instead of the previous English-style left side. This change would have a drastic effect on beef prices since the oxen of Nova Scotia had been trained to keep to the left. Once trained, the oxen could not be retrained to walk on the opposite side of the road culminating in many accidents and dying oxen. Many previously trained oxen would also be sent to slaughter and 1923 became known as *"The Year of the Free Beef."* For Black subsistence farmers, this was another economic blow that they could not afford.

CHAPTER NINETEEN

FROM THE ASHES TO THE ASHES

During the 1920's, Black hockey players returned to the Nova Scotia ice arenas but by this time Kinney was no longer involved. New teams emerged. Once again the Colored Hockey League would be recognized in the local media. Some teams had continued the tradition of dual meaning team names. For example, the *Halifax Diamonds* name referred to the North Star Constellation, which had served as a directional beacon of hope in the night for fleeing slaves moving northward to Canada in the days of the Underground Railroad.

On the Diamonds team there was Charles Adams, the son of the store clerk, John Adams, and cousin of Gus and George of the Eurekas. The letter carrier, Matthew Collins had his son, Ralph, playing on the Diamonds, stevedore, Thomas Taylor of Gottingen Street had his son Joe also wearing the Diamonds uniform. Additional teams included the *New Glasgow Speed Boys* and the *Africville Brown Bombers*. The name *"Bombers"* being old English slang for *"the successes."*

Over the years the rules of hockey had changed. Now Black teams, like all Canadian hockey teams, began to play six men aside hockey with three 20-minute periods. On March 9th of that year the Amherst Royals and the New Glasgow Speed Boys would meet in Amherst with the teams battling through two overtime periods finishing in a 1 to 1 draw. The next night the Royals would travel to Charlottetown to play the West End Rangers, losing by a score of 7 to 5.

Two days later it would be reported that the Halifax Diamonds Manager Donald "Skinner" Maxwell, had arranged for the Diamonds to play the Truro Victorias at the Arena in Halifax on March 16th. Due to the mild weather, the ice was in such poor shape that the game would have to be called off. No further games would be played until the following year.

1921 Halifax Diamonds Championship Baseball Team.

Team members include Charles Adams, Henry Nat Bunyon, Ralph Collins, Al DeLeon, C. Gibson, Harold G. Lambert, T. "Pop Corn" Lambert, George Richardson, Joe Taylor, and John "Jack" Turner.

Photo courtesy Public Archives of Nova Scotia.

On January 27, 1922, an announcement would appear in the *Acadian Recorder* promoting an upcoming game between the Truro Victorias and the Halifax All-Stars, a team of the top players from the Diamonds and the Eurekas. Unfortunately, the results of the game would not be reported but the outcome had resulted the Victorias (later to be renamed the Sheiks) earning the right to play Amherst on March 4th for the title of Colored

Hockey Champions of Nova Scotia. It was reported the game had been sloppy due to water on the ice, but considering the poor conditions that both teams played under, they were still able to put on a surprisingly good brand of hockey. In the end, Amherst's Lousey Williams would score in overtime giving Amherst a 2-1 victory.

Africville Sea- Sides, c.1922. Possibly their final year in existence.

Team members in photo: Aaron "Pa" Carvery, Fredrick Carvery, James Carvery, Richard Carvery, William Carvery, Jr., James E. Dixon, Richard "Dixon, James Paris Jr., (?) Mantley, William Carvery, Sr., and Treasurer T. G. MacDonald.

Photo courtesy Public Archives of Nova Scotia.

Possibly the most interesting games played that year took place after the Championship match, when the Halifax All-Stars played the Africville Sea-Sides. Listed on the Sea-Sides roster was 39 year-old James Dixon and his 38 year-old brother Richard "Dick" Dixon, 43 year-old James Carvery, 41 year-old Richard Carvery, 38 year-old Fredrick Carvery, along with

William Carvery's 24 year-old son, William Jr. and James Paris' 26 year-old son, James Paris Jr. Aaron "Pa" Carvery would also play. It would be Pa Carvery who would later become known for fighting the City of Halifax during the 1960's when they tried to relocate Blacks from Africville. He would become known as "the last man standing" in Africville.

Playing a team significantly younger, the Sea-Sides would take a 3 to 0 lead into the second period only to end up losing by a score of 7 to 4. It was reported that each team had *"some excellent players"* and that *"both squads showed a good knowledge of the game."* Three weeks later, the two teams would meet again and the Sea-Sides dominated, winning by the score of 8-2.

The Sea-Sides performance would be a testimonial to how great the original players of the league had been. Over twenty years had passed since many of these members first began to compete against other all-Black clubs, and despite their age, they still had the ability to defeat an All-Star team from Halifax. These men had been some of the best athletes in Canada. Sadly, only a few hundred people would be in attendance to witness the Sea-Sides last known game. No games would be reported in 1924 and only two games would be mentioned the following year, both of which involved the New Glasgow Speed Boys.

Although the league had reemerged to some prominence by 1921, the Colored Hockey League was essentially dead as far as its social significance. Racism, the war, the Halifax Explosion and economic factors had all played their part in the league's demise. From this point on only scattered mention of the all-Black teams would appear in the newspapers. Of the few accounts that were mentioned, the most significant would be the signs of an American hockey link to the Colored League. With the influx of Black Canadians to the Boston region in the 1920's, it is apparent that teams comprised of former players from the Maritimes were now playing in and around Boston.

Truro Sheiks 1930.

During the 1920's the Truro Victorias changed their name to the Truro Sheiks. It is likely the Sheiks continued the Colored Hockey League until the start of the Second World War although records of their play during this period remain largely unknown.

Photo courtesy of Stryker-Indigo, New York.

In a February 13, 1929 *Boston Daily Advertiser* article entitled: *"Colored Panthers on Arena Hockey Bill Tomorrow,"* the newspaper reported:

The Colored Panthers, the comedy hockey team who created so much fun in the Arena last season, are on the bill at the St. Botolph Street rink tomorrow. The Negro team will play the St. Joe's of East Boston . . . This will be the first appearance of the Colored Panthers in the Arena this season. They have won five out of six games this season and hope to get revenge for the defeat suffered in a game with the St. Joe's last season. The Negro team has a new defense player who weighs more

*than 200 pounds. Talbert, States, Mills, Gibson and
other players, who were favorites last season, are with
the team again.*

The history and eventual fate of this team is unknown. Though
there is little doubt, from some of the surnames listed, that the
team had historical and/or family links to both Halifax and the
Bog.

During the 1930's other all-Black teams emerged throughout
the United States. On August 6, 1934 the Colored Monarchs of
Hockey issued a press release where they challenged any and all
American and Canadian amateur and professional teams willing
to play them in exhibition. The challenge was in the form of an
8" by 11" poster and letter. The poster (having been previously
issued a year earlier) reads:

**RUSSELL VOELZ'S
COLORED MONARCHS OF HOCKEY**
Members of this club picked from the U.S. and Canada. Each
player is a star by reputation and playing ability.

High Lights of the Club
The only colored hockey team in the world.

The only colored professional hockey team in the world.

**Will play any team any place on one weeks notice if not
booked on date desired.**

Has Taken Two Years to Assemble a Good Colored Hockey
Team.

MANAGEMENTS PLEDGE TO PUBLIC

Whether your club be the Chicago Black Hawks or America's
weakest Club, we still guarantee to give you the greatest hockey
show on earth.

194

RUSSELL VOELZ'S

COLORED MONARCHS OF HOCKEY

Members of this club picked from the U. S. and Canada. Each player is a star by reputation and playing ability.

High Lights of the Club

The only colored hockey team in the world

The only colored professional hockey team in the world.

Will play any team any place on one weeks notice if not booked on date desired.

Has Taken Two Years to Assemble a Good Colored Hockey Team.

MANAGEMENTS PLEDGE
TO PUBLIC

Whether your club be the Chicago Black Hawks or America's weakest club, we still guarantee to give you the greatest hockey show on earth.

The poster was accompanied by a letter written by R.L. Voelz on The Colored Monarchs of Hockey official letter stationary from the Booking Office in Robbinsdale, Minnesota, a suburb of Minneapolis. The letter read:

Attention Sport Editor:

You know doubt have heard of the great colored base-ball club the Kansas City Monarchs and the colored basketball club the Globe Trotters. Now Comes one of the most outstanding sensations in the sport world, the colored Monarchs of hockey. We have the greatest array of colored hockey talent and many of these boys would be playing major league hockey if white.

Most of these lads are Canadian born, but are recruited from New York, Boston, Pittsburgh, Chicago, Quebec and Nova Scotia. I have spent a great deal of time promoting sports, but I have never seen a finer bunch of athletes (colored) on one team. It was my pleasure to organize the Northern league of Professional Baseball and served as its President during the 1933 season.

I am making arrangements to come to your city next winter for a four

Game series. Two on our way to the coast and two on our return. We have seventy games up to date.

Thanking you for publicity you may give I am,

Yours very truly,

R.L. Voelz

The letter and mini-poster were sent to clubs across Western Canada. Voelz had apparently envisioned a multi-game exhibition swing from Minneapolis to Vancouver, British Columbia and back. Among the teams responding to his letter was the Quakers Hockey Club of Saskatoon. In a letter dated August 20, 1934 the club's Secretary-treasurer wrote Voelz stating:

Dear Sir:

We have been informed by the Rink Manager and the Sporting Editor of this city that you would be making a tour of Canada with the Colored Hockey Club called the "Monarchs". We would be very much interested in making arrangements to play you a series of four games this winter.

We might mention that in 1932-33 we were Western Canada Champions and in 1933-34 World's Amateur Champions at Milan, Italy.

Of course, we would have to get sanction of the president of the C.A.H.A., Mr. Hewitt of Toronto.

We would advise you, if you are going to play in Canada, to get a permit to play Amateur Clubs during your tour as there are very few Professional Clubs in Western Canada.

Trusting to hear from you at an early date, we are

Yours very truly,

The QUAKER HOCKEY CLUB

PER: (name blank)

SECRETARY-TREASURER

The idea that a Black hockey team was capable of playing the Quakers must have appeared as a shock to the Canadian Amateur Hockey Association. There is no record of further correspondence between the Quakers and Monarchs. Nor is it known if Voelz sent a letter to C.A.H.A. President William Hewitt. Given the time and the difficulties associated with such an undertaking, it is unlikely that the Monarchs achieved their goal of touring Western Canada. One thing is certain however, by the Summer of 1934, the small suburb community of Robbinsdale, Minneapolis was the home to the first professional black hockey team ever assembled. A team comprised of young Black-Nova Scotians, the likely son's of men who would have played in the original Colored Hockey League.

In her book *Halifax: Cornerstone of Canada,* Joan M. Payzant makes mention of the existence of four Black hockey teams in Halifax during the 1930's. She writes:

There were many amateur teams on both sides of the harbour at this time, including four all-Black teams -- the [West End] Rangers, Cherry Brook, Halifax Hawks, and Africville [Brown Bombers]. Dartmouth was limited to playing on the lakes or outdoor rinks because its second rink, the Marks Cross Arena, burned in the late 1920's, but Halifax had good ice at both the Arena and Forum in the Exhibition Grounds.

The reference to the Rangers is of interest since the team would have been the West End Rangers of Charlottetown, making them the longest running Black hockey team in existence.

In the book, *The Spirit of Africville,* written and edited by members of the Africville Genealogical Society, we learn an intriguing bit of information as to the game of hockey during this period. Of the Africville Brown Bombers, they write:

There's Dick Killum's house. Look past it, and you'll see a level field. We call it the Southwestern. It's a sports field, mostly. There's some buddies out there playin' softball. We play horseshoes there, too. In the Wintertime, the whole thing freezes over, and you can play hockey on it. You ever hear of the Africville Brown Bombers? The team Gordon Jemmott coached? That's where they practiced. Back in the old days, the Basin used to freeze over, and they played hockey out there. Imagine playin' hockey on part of the Atlantic Ocean! Can't do that nowadays. Winter aint what it used to be. Nothing is. Fellas here play hockey for the fun of it. Aint

198

lookin' to get into the NHL. NHL aint ready for no
Jackie Robinson yet, so they say.

What the statement fails to mention is that Bedford Basin would occasionally freeze over as late as the 1920's. By the 1930's, however, the Basin had become the major dumping pond for the City of Halifax's household sewage and as a result the water temperature had increased to levels that prevented the Basin from freezing. Sewage also destroyed the local fishery, depriving Blacks and others a constant source of income. The first casualty of the advent of indoor plumbing in Halifax was Atlantic Ocean Hockey.

CHAPTER TWENTY

THE DEPRESSION YEARS

In 1933, Gordon T. C. Jemmott, the star and coach of the Africville Brown Bombers, became the new headmaster at the Africville School. Gordon replaced his father M. Fitzgerald Jemmott who had served as headmaster for thirty years. The elder Jemmott worked with Kinney and Johnston for an end to school segregation during the early years of his tenure, but with only limited success. Now the young son was in charge. What made Gordon Jemmott unique was the level of education he had obtained. Within a year of taking over the school he had earned a Class A education license from the Board of Education as well as a Bachelor of Arts degree from a local university. This meant that Jemmott, one of the last of the Colored League hierarchy, was now taking on a role as educator and moral example to a new generation of Africville children. In the first year Jemmott ran the school on his own, attending to fifty children of various ages.

However, by the second year he had successfully lobbied to have a teacher's aide hired so that the younger children could be taught separately from their older peers. The teacher's aide was Portia White who was the daughter of Colonel William White the chaplain of the No. 2 Construction Battalion. Portia White oversaw the early childhood classes while Gordon Jemmott worked with the older students. On average Portia had a class of 21 children while Jemmott had 28.

What these two individuals represented to the community, as well as local history, was unmistakable. They were the first generation raised in the shadow of men who had stood tall in the face of discrimination. Young Jemmott had seen his father struggle for three decades to educate the local Blacks with little if any real support from the Halifax School Board.

For decades the older Jemmott had fought to increase services for the Black children of Africville. For three decades the school had existed in the building and the yearly allotment of $100 for supplies and furnishings had remained constant. Given the degree of inflation and wear-and-tear on the equipment and facility, it was a wonder there were any chairs or desks. It was apparent to anyone who took the time to examine the Africville School in detail that the Halifax Board of Education was deliberately trying to squeeze the school out of existence.

As late as 1939 little had changed, the budget and contents of the school were valued at $300 and the building itself was valued at $3,000. Compared to other White area schools, the building had only $1/17^{th}$ of the value of typical schools. In terms of yearly budgetary allotments, the school received only $1/7^{th}$ that awarded to comparable White schools. So dilapidated was the school building that the school board's own parking garage was valued at $800 more than the school. If the Black children of Africville had attended classes in the parking garage they would have been housed at a better facility. Such discrepancies were a form of hidden racism. Though the provincial laws mandated that Black children receive equal educational opportunities, the laws never mandated budgetary allotments or school building standards. Yet, these figures alone do not adequately record the degree of underfunding that existed. For the 1939 report fails to note that in 1933, when Jemmott had taken over the Africville School, the building had been in far worse shape – valued at only $900 – and it was only through constant petitioning that the young Jemmott had succeeded in having repairs made. The fact that he and Portia White had increased the yearly allotment for supplies three-fold was a major achievement.

During the first decade of Fitzgerald Jemmott's tenure, the Africville School averaged 50 percent absentee rate among the students. Though the older Jemmott had worked with Kinney and Johnston, as well as Church Officials, to increase attendance, he had only been able to cut the absenteeism to thirty percent. The younger Jemmott and White faced a similar problem, however, during their worst years of the Depression, class absenteeism seldom exceeded 30 percent.

W. P. Oliver in a December, 1949, article entitled, *"The Negro in Nova Scotia"* which appeared in the *Journal of Education,* wrote:

> *During the 135 years of their settlement here, there is a record of only nine Negro University graduates, and of these nine only three can really be called direct descendants of the early settlers, for one was born in the United States and brought here for his education, while the remaining five were children of West African families who came to this country after 1900. It might be well to observe that the three described as direct descendants of the early settlers were educated in urban mixed schools and all three were in close contact with White culture, in that the education of two of them was sponsored by wealthy White individuals, while the third was practically born on a university campus.*

Oliver went on to report the story of a letter he had received from a young Black girl on May 30, 1949. When he recounted the letter he removed reference to the community where she resided and the name of a nearby factory for fear that the young woman's identity would be revealed. In the letter the young girl wrote:

> *Dear Mr. Oliver:*
>
> *I am writing to ask you to find me a job in Halifax for the summer. It is such a problem to get enough money to go through High School and jobs are scarce down here. There is simply no place in _____ [12]for*

---

[12] Names intentionally blanked out.

girls to work at all, and I want to take my "eleven" next term, which will take some money.

If you know where I can get a job in Halifax, would you please let me know! I read the ads in the paper but I don't suppose they hire Coloured girls. Like in ____ factory, they wanted girls there for different kinds of jobs, well, I don't suppose they would want Coloured girls.

Well, could you find out if you can place me please, and thank you very much.

Yours truly . . .

Oliver ends his article with the words:

Need I say anything further regarding the racial influence? Its results are very evident in this letter: The optimism, confidence and positiveness of purpose -- the essentials of live -- have been destroyed by this sinister evil. Yet is there not a greater danger: is not this child, like many others of the race who all struggling outside that leads to life, an easy prey to any false philosophy of life that will offer freedom from the stigma of race? A people of a rich spiritual nature born to be free, how long will they cling to the Old Rugged Cross, while they suffer shame and reproach at the hands of those who claim to be their saviors?

CHAPTER TWENTY–ONE

THE LION SLEEPS TONIGHT

It was often said Kinney was a perfectionist and that he expected all Blacks to live by the same high standards that he himself adhered to. Through his public speeches, it becomes apparent that the concepts of race and injustice weighed heavily upon his soul. For he was one who understood his place within Canadian and Nova Scotian society and with it, all of the benefits and limitations such a placement held. He also understood quite well that his was the first generation of Canadian Blacks permitted to speak out and demand change. No one needed to remind Kinney that many of the Black elders were either former slaves or the children of former slaves, and that their suffering and determination had afforded him his opportunity to be a Canadian to enjoy limited freedoms. He also understood that freedom was not free, and that it had been bought with a price. In order for Blacks to gain true equality, more effort and self-sacrifice would be required.

In a speech, late in his life, he reflected upon the history of the early Black settlers and their struggle. He said:

With traits of character and mannerisms so much different from the other settlers, they must have been greatly misunderstood – prejudice was rife, and for many years every door of opportunity opened to them reminded one of that old cartoon of the Boxer Rebellion – the open door of China – that bristled with bayonets, which must be faced by any who dare enter . . . Many that came from the United States were tradesmen – carpenters, Blacksmiths, stone-masons, coopers, etc., and even to this day some of these trades are carried on – but they were looked upon as scab labour, a position which could not be bettered as trade unions would not admit them to membership, so they could do little than job around . . . The thoughts I wish to advance are, with climatic conditions altogether different, with no knowledge of procedure, with no money, with no education, no sympathy, little patience and helpfulness, how could they quickly acquire an equal status with the dominant race? Yet their brains were just as fertile, as is clearly proved by their quick response to encouragement.

James A. R. Kinney as he appeared late in his life.

Photo Courtesy of the Black Cultural Centre for Nova Scotia.

By 1928, the Home for Colored Orphans was facing its greatest challenge. The wells were running dry. Without water, and basic sanitary conditions, everyday tasks could not be accomplished. Without water, seven years accomplishments would cease. Desperate to raise the required $25,000 necessary to ensure the home's survival, through the drilling of new wells and the implementation of a sewage system, Kinney made a public plea to the citizenry of Nova Scotia and Canada:

The gravity of the situation is too clearly apparent in the fact that on immediate action depends the continuity of the Home which has done so much for these dark-

skinned little ones in training them to take their places as citizens of the future. Is this magnificent work to continue, or must it close its doors as the fruits of its efforts are ripening. Imagine your own kiddies with a meager supply of water, then do your very utmost, if that utmost is only a little, for these colored little ones are God's as much as your children.

Again Kinney's words would cut like a knife through the bureaucracy that was White Canada. Canadians of all colors sent funds to help the Home. Wells were drilled and modern plumbing installed. The Home lived on.

In 1939, as the storm clouds of war again touched Canada's shores, Kinney took the time to reflect on the first twenty years of the Home. He wrote:

In all these years, there has been but one death, and no epidemics. None of the children who have left us (to our knowledge) has ever been brought before a court on a major charge. A number of the first ones are married and have families, others are scattered over the province and Upper Canada, some even in the United States. There are 45 in the Home this winter.

A tireless worker, by 1940, years of struggle and worry had taken a toll on Kinney. By the age of 61, his had been a life scarred by battles and opposition. He had faced many obstacles: personal handicaps, loneliness, racism, politics, the Halifax Explosion, the Great War, and the Depression. He defeated them all. In doing so, his body could endure no more. In early October, he was admitted to Victoria General Hospital suffering from a fever. Three weeks later, he died. The man that had given Black Nova Scotians self-pride, purpose and goals for a better future was gone. Almost immediately those who had spent a lifetime ignoring his efforts, or doing little to help, proclaimed eulogies espousing his greatness. In death he was a hero. In life, he had been an unbending Black man – a threat to the status quo -- a man who had set high standards few could or were prepared to achieve.

206

Eulogies to Kinney:

The colored people of Saint John are mourning with people of their race throughout this Dominion the passing of J.A.R. Kinney, secretary, treasurer, and superintendent of the Nova Scotia Home for Colored Children which was established, largely through his efforts, in 1921. The institution took care of many little ones and it was said today some Saint John children had enjoyed the privileges. – Saint John Newspaper, November 1940.

The present high standards of the Home is almost completely due to his untiring efforts extended over 20 years. It will stand as a monument to his memory. – Henry G. Bauld.

I have known the late James A.R. Kinney for a long number of years and have always admired him for his energy and enthusiasm in his work for the benefit of his race and the public generally, throughout the Province and often for the whole Dominion. He spent years of his time in the interest of the Nova Scotia Home for Colored Children, and its present success is very largely due to his efforts. – B. A. Husbands. Founder of the Nova Scotia Association for the Advancement of Colored People.

Thirty-two years had passed since James Johnston first presented the idea of a Home. Kinney had been involved with the home from its inception, and after the catastrophic Halifax Explosion destroyed the first incarnation of the dream, he was the one who had presided over its rebirth and subsequent development. – George P. Saunders, Author, "Share and Care".

CHAPTER TWENTY–TWO

THE DEATH OF AFRICVILLE

During the 1950's, social advocates found little support in their efforts to create job opportunities in and around Black communities.   On one occasion the Nova Scotia Provincial Government allocated funds for the planting of 500 trees by school children at Hammond Plains.   This modest attempt at reforestation was more to give the impression that *"jobs"* were being created, whereas, in reality, nothing was further from the truth.   By having Black children planting the trees allowed for the possibility of photo opportunities giving White politicians a chance to stand beside a Black child and give the impression of racial harmony - a caring face of government.   Like *"babes in the woods"* the children planted the trees and the politicians scanned the horizon proclaiming a new day dawning.   Later the Federal Government donated high-brush blueberry plants. Unable to find root, they died.   At a loss and not knowing what else to do, the politicians retreated back into their halls of power, knowing that a tree requires 20-years to reach maturity in Nova Scotia.   It would be a long time before another photo opportunity could be organized.

By the 1950's such had been the destruction of the Black middle classes of Nova Scotia that Gwendolyn V. Shand in her report, *Adult Education Among the Negroes of Nova Scotia,* wrote:

> *The problem of the Negro is so complex that it would seem that the Adult Education Division needs the active co-operation of other groups, especially those concerned with health, welfare, and education.*

Shand could not have known the history of Blacks in Nova Scotia. For if she had, she would have understood that theirs' was not a story of an underclass denied opportunity, but rather a proud race that had survived economic, political, and cultural genocide. The Black man's problems were never complex. The problem had always been the forces within the White upper classes of Nova Scotian society who were aligned against them.

In 1956, University of Toronto Professor Gordon Stephenson conducted a study entitled: *A Redevelopment Study of Halifax, Nova Scotia (including Supplementary Volume).* Funded by the City of Halifax, the purpose of the Stephenson study was to assess the harbor situation and to identify possible options for harbor expansions. The 1956 report was to the point:

> *There is a little frequented part of the City, overlooking Bedford Basin, which presents an unusual problem for any community to face. In what may be described as an encampment, or shack town, there live about seventy negro families. They are descendants of early settlers, and it is probable that Africville originated with a few shacks well over a century ago. Title to some of the land will be difficult to ascertain. Some of the hutted homes are on railway land, some on City land, some on private land. There will be families with squatter rights, and others with clear title to the land which is now appreciating considerably in value.*

The report had its effect. The last thing the City officials wanted to do was to pay large amounts of taxpayer funds for lands owned by Blacks. Underscored in the report was the realization that having the Blacks relocated would not be without a certain degree of social and cultural upheaval. According to the report:

> *The citizens of Africville live a life apart. On a sunny, summer day, the small children roam at will in a spacious area and swim in what amounts to their private lagoon. In winter, life is far from idyllic. In terms of the physical condition of the buildings and sanitation, the story is deplorable. Shallow wells and cesspools, in close proximity, are scattered about the slopes between the shacks. There are no accurate records of conditions in Africville. There are only two things to be said. The families will have to be rehoused in the near future. The land which they now occupy will be required for future development of the City. A solution which is satisfactory, socially as well as economically, will be difficult to achieve. Africville stands as an indictment of society and not of its inhabitants. They are old Canadians who have never had the opportunities enjoyed by their more fortunate fellows.*

In a purely sociological sense, the report was profound, identifying the historic plight of the people of Africville and the uniqueness of the settlement. Unfortunately, economic realities would upstage cultural, social, and even legal factors. At the time of the study the city possessed only 19.3 acres of land suitable for industrial shoreline development within its city limits. If they could acquire the lands around Africville they could add an additional 150 to 160 acres of shoreline lands under their control. This would give the City enough land necessary to attract corporate development and to afford the expansion of harbor facilities. The problem facing the City was how to pay for the land? If the City officials implemented a *"fair value"* policy for the land the cost would be enormous. At the time, the average home in Halifax was valued around $4,000 to $6,000. The Africville homes, in large part, were valued in the low $4,000 to $5,000 range. However, the land those homes sat on was worth millions. In the end, the City of Halifax would resort to a time proven formula designed to obtain the lands without adequate reimbursement. They would make a number of *"low-ball"* offers to buy the homes, but conveniently fail to inform the residents as to the true value of the property. At the same time, they would argue that many of the homes sat on City and railroad property, or that the homeowners could not prove land ownership because few having deeds to the land, effectively implying that the land was not theirs to begin with.

By the 1960's Africville had become a social embarrassment for many in Halifax. In his study, *"The Condition of Negroes of Halifax City, Nova Scotia"*, Guy Henson wrote:

> *The problems of Africville are not readily evident visually as those of mid-city Negroes. One must journey to the far north of the city to see the place, and it is not even located on any main access route from the city. But in its way it too is a source of embarrassment to Haligonians. Among the first things a visitor notices on a tourist map of the city is that one district is called Africville. Why it is called that, he wants to know, and what is the place like? Africville provides a convenient subject for newspaper pictures whenever a movement for better housing gets under way . . . In addition, almost two-thirds of those interviewed claimed that they liked living in Africville, citing as reasons the freedom of the place, the cleaner air, the view, the open spaces, the opportunities for fishing, and congenial neighbours . . . while a few families, perhaps twenty at most, appear to have deeds to their land, the majority of families seem uncertain of their title position. Many claim that Queen Victoria granted the land to their ancestors, a claim that may have more social significance than legal validity.*

Henson and the Africville Blacks failed to realize why many of the families did not hold land deeds to the property. Africville was a designed to be a Maroon Colony. As such, the land had been under the legal protection of the British Government and the Government of Jamaica not the Governments of Canada, Nova Scotia, nor the City of Halifax - governments that had not even existed at the time of Africville's founding. Generations

211

had past and this key legal point had been forgotten. So too had the reality that the reason the Blacks did not have *"land deeds"* was due to the lands being deemed a *"territory"* or *"autonomous reservation"* outside of the jurisdiction of the British and Canadian legal and political authorities. Africville Blacks claimed that Queen Victoria had awarded them the lands for military service. They were in part correct. In fact, the lands had been awarded to their ancestors by King George III as part of a Peace Treaty following the Second Maroon War in Jamaica and subsequent Maroon participation in the defense of Halifax from Napoleon's French Naval Fleet. The Maroons had never surrendered to the British nor to the Canadians and as a result, any movement on Maroon-held Nova Scotian territory (including the Maroon settlement at Preston) was not only in violation of previous treaties but tantamount to a hostile invasion or occupation. This is important, for as late as 1962, when Jamaica obtained its independence from England, Maroon lands were deemed *"separate"* from British Jamaica and as such only became part of the independent nation of Jamaica after much negotiation and promises of economic and social support for the Maroons living within these tribal lands. At the time of the Halifax City annexation of Africville, a number of Maroon families were still living on the lands. Had the City wished to negotiate in good faith they simply would have had to look at early Nova Scotian histories from the nineteenth century to find proof of Black family ownership.

The legal precedent established by the Maroon settlement in Canada sits at the heart of modern Canadian land claim issues Simply put, the citizens of Africville were not only forcibly evicted from their lands in the 1960's but were also *"conquered"* by a foreign government. *"Africville Justice,"* if it is ever to be achieved, will never be determined independently by the Governments of Canada, Nova Scotia, nor the City of Halifax, but instead only through either direct treaty negotiations between the three Governments of Canada, the United Kingdom and Jamaica, or through a Black legal petition to the World Court in The Hague for financial and territorial compensation. The ramifications of such moves would be tremendous and the financial windfall for Black Africville citizens would be in the billions of dollars since the Africville Blacks would have a right to their old lands as well as claims to a percentage of the financial proceeds generated from railroad tariffs and port duties. Not only were all lands seized by the railroads as far back as the mid-1800's in question, but the lands taken from the Blacks in the 1960's would also be subject to International or World Court review.

By the 1960's the plight of Black Nova Scotia communities was becoming a national embarrassment to Canadians. Victims of social and economic repression, many Blacks had assumed the status of strangers in their own land. Misunderstood and repressed, their heritage was deemed to be of little importance or value in the face of modern Canadian society. In 1964, the Reverend W. P. Oliver, in an article in the Journal of Education, entitled: *"The Negro in Nova Scotia"* lambasted Nova Scotian White society when he wrote:

> *There has been very little in the attitude of society and in the racial structure over the past 100 years to encourage Negros to aspire to the better things in life. Usually, if he endeavors to buy a house outside of his local community he is refused. He is reluctant to ask for lights, decent roads or other improvements to his community because so often his voice has gone unheard. He has ceased to realize that he has a right to a decent standard of living. He is refused rental accommodations and is often denied the opportunity to work at the skills he has trained for.*

During this period Halifax City, at the height of post-war economic renewal and development, moved aggressively to eliminate the area known as Africville. The City planners, in search of cheap land, ignorant of history and desiring to rid themselves of a Black economic burden they had, for the most part, created themselves, moved to reestablish the area residents in so-called *"better neighborhoods"*.

Offering the residents far less than the true value of their homes, properties and businesses, and using the implied threat of forced eviction, the City of Halifax, amid national outrage and calls of injustice, succeeded in forcibly resettling part of the Black population to isolated locations chosen by Whites.

By decade's end, under constant threat and harassment by City officials, only a handful of Africville residents remained. In 1969, determined to rid themselves of Africville, the City ordered its work crews, under a veil of early morning darkness, and armed with bulldozers and dump trucks, to converge on the area and to forcibly evict the remaining inhabitants from their homes. In all, nearly 1,000 people were evicted. Given only minutes to pack up belongings and personal memories, which were thrown into bags and hand, tied blankets, frantic and frightened residents stood in horror awaiting forced resettlement. Some, away at the time, would return to discover that the City had simply bulldozed their homes, destroying a lifetime of hard work. It was a brutal action in the name of progress. Economic theft designed to benefit White business interests. The lands around Africville were a developer's dream. Located on the shores of one of the world's finest natural deep harbors, the land was an economic gold mine, the value of which was impossible to estimate. Rather than preserve the region, or to pay true market value for the land, the City chose to steal it.

Those who perpetrated the destruction of Africville and the forced resettlement of the local Black population could be described as *"barbarians in suits."* However, such was not the case. These individuals were nothing more than ordinary citizens and businessmen who possessed modern values and a sense of self-proclaimed moral right in a society that places capitalist interest above community needs. Their greatest flaw was their inability to recognize the historic and cultural importance of Africville and the important role the community had played in Nova Scotian and Canadian history. In a society that is to this day culturally overshadowed by the influences of the United States, it is not surprising that White Canadians, unable and unwilling to preserve their own history and culture, have had even more difficulty recognizing and preserving the history and culture of Black Canadians. The destruction of Africville was not a Haligonian action, but rather, it was a modern Canadian action, the roots of which lie in the nations own sense of cultural and historic inadequacy and sense of unimportance.

Among the families who decided to fight the hostile takeover of Africville by the City of Halifax, none were more determined than the Carvery clan; a family whose ancestors had been the heart of the Colored Hockey League. A review of the records of the late eighteenth and nineteenth century implies that the Carverys were descendants of the first Maroons to settle at Africville. Their name does not appear on Loyalist or Chesapeake Black ship logs. And on account of their historic social standing within the Black community, as indicated by the respect that this family held within the Black Nova Scotia communities, they were likely one of the original Maroon Captain or Chieftain families recognized by the British as the legal spokesmen of the people.

Not prepared to accept the City's offer, Aaron 'Pa' Carvery decided to fight. During the 1920's Aaron had been one of the stalwart defensemen of the Sea-Sides and often had been the last man standing when the opposition had charged for the Sea-Sides goal. Pa Carvery had always been an obstacle in the face of opposition, and the idea of standing his ground against shadowy politicians and City officials was not something he shied away from. Early on, City officials realized that Carvery was the greatest obstacle in their path and as a result, they made moves to buy his silence; rid themselves of his determined opposition. *"As Pa Carvery goes, so goes Africville"* could have been the catch phrase of many Haligonian officials who realized the respect the man held within his community. On one occasion, he was invited to the Mayor's office and shown a briefcase containing 5,000 one-dollar Canadian bills. He was told *"all this can be yours if you decide to sell."* Carvery had angered his hosts by refusing to accept the gesture and from that time on the City worked to defame his character and to drive a wedge between the Carvery family and other Black families who had agreed to the buy-out offers. By defaming the man, implied that he was *"crazy"* and *"senile,"* and by harassing the family, the City was able to garnish local support for their expropriation efforts. That such efforts occurred is an indictment of the Canadian political and legal system.

In the end, Aaron Carvery would be given a day to vacate his property. He was forced to watch the City move on his home with bulldozers destroying a home in which he had lived in for over seventy years. One of the last known pictures of Africville is a photo of Aaron Carvery among the ruins of his house searching for kitchenware that had survived the demolition. The man who had often been noted for his defensive and determined play during the twilight years of the Colored Hockey League is today remembered as the last man standing in the final moments of Africville's destruction. Just as his ancestors had done nearly two hundred years earlier, he had fought to the end. His children continue his fight to this day.

**Aaron "Pa" Carvery surrounded by rubble
on the site of his former Africville home.**

Photo courtesy Black Cultural Centre for Nova Scotia.

The outright theft and destruction of Africville in the mid-to-late 1960s remains one of the most shameful chapters in modern Canadian history. Though numerous Federal government officials in Ottawa and scores of Provincial and community politicians in Nova Scotia seemingly given support to the Black fight for retribution, their words are only designed for political benefit and carry little if any substance. The politicians say what they feel their audience wants to hear and few are ever called to task for their statements. It is a game that is played well by those who are only interested in securing their own social status and economic being. Africville is more than a Black Canadian tragedy. It speaks volumes about the social character of Canada and all Canadians. For by allowing the weak to be crushed by the strong we set the precedent where actions and not the rule of law determines the definition of democracy and justice. By allowing the powerful to deny justice and dignity to those within our society who cannot fight back we set a standard for which future disputes. Laws and democracy can only be protected if people are willing to fight for them. Unfortunately, as it stands today, if one is not part of a powerful elite then one fails to have a voice in one's own future. Today, because of the destruction of Africville, Canadian property laws and democracy are not worth the paper they are written on. Justice is only justice when it is enforced. *Tyranny is the heritage of the silent.*

In a paper entitled: *From Slavery to the Ghetto: The Story of the Negro in the Maritimes,* and presented in 1968 to the New Brunswick Human Rights Commission, H.A. Wedderburn, a member of the Nova Scotia Human Rights Commission, and President of the Nova Scotia Association for the Advancement of Colored People, wrote:

> . . . *by the time a negro child is four years old, he has developed negative attitudes towards himself and his race, attitudes can persist for the remainder of his life.*

Weddeburn went on to add:

> *The negro . . . regardless of his education, upbringing*

217

and religion, remains foremost a negro, with his being a human being of secondary importance.

Racism is so instilled in Canadian culture that Canadians fail to recognize it for what it is. An old Indian prophet once wrote that *"a valley is clearer from an adjacent mountain top than from the valley itself"* and such is the case in Canada where the struggle of the non-White Canadian is much clearer from the distance of time and history than from the day-to-day examination of the lives of individuals.

Following the destruction of Africville, most of the families were relocated to the Mulgrave Park area of Halifax and placed into public subsidized housing. The total cost to the City of Halifax was $800,000, a far cry from what the cost would have been had a fair market value for the homes and property been offered. Today this site is a City park, a chilling monument and legacy to the Black struggle for historic recognition and acceptance in Canada as well as a lesson to all Canadians of the vulnerability of minorities at odds with non-representative government.

Today, on the North Side of Halifax, on the site that was once Africville, is Seaview Park. In the park stands a sun dial monument bearing the names of the original families whom settled Africville. The monument is designed to show the slow movement of time by the position of the sun. It is a haunting epitaph to the historic Black struggle in Canadian society. During the nineteenth century, bigoted Whites would often mutter the expression; *"Nigger don't let the Sun set on your back in this Community."* It is an expression understood by all men of color who have witnessed the anger of White mobs determined to rid their neighborhoods of people they deemed "inferior". It is a haunting expression that echoes in the final memories of hundreds of Blacks who themselves were the victims of White lynch mobs and racists. The sun dial takes on a greater meaning when it is viewed in context of Black history. For the Blacks of Africville its meaning is clear: *"You are not welcome here."*

At the height of the Africville controversy, on December 16, 1968, a letter to the Editor appeared in *The Halifax Chronicle-*

Herald newspaper. Though anonymous, it represented the views of many Blacks.

> *I am a Black (with a capital B) . . . I harbor no inferiority complexes about my beautiful Blackness. "Negro" is a polite way of saying "Nigger." I am no Negro, nor am I colored; for Black is an absence of color. I am a Black Canadian; I am Black and I am proud.*

In the early 1970's, following the forced relocation of the Black Africville families to Mulgrave Park, Frances Henry, in her book entitled: *Forgotten Canadians: The Blacks of Nova Scotia,* wrote:

> *Black communities are under-organized and do not show any strong viable institutional support. This is manifested by the lack of leaders and of voluntary associations in the communities, and by the lack of economic organization of any kind, which makes such Black communities dependent on neighbouring White towns for their goods and services. Institutionalized religion in these Black communities is not binding or influential, and it lacks any symbolic or ideational system, as that folklore, music and the like are almost non-existent. The family system, while nuclear and stable as far as the male presence in the home is concerned, is frequently conflict-ridden.*

Henry apparently was unfamiliar of the story of Williams, Kinney, Johnston and the others. She could not have guessed to what extent Black efforts to obtain a dignified level of existence had been crushed. All of the points that Henry argues were once the cornerstone of late-nineteenth century Black Halifax. So much had been destroyed could only be described if seen in the context of a slow and methodical socio-economic policy of planned genocide.

During the 1960's self-awareness and pride re-emerged from the shadows of Campbell Road and the community of Africville.

No longer willing to allow themselves to be seen as outcasts or second-class citizens, in a city that they and their ancestors had built, the Black population began to organize, determined to fight for the culture that few outsiders understood. This fight continues to this day.

The history of Black Canadians has been forgotten, deliberately destroyed, or conveniently ignored. Most historians have or have viewed it as irrelevant. When it has been discussed, it has often been presented in relation to the cause and effects of American and New World Slavery. If the truth were known, Canadian Black history is as complex and intriguing as that of any European race or nation that has shaped the modern world. It is a history rich in its telling, one that evokes heroism, determination and dignity, a legendary story supplanted by modern bias and myths.

Canada, five hundred years in the making, is a complex and successful nations. The second largest country in land area, its population numbers less than 32 million. It is a nation in the shadow of the United States, one that officially prides itself as a cultural mosaic of over two hundred cultures, living for the most part, at ease with one another. Yet, historically, it is a country whose existence is a direct result of the influences and efforts of four great peoples and races – the French, the English, the Native Americans, and the Blacks.

The creation of the Colored Hockey League and the role played by the Baptist Churches and their leadership within the Maritimes cannot be appreciated unless it is seen in its true historic and religious context. With the publishing of Charles Darwin's book *"On the Origin of Species by Natural Selection,"* in 1859, creationists and bigots alike espoused the theory that Darwin's thesis pertained only to Blacks and other races. Portraying Blacks as non-human, an evolutionary link between Apes and Man. By denigrating Blacks and other minorities, these proponents of *White Supremacy* found justification in their actions as well as explanation for the Biblical scripture.

Man is a distinct creation, in the image of God . . . of which the White is the highest, and the Negro the lowest

220

race, with the browns, reds and yellows as intermediate races, in different stages of development.

With the growing popularity of White-based sports and team concepts and extreme religious beliefs gave fuel to the arguments and theories espousing that Blacks were neither suited physically or mentally for sport, and that at best, they could only be trained to mimic the actions of Whites. Such concepts received widespread legitimacy and promotion throughout North America at a time when Blacks and their leadership were attempting to make inroads for equality and social acceptance. Thus, by creating teams of Blacks, skilled in hockey, and led by respected Black religious leaders, the Colored League was not only challenging the traditional Canadian hockey status quo, but was also challenging both religious and scientific extremism as well. The League, by its very existence, gave Blacks hope, setting itself up as a symbolic target for anyone who sought its failure or demise. The Colored Hockey League of the Maritimes changed the way hockey was seen and played in early Canada.

Hockey permeates all levels of Canadian society, impacting on social status, ethical values, language, hero worship, and race. It is a record of who Canadians are; what they aspire to; and what they have achieved. For many, the sport is a source of wonder, beauty and passion. Hockey, when performed at its highest level and skill, achieves timelessness.

Today there are no monuments to the Colored Hockey League of the Maritimes and few hockey books even recognize the league. Names of hockey pioneers like Henry Sylvester Williams, James Johnston, James Kinney or the scores of players who wore the Colored League uniforms are nowhere to be found. There is no mention in the Hockey Hall Of Fame of the impact that Blacks had in the development of the modern game of hockey. There are no references to the Black origin of the slap shot or the innovative style of goal play exhibited by Franklyn. There is no reference to the Black origin of goalies going down on ice in order to stop the puck. It is as if the league had never existed. For hockey is today a sport whiter in history than a Canadian winter.

In Canadian history, as it is in winter, the landscape is that of bleached white. It is a white world of seeming beauty, yet one without color. It is a sterile landscape, deadened by cold and time, blinding to all who are lost within its blanketed form.

Yet, a Canadian winter is deceptive for we need only to scrape away the season's covering to find its brown soil. For in Canadian history and hockey, as with the seasons, between the time of the last white winter snows and the first brown spring soils, there inevitably will always be a period we call *Black Ice*.

TEAM ROSTERS & PLAYER BIOS

AFRICVILLE SEA-SIDES

Brown, John Jr.: born Sept 1, 1860. Year known to play: 1899 (Forward).

Cassiday, John: born March 14, 1878. Years known to play 1899-1904 (Point - Goal). Mainly a defenseman, Cassiday was one of the better players in the league. He only briefly played some goal when Eddie Martin was on the team. He was a boarder renting from Joseph Carvery during the time of the league.

Carvery, Aaron "Pa": Year known to play. 1922 (Defense). Fought the City of Halifax during the 1960's when they tried to relocate Blacks from Africville. Last man to leave Africville in 1970.

Carvery, Fredrick: born Feb. 20, 1884. Year known to play 1922 (Sub). It is clear he was a substitute with the team possibly as early 1902 (substitutes were not listed on the starting roster until the 1920's). He was still playing at age 38.

Carvery, James: born Feb. 19, 1879. Years known to play 1899-1922 (Forward, Center, Goal). Named the team Vice President in 1899, he was described as *"the star player of his team and the fastest man on the ice"* by the *Acadian Recorder* in 1899 and quite possibly the fastest skater in the league. He was listed as the teams starting goaltender in 1922 at the age of 43.

Carvery, Richard "Dick": born Feb. 16, 1881. Years known to play 1900-22 (Forward, Right Wing). Remarkably was still listed as a substitute in 1922 at age 41.

Carvery, William Sr.: born Aug.8, 1875. Years known to play 1899-1904 (Goal). He was the uncle of James, Richard, and Fredrick. It was noted in the Acadian Recorder *"he stopped shot after shot, and even in the senior* [White] *league better work would not be seen."* - 1902.

Carvery, William Jr.: born Dec. 15, 1898. Years known to play 1922 (Sub). He was the son of William Sr.

Dixon, Allen: born March 23, 1878. Years known to play 1899-1904 (Forward-Point - Rover). He is the brother of James and Wallace and cousin of world famous boxer George Dixon. He did play one game for the Eurekas 1899 (vs. Jubilees). His father was Rev. Edward Dixon.

Dixon, James E.: born June 3rd, 1882. Years known to play 1898-1922 (Forward - Point - Goal- Left Wing). He was the team Captain and the other half of the offense with James Carvery. His first recorded game came in 1898 playing goal for the Eurekas (vs. Dartmouth). The next year, the Sea-Sides were formed with James as Team Secretary. Him and his brother Wallace owned their own Grocery store in the 1920's - J. W. Dixon Groceries. He was still playing competitive hockey until at least age 39.

Dixon, Wallace: born Aug. 6th, 1879. Years know to play 1899-1904. (Forward - Cover Point). He severed in the No.2 Construction Battalion WWI.

Dixon, Richard "Dick": born Feb. 1st, 1872. Years known to play 1922 (Forward). Richard was likely a substitute with the team possibly as early 1899. He was still playing at age 38.

Howe, William G. Jr.: born Jan 11, 1880. Listed as Sea-Sides executive, no record of playing.

MacDonald, T.G.: Listed as Sea-Sides Team Treasure and Manager.

Mantley, __: years played: 1922 (Forward).

Paris, James: born Aug. 20, 1871. Years known to play 1899-1900 (Point-Goal). He is listed as the team's first President.

Paris, James Jr.: born July 8, 1895. Year known to play 1922 (Defense-Wing). He also played a game for Truro in 1922 and he served with the No 2 Construction Battalion WWI.

AMHERST ROYALS

Cook, __: year known to play 1903 (Point).

Cook, Frank: year known to play 1922 (Wing).

Cummins, __ : year known to play 1903 (Point -Left Wing).

Halfkenny, Robert: year known to play 1922 (Sub).

Izzerd, __:

Jackson, __: year known to play 1903 (Rover).

Jones, Frank: year known to play 1922 (Wing).

Jordan, __: year known to play 1922 (Defense).

Lee. L: year known to play 1903 (Rover).

Martin, David: year known to play 1922 (Defense).

Martin, R.: year known to play 1922 (Sub).

Martin, L: year known to play 1903 (Center-Goal).

Parsons, Joe: year known to play 1903 (Goal). Played on Championship Royals baseball team 1907.

Riley, __: year known to play 1903 (Left Wing).

Ross, H: year known to play 1903 (Cover Point).

Ross, George: year known to play 1903 (Right Wing). Played on Championship Royals baseball team 1907.

Tankard, H.: year known to play 1922 (Sub).

Williams, David "Louse": year known to play 1922 (Center).

Williams, Oscar: year known to play 1922.

DARTMOUTH JUBILEES

Borden, Charles: born Jan 5, 1875. Years known to play 1895-98. (Forward & Point) Relative of Fred Borden and Pastor James Borden of the Dartmouth Lake Church.

Borden, Fred "Freddie": born July 1864. Years known to play 1899-1900. (Goal & Forward) Freddie Borden apparently played much longer. In 1900 he played one game in goal for Eurekas (vs. Sea Sides) as a replacement. Acadian Recorder: *"Freddie Borden at goal gave an exhibition of goal keeping that has seldom been seen here . . . He was carried off the ice by his admirers after the game for his splendid defence."* A relative of Charles and James Borden.

Brown, John "Cut": born Aug. 27, 1860, Years known playing years: 1895 & 1899. (Forward). Also played one game for Sea-Sides (vs. Eurekas) as a replacement (1899).

Collins, George: born Sept 7, 1878. Year known playing years 1898.

Flint, Charles: Years known playing years 1895-99. (Forward).

Flint, F.: Years known playing years 1895 (Point).

Franklyn, Henry "Braces": Years known playing years 1895-98 (Forward & Goal) (Captain in 1895). He was said to be only 3' 6" tall and is recognized as the first recorded goalie to go down on ice during a game. Franklyn dies c. 1899 at the approximate of age 38.

Green, B.: Year known playing years 1895 (Cover Point).

Johnson, C.: Years known playing years 1898-1904, (Forward). Named team Captain in 1899.

Johnson, Edward: born: March 31, 1874. Year known playing years: 1898. Died in Halifax Explosion, Dec. 6th 1917.

Johnson, Oscar: Year known playing years 1898.

Kelly, Albert: born July 8, 1880. Years known playing years 1904 (Center).

Lattimore, Gilbert Richard: Years known playing years 1902-04 (Point). A top player for Dartmouth, he was a last minute pick-up for the Eurekas (vs. Truro) in 1902. Involved in *"Dynamite Love Affair"* incident in 1914 and served with the No. 2 Construction Battalion.

McCann, T.: Year known playing years 1898. Killed in the Halifax Explosion.

Reilly, R.: Year known playing years 1895 (Forward).

Tynes, Thomas "Tommy" Jr: born June 21, 1856. Years known to play pre-1895, 1899. (Forward – Cover Point). Only listed as not being present for a game. He was considered one of the finest hockey players in the region although no accounts of his play exist. His father, Thomas Tynes Sr. was a Deacon at the Dartmouth Lake Church.

Williams, George: born Sept. 15, 1878. Years known to play 1899 -1904 (Point & Goal). Played for the Jubilees from 1899-1902 and the Truro Victorias from 1903-04. Believed to be killed in the Halifax Explosion.

DARMOUTH VICTORIAS

Saunders, Walter: born. Sept.1878. Years known to play 1895, 1899, 1902, 1904 (Forward). Captain of the Dartmouth Victorias (1902), Sauders first appeared on the Halifax Stanleys (1895). He also played for the Dartmouth Jubilees (1899), and the Eurekas (1904).

Lee, ____: Year known to play 1902 (Cover Point).

HALIFAX DIAMONDS

*Provincial Baseball Colored Champions 1921

Adams, Charles: born July 10, 1879. Year known to play 1921 (Sub)

Bunyon, Henry Nat.: born. Feb. 4, 1888. Year known to play 1921 (Point).

Collins, Ralph: born Jan 25, 1898. Year known to play 1921 (Center).

DeLeon, Al: Year known to play 1921 (Wing).

Gibson, C.: Year known to play 1921 (Goal).

Lambert, Harold G.: born Aug 8 1895. Year known to play 1922 (Forward)

Lambert, William T. "Pop Corn": born Feb 19, 1894. Years known to play 1921-22. He is the son of George Lambert.

Richardson, George: born. Feb. 6, 1891. Years known to play: 1921 (Sub)

Taylor, Joe: born 1895. Years known to play 1922 (Cover Point).

Turner, John "Jack": born June 6, 1888. Years known to play 1921-22 (Sub).

HALIFAX ALL-STARS

Team comprised of the best players from the Halifax Diamonds and Halifax Eurekas.

HALIFAX EUREKAS

Adams, Agustus "Gus": born April 5, 1876 - known playing years 1898-1903 (Forward). Older brother to George and a speedy skater.

Adams, George: born June 5. 1879 - known playing years 1885-1904 (Forward - Cover Point -Center). He is the brothers of "Gus" Adams and was known as a fast skater.

Allison, Charles: born June 27, 1882 - known playing years: 1898-1902 (Forward). Known for his goal scoring, Allison along with the Adams brothers was the top forward line in the league. His father, James Allison, was killed in Halifax Explosion.

Allison, Herbert W.: born July 28, 1876 - known playing years: 1902-1904(Goal). Older brother to Charles, Herbert was a good goaltender who was also know to go down on the ice to make a save. *"Allison, goal for the Eurekas, put up a star game, stopping the puck in every conceivable way, standing up or sitting down positions was nothing to him."* 3-9-04, Acadian Recorder.

Barton, ____: known playing years: 1922 (Goal).

Brown, George: born Jan. 24, 1895 - known playing years 1922. (Sub). Served with No. 2 Construction Battalion.

Brindley, ____: known playing years: 1922 (Sub).

Carter, Herbert S.: born Dec. 30, 1899 - known playing years: 1922. (Defense).

Davidson, John "Harley": born Oct. 16, 1867 - known playing years: 1900. (Point).

DeLeon, (either Herbert or Frank): Herbert born: July 9, 1897 or Frank born Sept. 25, 1900 - known playing years 1922 (Forward).

Flint, William "Harry" A.: born Nov. 1, 1872 years known to play: 1895,1902,1903 (Goal & Point). He played two games for the Eurkas (1902 & 1903) as an injury replacement. *"Adopted the double goaltender positon"* (two players in the net at one time) vs West End Rangers in 1902.

Johnson, Stanley: born April 24, 1877: years known to play 1898-99 (Goal) Related to Edward Johnson of the Jubilees.

Mansfield, John: born Feb. 20, 1869, years known to play: 1904 (Sub)(**Mansfield, John:** 1904). He was a boarder living with the Brown family.

Martin, A. Edward "Eddie": born Nov. 1876: years known to play. 1899 -1902 (Cover Point). Was the Captain of the Eurekas in 1899. Began to play some games for the Sea-Sides and led Africville to the 1901 Maritime Championship. In 1902 Eurekas refused to play the Sea-Sides and walked off the ice. The two teams would not play again until 1904, and Martin, a star of the league would not play again.

Saunders, Laurence: born Feb. 18, 1879: years known to play 1904 (Sub).

Symonds, Frank L.: - Halifax Eurekas.: born April 8, 1971. Years known to play: 1895. He was a boarder.

Skinner, Adophus Francis: born Aug. 9, 1869: years known to play 1902-04. Became Captain after Eddie Martin left the team. 1905 became the coach and captain of the Amherst Royals baseball and hockey team. He served in the No. 2 Construction Battalion.

Taylor, George: years known to play: 1902-1904 (Cover Point). Became team Captain in 1904 and a stand out player.

Thomas, Walter "Jack": born March 7, 1873: years known to play: 1898-1900 (Forward -Point). He was a domestic, living at the home of William (age 71) and Elizabeth Brown (age 69) helping the family.

Tolliver, George "Charlie": born Feb. 14, 1865: years known to play: 1899-1906 (Point - Forward) - A top player, he was known for his physical play, *"introduced his flying body check"* Acadian Recorder 1906. Both his sons served with No. 2 Construction Battalion.

Tynes ____: years known to play: 1922 (Forward). It isn't clear which Tynes he was but it is almost certain he was one of the Tynes who had served with No. 2 Construction Battalion.

Wilson ____: years known to play: 1898 (Forward).

HALIFAX STANLEYS

Adams, Agustus "Gus": (Point) - played for Eurekas (see Eurekas for bio)

Allison, Charles: (Point) - played for Eurekas (see Eurekas for bio)

Carter, Alfred: born April 8, 1872 - (Forward) - no record of playing again.

Clyke, George: (Goal) started Truro Victorias (see Victorias for bio)

McKerrow, B.: (Forward) - Relative of Rev. Peter McKerrow and a replacement referee for one game in 1898.

Saunders, Frank: (Captain) - no record of playing again, killed Halifax explosion Dec. 6, 1917.

Saunders, Walter: see Dartmouth Victorias for bio.

HAMMOND PLANS MOSS BACKS

Only mention of a team in 1904. No games recorded.

Emmerson, Albert: years known to play: 1904. Team Captain 1904, his father is Alexander Emmerson Hammond Plains Baptist church clerk.

TRURO VICTORIAS

Ash, Alex: years known to play: 1899.

Bard _____: years known to play: 1922 (Sub).

Buchanan, D: years known to play: 1899.

Cassidy, J.: years known to play 1902 (Point).

Clyke, Ansel: born April 8, 1891: 1910, 1922, 1930 (Forward). Played for 1930 Truro Sheiks.

232

Clyke, Alexander: born Feb. 12, 1896 years known to play: 1922 (Goal).

Clyke, George: born April 25, 1877: years known to play: 1895-1904 (Center-Point). George Clyke is first mentioned as a player for the Halifax Stanleys in 1895. He is the founder of the Victorias an team Captain from 1899 -1904. He was the star player of the team and one of the top players in the league.

Clyke, James A.: born Feb, 20, 1889: years known to play:(Goal)(1903)(1904)

Clyke, Joesph Palmer: years known to play: 1922 (Sub). He served with the No. 2 Construction Battalion.

Clyke, Oscar: born April 27, 1881: years known to play: 1899.

Clyke, William H.: born Feb 10, 1883: years known to play: 1903 & 1910

Connolley, Willie: years known to play: 1899.

Mantos, _____: years known to play: 1922 (Defense).

Martin, Marty: years known to play: 1903-10 (Left Wing). The Victorias became a much better team once Martin arrived in the lineup. It is apparent he was one of the stars of the Victorias. *"some of the (Martin's) stunts . . . were thrilling . . . he electrified the audience by a sensational double somersault winding up with a vicious swing at an opponent, who wasn't there"* Truro Daily News, 1910.

Parris, Arthur: years known to play: 1899.

Paris, Alexander Joseph: unknown date of birth: years known to play: 1903-04 (Rover). He served with the No. 2 Battalion.

Parris, O.: years known to play: 1903-04 (Right Wing).

Paris, Norman: born Aug. 14, 1874: years known to play: 1899.

Parris, T.: years known to play: 1922 (Center).

Shepard, Wilbert: born Sept. 29, 1897 - years known to play: 1922 (Sub).

Talbot, Tude. : years known to play: 1922-30 (Wing-Center). He is listed as a Center on the 1930 all-Black Truro Sheiks (successor of the Victorias)

Taylor, Joe: years known to play: 1904. He was the uncle of Eureka's cover-point (defenseman) George Taylor.

WEST END RANGERS

Byers, Edmond: years known to play: 1900-03 (Point). Weighing over 200 pounds, Byers was a physical defensive presence. The "big fellow" was a cousin of the boxer "George 'the Budge' Byers (the Champion Colored boxer of New England who fought in three World Champion title fights, lost all three).

Crosby, E.: years known to play: 1903 (Goal).

DeCourcey: years known to play: 1902 (Forward). He replaced one of the Mills after they moved.

McNeill, A. "Harry": years known to play: 1900-03 (Goal - Center).

Mills, George "Hurley": years known to play: 1900-03 (Cover Point). Played for the Eurekas in 1903-4.

Mills, John "Jack" T.: years known to play: 1900-04 (Rover). Captain. In 1947, former West End Rangers star Jack Mills died with obituary was published in both the Charlottetown Guardian and New Glasgow Clarion: *"The death occurred at the Charlottetown Hospital last night of a well known and highly respected citizen of Charlottetown, John T. Mills. The deceased was born in Charlottetown on February 24th, 1873, and spent most of his life in this city. For a number of years he followed the sea acting as cook on many different ships. The late Mr. Mills was also employed in a similar role at the Victoria and Queen hotels here, as well as for various units of the militia during their training periods. He was keenly interested in sports and was a speed skater of distinction; his record of 18 miles in 50 minutes established on the East River ice on April 10, 1892 still remains unbroken. He was a member of the famous West End Rangers hockey squad, five members of which bore the Mills name. He, with his father and brothers, was a member of the "West End colored brass band" of some years back. The late Mr. Mills is survived by four daughters and two sons . . ."*

Mills, Albert "Bert": years known to play: 1900-03 (Left Wing).

Mills, Lemuel "Lewis": born Aug. 24, 1882: years known to play: 1902-04 (Right Wing). Played for West End Ranger in 1903 and Eurekas in 1904.

Mills, Oliver: born. Nov. 25, 1883: years known to play: 1904 (Point) - played for Eureka's.

Ryan, Al: years known to play: 1902 (Center).

Stanley, _____: years known to play: 1903 (Cover Point).

OTHER KNOWN TEAMS AND ROSTERS

THE RALPH WALDO EMERSONS

Believed to have been in existence in the latter half of the 1890's in Saint John, New Brunswick. Team named in honor of the American Philosopher, Religious Leader and Abolitionist Ralph Waldo Emerson. Team and player statistics unknown.

THE ST. JOHN ROYALS

Believed to have been in existence in the latter half of the 1890's in Saint John, New Brunswick. Team named in honor of the Kingdom of Heaven. Team and player statistics unknown.

THE CELESTIALS

Believed to have been in existence in the latter half of the 1890's in Fredericton, New Brunswick. Team name derived from the North Star, Polaris. Team and player statistics unknown.

THE BLACK PANTHERS

Team existed in the late 1920's to early 1930's in Boston, Massachusetts. The team was renowned for its entertaining circus-like play. The Panthers were the hockey equivalent of the Harlem Globetrotters. Team and player statistics unknown.

THE COLORED MONARCHS

Team existed in 1934 in Robbinsdale, Minnesota a suburb of Minneapolis. It was run by Russell Voeltz a grain salesman of Swedish descent. Detailed information on this team is unknown. This appears to have been the first professional all-Black hockey team ever formed.

CHERRY BROOK

Team existed in the Halifax -Dartmouth, Nova Scotia region in the 1930s. Team information and player statistics unknown.

HALIFAX HAWKS

Team existed in the Halifax, Nova Scotia region in the 1930s. Team information and player statistics unknown.

NEW GLASGOW SPEED BOYS

Indication is that there was a team in New Glasgow unclear what their original name is in c.1904 since there are no records of any games. It is uncertain, but it is believed the original name was the Rovers, and they changed their name to the Speed Boys due to confusion with an all-White team with the same name.

AFRICVILLE BROWN BOMBERS

Jack Desmond
Freeman Johnson
Harold Colley
Elmer Jones
Vic Jones
Gordon Jemmott
Leo Adams
Bess Husbans
Chink Tynes

Billy Parker
Lewis Jones – Boxer "Snook" Jones father
Max Halfkenny
Bobby James
Frank Adams – Goaltender

TRURO SHEIKS – 1930

Edward Clyke
Buster Clyke
Joe Paris
St. Claire Byard
Tude Talbot
Wilfred Jordan
Ansel Clyke
Fred "Ted" Dorrington
Simmonds Clyke

LEAGUE OFFICIALS

James R. F. Johnston born March 12, 1876
Henry Sylvester Williams - An organizer/spokesman 1895.
James A. R. Kinney born Feb. 25, 1879, Eureka Manager
Pastor James Borden - An organizer of Dartmouth Jubilees hockey.
Albert R. Tabbe, Sea-Sides Manager 1900-1905. His son served in the No. 2 Construction Battalion.
David N. Maxwell: Halifax Diamonds/Halifax All-Stars Manager.

PLAYERS BORN BY DECADE

BORN 1850's

Thomas "Tommy" Tynes Jr. - Jubilees - born June 21, 1856

BORN 1860's

James "Cut" Brown - Dartmouth - born Sept 1, 1860
Fred "Freddie" Borden,- Jubilees- born July, 1864
George "Charlie" Tolliver - Eurekas - Feb. 14th 1865
John "Harley" Davidson - Eurekas born Oct. 16, 1867
John Mansfield - Eurekas - Born, Feb. 20, 1869
Adophus Francis Skinner - Eurekas - born Aug. 9, 1869

BORN 1870's

Henry "Braces" Franklyn - Jubilees - born, 1870
James Paris - Sea Sides - born Aug. 20, 1871
Richard "Dick" Dixon - Sea-Sides - born Feb. 1, 1872
Alfred Carter - Stanleys - born April 8, 1872
William "Harry" A. Flint - Jubilees - born Nov. 1, 1872
John "Jack" T. Mills - West End Rangers - born Feb. 24, 1873
Walter "Jack" Thomas - Eurekas - born March 7, 1873
Edward Johnson - Jubilees - born: March 31, 1874
Norman Paris - Victorias - born Aug. 14, 1874
Charles Borden - Jubilees Jan 5, 1875
William Carvery - Sea Sides - Aug. 8, 1875
James R. F. Johnston - League Official - born March 12, 1876
Agustus "Gus" Adams - Eurekas - born April 5, 1876
Herbert W. Allison - Eurekas - born July 28, 1876
Edward A. E. Martin - Eurekas - born Nov. 1876
Stanley Johnson - Eurekas - born April 24, 1877
George Clyke - Victorias - born April 25, 1877

John Cassidy - Sea-Sides - born March 14, 1878
Allen Dixon – Sea-Sides - born March 23, 1878
Walter Saunders - Stanley/Jubilees- born. Sept. 1878
George Collins – Jubilees - born Sept 7, 1878
George Williams – Jubilees/Victorias born Sept. 15, 1878:
Laurence Saunders - Eurekas - born Feb. 18, 1879
James Carvery - Sea Sides - born Feb. 19, 1879
James A. R. Kinney - Manager Eurekas - born Feb. 25, 1879
George Adams - Eurekas - born June 5. 1879
Wallace Dixon - Sea-Sides - born Aug. 6, 1879

BORN 1880's

Albert Kelly - Jubilees - born July 8, 1880
Richard "Dick" Carvery – Sea-Sides - born Feb. 16, 1881
Ansel Clyke - Victorias - born April 8, 1891
Oscar Clyke - Victorias - born April 27, 1881
James E. Dixon - Sea Sides - born June 3, 1882
Charles Allison - Eurekas - born June 27, 1882
Lewis Mills - Eurekas - born Aug. 24, 1882
William H. Clyke - Victorias - born Feb 10, 1883
Oliver Mills - Eurekas - born Nov. 25, 1883
Fredrick Carvery - Sea Sides - born Feb. 20, 1884
Henry Nat. Bunyon - Diamonds -born. Feb. 4, 1888
James A. Clyke - Victorias - born Feb, 20, 1889

BORN 1890's

William T. "Pop Corn" Lambert - Diamonds - born Feb 19, 1894
George Brown - Eurekas - born Jan. 24, 1895
James Paris, Jr. - Victorias - born July 8, 1895
Harold G. Lambert - Diamonds - born Aug 8 1895
Joe Taylor - Diamonds - born 1895
William Carvery Jr. - Seas Sides - born Dec. 15, 1898
Herbert S. Carter - Eurekas - born Dec. 30 - 1899

NO. 2 CONSTRUCTION BATTALION

Gilbert Richard Lattimore - Dartmouth Jubilees- 1904
Adophus Francis Skinner - Halifax Eurekas - Captain -1902-04
George Brown - Halifax Eurekas - 1922
Wallace Dixon - Africville Sea Sides - 1899-1904
James Paris Jr. - Africville Sea Sides - 1922
Alexander Joseph Paris - Truro Victorias - 1903-04
Joseph Palmer Clyke - Truro Victorias - 1922
John Mansfield – Halifax Eurekas – 1904

*George "Charlie" Tolliver had two sons serve with the No. 2 Battalion and Albert R. Tabbe had one son serve with the No. 2 Battalion.

*Note: a number of family names that correspond with known players in the league appear on the No. 2 Construction Rosters implying that a larger number of family members of league players were involved with the No. 2. Records for the battalion unfortunately are incomplete.

*The brothers, Herbert and Clinton Halfkenny of the Amherst Royals baseball team, may have played hockey and served with the 106th Battalion, CEF.

PLAYERS WITH LOYALIST HERITAGE

Adams, A. "Gus" - Halifax Eurekas/Halifax Stanleys
Adams, Charles - Halifax Diamonds
Adams, George - Halifax Eurekas
Borden, Charles - Dartmouth Jubilees
Borden, Fred "Freddie" - Dartmouth Jubilees
Brown, John "Cut" - Dartmouth Jubilees (Ethiopian Regiment Roster Name)
Brown, George - Halifax Eurekas (Ethiopian Regiment Roster Name)
Collins, Ralph - Halifax Diamonds
Collins, George - Dartmouth Jubilees
Cook, Frank - Amherst Royals
Davidson, John - Halifax Eurekas
Dixon, James - Africville Sea Sides
Dixon, Allen - Africville Sea Sides
Dixon, Wallace - Africville Sea Sides
Dixon, Richard "Dick" - Africville Sea Sides
Gibson, C. - Halifax Diamonds
Johnson, Edward - Dartmouth Jubilees
Johnson, Stanley - Halifax Eurekas
Jones, Frank - Amherst Royals (Ethiopian Regiment Roster Name)
Lambert, Harold W. - Halifax Diamonds
Lambert, John "Pop Corn" - Halifax Diamonds
Lattimore, Gilbert Richard - Halifax Eurekas/Dartmouth Jubilees
Lee, L. - Amherst Royals
Martin, David - Amherst Royals
Martin, Edward, A. E. - Halifax Eurekas/Africville Sea Sides
Martin, L. - Amherst Royals

243

Martin, R. - Amherst Royals

Maxwell, David N. - Halifax Diamonds/All-Stars (Manager)

Mills, Oliver - West End Rangers/Halifax Eurekas/

Mills, Lewis - West End Rangers/Halifax Eurekas/

Mills, George - West End Rangers

Mills, Albert - West End Rangers

Mills, John - West End Ranger/New Glasgow/Halifax Eurekas

Paris, Alexander Joseph - Truro Victorias

Paris, Arthur - Truro Victorias

Paris, James - Africville Sea Sides

Paris, James, Jr. - Africville Sea Sides

Paris, Norman - Truro Victorias

Paris, O. - Truro Victorias

Paris, T. - Truro Victorias

*Paris related to Black Loyalist leaders who established free state of Sierra Leone.

Saunders, Frank - Halifax Stanleys

Saunders, Laurence - Halifaxs Eurekas

Saunders, Walter - Dartmouth Jubilees/Halifax Stanleys

Skinner, Adophus Francis - Halifax Eurekas

Symonds, Frank L. - Halifax Eurekas

Talbot, Tude - Truro Victorias   (Ethiopian Regiment Roster Name)

Taylor, George - Halifax Eurekas

Taylor, Joe - Halifax Diamonds

Thomas, Walter "Jack" - Halifax Eurekas

Turner, Jack - Halifax Diamonds

Tynes, Thomas "Tommy" - Dartmouth Jubilees

Tynes, Abraham - Dartmouth Jubilees

Williams, David "Louse" - Amherst Royals

Williams, George - Dartmouth Jubilees

PLAYERS WITH MAROON HERITAGE

Carvery, Aaron "Pa" - Africville Sea Sides
Carvery, Fredrick - Africville Sea Sides
Carvery, James - Africville Sea Sides
Carvery, Richard "Dick" or "Harry" - Africville Sea Sides
Carvery, William - Africville Sea Sides
Carvery, William Jr. - Africville Sea Sides
*Note: The Carvery are descendants of a Maroon military Captain
Johnston, James R. F. - League Official
Johnston, Oscar - Dartmouth Jubilees

LEAGUE CHAMPIONSHIPS

1895 - Halifax Stanley
1896 - Halifax Eurekas
1897 - Halifax Eurekas
1898 - Halifax Eurekas
1899 - Halifax Eurekas
1900 - Halifax Eurekas
1901 - Africville Sea Sides & West End Rangers each claim share
1902 - Africville Sea Sides & West End Rangers each claim share
1903 - Halifax Eurekas & West End Rangers each claim share
1904 - Halifax Eurekas
1905 - Halifax Eurekas
1906 - Halifax Eurekas
1907-1913 – *No public records of games.*
1914 -1919 - League suspended due to War.
1920 - Truro Victorias
1921 - West End Rangers
1922 - Amherst Royals
1930 - Truro Sheiks

COLORED HOCKEY LEAGUE
DECLARATION OF FAITH

1. *We believe that there is but one living and true God, who is a Spirit, infinite, eternal, and unchangeable in his being, wisdom, power, holiness, justice, goodness and truth.*

2. *That there are three persons in the Godhead – the Father, the Son, and the Holy Ghost –who are but one God, the same in substance, equal in power and glory.*

3. *That the Holy Scriptures of the Old and New Testaments are the Word of God, in which He hath given us our only rule of faith and practice.*

4. *That God who is infinite in knowledge, and perfectly views all things from the beginning to the end, has foreordained that whatsoever comes to pass, either by His order or permission, shall work for the eternal glory of His great name.*

5. *That in the beginning God created the heavens and the earth, the sea, and all that in them are; and He upholds and governs all things by the word of His power.*

6. *That God made man in His own image, in knowledge, righteousness and true holiness; and made with him a covenant of life, the condition of which was perfect obedience.*

7. *That man being left to himself soon fell from that happy and glorious estate in which he was made, by*

eating the forbidden fruit, by which he brought himself and all his posterity into a state of death.

8. That man being thus dead, his help and recovery are wholly in and from God.

9. That God the Father has chosen a great multitude of the human family, whom no man can number, of all nations, and kindreds, and people, and tongues, and given them to His Son in covenant of His grace, that He might redeem them from all iniquity, and purify unto foundation of salvation for lost and helpless sinners; and thereby the Ministers of the Lord are encouraged to preach the Gospel to every rational creature, because the purposes of God, and the infinite value of Christ's atonement, secure the increase and establishment of Christ's kingdom, so that the kingdoms of this world shall become the kingdom of our Lord and of His Christ; and He shall reign for ever and ever.

10. That Jesus, the eternal Son of God, hath come, and taken on Him our nature, and in that nature hath yielded a perfect obedience to the law which we have transgressed, and suffered death from our sins, and hath brought in a complete and everlasting righteousness, and hath risen and ascended to the right hand of God, and ever liveth to make intercession for us.

11. That the Holy Ghost, and He only, can and doth make particular application of the benefits of the atonement made by Christ to every elect soul.

12. That the Spirit of God applies the benefit of this atonement, by convincing us of our sinful, lost, and miserable condition; and then discovering the glorious Saviour, as He is exhibited in the gospel, in his suitableness and sufficiency, and enabling us to embrace Him with our whole souls, by which He is made unto us wisdom, righteousness, sanctification and redemption.

13. That the life of religion consists in knowledge of God, and conformity to His commands, and brings us to live in obedience to His holy will in all our ways, and in our several places and relations.

14. That true believers being united to Jesus Christ, shall never perish, but live and reign with Him forever. They have communion with God, and by His Spirit they are united with each other, and have, other's gifts and graces.

15. That the first day of the week commonly called the Lord's day, is the Christian Sabbath.

16. That God hath appointed the ordinance of civil government for defending the poor as well as the rich, in their civil rights, without infringing upon the consciences of any, or attempting to dictate or govern in worship of the eternal God, which belongs only to Jesus Christ, the great lawgiver and head of His church.

17. That there will be a general resurrection, both of the just and the unjust; and that God hath appointed a day in which He will judge the world in righteousness, by Jesus Christ, and will reward every man according to his works; when the wicked will be sent away into everlasting punishment, and the righteous received into life eternal.

BIBLIOGRAPHY

Abucar, Dr. Mohamed. *Struggle for Development: The Black Communities of North & East Preston and Cherry Brook, Nova Scotia 1784-1987.* Halifax, Nova Scotia: McCurdy Printing & Typesetting Ltd. 1988.

Acadian Recorder Newspaper: 1895-1930.

Benedict, David, A. M. Pastor of the Baptist Church in Pawtucket, Rhode Island. *A General History of the Baptist Denomination in America, and Other Parts of the World. Vol. I.* Printed by Lincoln & Edmands, Boston, Mass, U.S.A.,1813.

Berton, Pierre, *Flames Across the Border, 1813-1814,* McClelland & Stewart, Toronto, Canada, 1981.

Bible, The King James Version. Published by Thomas Nelson, Inc., Nashville, TN., 1978.

Blockson, Charles L. *The Underground Railroad: First-Person Narrative of Escapes to Freedom in the North.* New York: Prentice Hall Press, 1987.

Bontemps, Arna, Ed., *American Negro Poetry.* Hill and Wang, New York, U.S.A.,1963.

Boyd, Frank Stanley Jr. Ed., Peter E. McKerrow. *A Brief History of Blacks in Nova Scotia (1783-1895).* Afro Nova Scotia Enterprises, Halifax, Nova Scotia, 1991.

Brathwaite, Keren S. & Carl E. James. *Educating African Canadians.* Toronto: James Lorimer & Company Ltd., Publishers, 1996.

Bird, Michael J. *The Town that Died: The True Story of the Greatest Man-Made Explosion Before Hiroshima.* Souvenir Press: London, 1962.

Calkin, J. B. Head Master of the Provincial Model School, Truro, Nova Scotia. *The Geography and History of Nova Scotia, With a General Outline of Geography and a Sketch of the British Possessions in North America.* A. W. Mackinlay: Halifax, Nova Scotia, 1866.

Canadian Colored Concept Company. Plantation Lullabies, *Songs Sung by the Famous Canadian Jubilee Singers. The Royal Paragon Male Quartette and Imperial Orchestra. Five Years' Tour of Great Britain, Three Years' Tour of United States,* Duncan Lithograph Company, Hamilton, Ontario, Canada. 1898.

Canadian Encyclopedia, The. Edmonton: Hurting Publishers, 1985.

Carroll, Charles, *The Negro a Beast.* (no publisher noted), Washington D. C., 1900.

Chapman, Harry. *Dartmouth's Day of Anguish: The Explosion, December 6, 1917.* Dartmouth Museum Society: Dartmouth, Nova Scotia, Canada, 1997.

Chapple, William. *The Story of Uncle Tom.* Uncle Tom's Cabin Museum, Dresden, Ontario, No Date.

Clairmont, Donald et al. *The Spirit of Africville.* Formac Publishing Company Ltd., Halifax, Nova Scotia, Canada, 1992.

Clairmont, Donald et al. *Africville: The Life and Death of a Canadian Black Community.* 3rd Edition, Canadian Scholars' Press, Toronto, 1999.

Clifford, Mary Louise. *From Slavery to Freetown: Black Loyalists After the American Revolution.* McFarland &

Company, Inc., Publishers: Jefferson, North Carolina, U. S. A. 1999.

Collections of the Nova Scotia Historical Society for the Years 1896-98, Volume X. Halifax, Nova Scotia: Nova Scotia Printing Company, 1899.

Conditions of the Negroes of Halifax City, Nova Scotia, The Dalhousie Institute of Public Affairs, Nova Scotia, Halifax, 1962.

Cornall, James. *Images of Canada: Halifax South End.* Arcadia Publishing: Charleston, South Carolina, 1998.

Dorrington, Aubrey, *History of Stellarton.* The Advocate Printing & Publishing Co., Ltd., Pictou, Nova Scotia, Canada, 1976.

Drew, Benjamin, *The Refugee: Or the Narratives of Fugitives Slaves in Canada. Related by Themselves, With an Account of the History and Condition of the Colored Population of Upper Canada.* Boston: John P. Jewett and Company, 1856.

Executive Council, The, *Record of the Proceedings of the First Universal Races Congress Held at the University of London, July 26-29, 1911,* P. S. King & Son, Westminster, England, 1911.

Falk, Lilian et al, Ed., *The English Language in Nova Scotia.* Roseway Publishing, Lockeport, Nova Scotia.

Fingard, Judith, *The Dark Side of Life in Victorian Halifax,* Pottersfield Press: Potters Lake, Nova Scotia, 1991.

Forsey, Eugene, M. A., *National Problems of Canada. Economic and Social Aspects of The Nova Scotia Coal Industry*, 1926.

Foster, Cecil, *A Place Called Heaven The Meaning of Being Black in Canada.* Harper Collins Publishers Ltd., Toronto, 1996.

Fosty, George and Darril, John Jelley. *Splendid is the Sun: The 5,000 Year History of Hockey.* Stryker-Indigo Publishing Company, Inc. New York, NY., 2003.

Frank, Lilian & Margaret Harry ed., *The English Language in Nova Scotia.* Rosway Publishing, Lockeport, Nova Scotia, 1998.

Gillis, Sheldon. *Putting It On Ice: A Social History of Hockey in the Maritimes, 1880-1914.* Masters Thesis, 1996.
Greaves, Ida, *National Problems of Canada. The Negros in Canada,* (McGill University Economic Studies, No. 16). McGill University, Montreal, Canada, 1930.

Greaves, Ida, *National Problems of Canada. The Negros in Canada,* (McGill University Economic Studies, No. 16). McGill University, Montreal Canada, 1930.

Gospel Sermons by Clergymen of the Anglican, Baptist, Methodist, and Presbyterian Churches. Halifax: British American Book and Tract Society, 1889.

Gordon, Grant, *From Slavery to Freedom: The Life of David George, Pioneer Black Baptist Minister.* Lancelot Press Limited, Hantsport, Nova Scotia, Canada, 1992.

Grant, John N., *Black Nova Scotians.* Nova Scotia Museum, Halifax, Nova Scotia, Canada, 1980.

Greig, Murray. *Going the Distance: Canada's Boxing Heritage.* Toronto: Macmillan Canada, 1996.

Halpenny, J., M.A. M.D. and Lilian B. Ireland. *How To Be Healthy.* Western Canada Series, Authorized for use in the schools of British Columbia, Alberta, Saskatchewan, Manitoba,

Quebec, Nova Scotia and Prince Edward Island. Toronto: W. J. Gage & Company, Limited, 1911.

Hammond, M. O., *Canadian Footprints: A Study in Foregrounds and Backgrounds.* Toronto: The MacMillian Company of Canada Limited, 1926.

Henson, Josiah. *The Life of Josiah Henson Formerly a Slave Now an Inhabitant of Canada as Narrated by Himself,* Arthur D. Phelps, Boston, Mass., U.S.A., 1849.

Henry, Frances, *Forgotten Canadians: The Blacks of Nova Scotia,* Longman Canada Ltd., Don Mills, Ontario, 1973.

Hill, Daniel G. *The Freedom – Seekers: Blacks in Early Canada.* Toronto: The Book Society of Canada Limited, 1981.

Hill, Lawrence, *Trials and Triumphs: The Story of African-Canadians,* Umbrella Press, Toronto, Canada, 1993.

Hodges, Graham Russell, Editor, *The Black Loyalist Directory,* Garland Publishing, Inc., New York, U.S.A., 1996.

Hooker, J. R. *Henry Sylvester Williams: Imperial Pan-Africanist.* Rex Collins: London, 1975.

Hopkins, J. Castell, F.S.S., F.R.G.S. *Canada at War: A Record of Heroism and Achievement 1914-1918.* Toronto: The Canadian Annual Review Limited, 1919.

Hornby, Jim, *Island Studies: Black Islanders Prince Edward Island's Historical Black Community.* Institute of Island Studies: Charlottetown, Prince Edward Island, 1991.

Hubbard, Stephen L. *Against All Odds: The Story of William Peyton Hubbard Black Leader and Municipal Reformer.* Dundurn Press Ltd., Toronto, Ontario, 1987.

Humber, William. *Diamonds of the North: A Concise History of Baseball in Canada.* Toronto: Oxford University Press, 1995.

Hunt, M. Stuart. *Nova Scotia's Part in the Great War.* Halifax, The Nova Scotia Veteran Publishing Company Limited, Halifax, Nova Scotia, 1920.

Jenson, L. B. *Vanishing Halifax, Drawings by L. B. Jenson.* Petheric Press: Halifax, Nova Scotia, Canada, 1968.

Jobb, Dean, *Bluenose Justice True Tales of Mischief, Mayhem and Murder*, Lancelot Press, Hantsport, Nova Scotia, 1996.

Johnston, A. J. B., *Defending Halifax: Ordnance, 1825-1906,* National Parks and Sites Branch, Parks Canada, Environment Canada, 1981.

Johnson, James Weldon, Editor, *The Book of American Negro Spirituals.* New York: The Viking Press, 1925.

Kaulback, E. C.A., Proprietor. *The Maritime Halifax & New Glasgow, The Maritime Business College Complete Course of Study, 73 College St., Halifax, Nova Scotia. 1921* (The Herald Press Limited, Montreal-Printers).

Kerr, A. E., President Dalhousie University. *The Condition of the Negroes of Halifax City, Nova Scotia: A Study Conducted by Institute of Public Affairs Dalhousie University.* Dalhousie University, 1962.

Kimball, R. Andrew. *The Silent Ending: The Death of Community Hockey Tradition in Nova Scotia.* History Department Thesis, Acadia University, April 1, 1986. Faculty Advisor Dr. Cross.

Konczacki, Janina M., *Victorian Explorer: The African Diaries of Captain William G. Stairs,* Nimbus Publishing Ltd., Halifax, Nova Scotia, 1998.

Lawrence, Catherine S., *Autobiography, Sketch of Life and Labors of Miss Catherine S. Lawrence.* Revised Edition, James B. Lyon, Printer, Albany, New York, 1896.

Lovell's Canadian Dominion Directory for 1871, *Nova Scotia Directory for 1871 The Names of the Professional and Business Men and Other Inhabitants in the Cities, Towns and Villages Throughout the Province of Nova Scotia, Canada in 1871.* Reprinted by Noel Elliot, January 1985.

MacDonald, Helen G. Ph. D. *Canadian Public Opinion on the American Civil War. Studies in History, Economics and Public Law Vol. CXXIV No. 2.* New York: Columbia University Press, 1926.

MacMillian, Hon. A. S. Minister of Highways Nova Scotia. *Historic Nova Scotia: A Land of Pilgrimage for all Time, Beloved for its Material Beauty and the Romance of its History.* Government of Nova Scotia, Halifax, Nova Scotia, 1935.

Mahar, James and Rowena. *Too Many to Mourn One Family's Tragedy in the Halifax Explosion.* Nimbus Publishing Limited, Halifax, Nova Scotia, 1998.

McKay, Karen E., C.G., *The 1838 Census Index of Pictou County Nova Scotia.* Publication No. 18, Genealogical Association of Nova Scotia, Halifax, Nova Scotia, 1985.

Metson, Graham & Archibald MacMechan. *The Halifax Explosion December 6, 1917.* Toronto: McGraw-Hill Ryerson Limited, 1978.

Miller, Kelly, A.M. LL.D. *Kelly Miller's History of the World War for Human Rights Being an Intensely Human and Brilliant Account of the World War and Why and for What Purpose America and the Allies are Fighting and the Important Pact Taken by the Negro.* Austin Jenkins Co. : Washington, D. C., 1919.

Minutes of the Twenty-Ninth Session of the Western New Brunswick Baptist Association, Held at Germain Street, Saint John, on Tuesday, Wednesday, and Thursday, 27th, 28th and 29th June, 1876 with the Annual Reports of the N.B. Baptist Home Missionary and Education Societies. Saint John, New Brunswick. Printed by Barnes & Company, Prince William Street, Saint John, New Brunswick, Canada, 1876.

Monnon, Mary Ann. *Miracles and Mysteries: The Halifax Explosion December 6, 1917.* Nimbus Publishing Limited, Halifax, Nova Scotia, 1977.

Morton, Desmond and J. L. Granatstein. *Marching to Armageddon: Canadians and the Great War 1914-1919.* Toronto: Lester and Orpen Dennys Limited, 1989.

Nova Scotia Historical Society. *Collection of the Nova Scotia Historical Society for the years 1878-1884.* Belleville, Ontario: Mika Publishing Company, 1976.

Nova Scotia's Industrial Centre New Glasgow Stellarton Westville Trenton, The Birthplace of Steel in Canada 1916, Issued Under the Approval of the Cormals of New Glasgow, Stellarton, Westville & Trenton, 1916.

O'Ree, Willie, *The Autobiography of Willie O'Ree Hockey's Black Pioneer,* Somerville House, New York, U.S.A., 2000.

Oliver, Grace A. *Arthur Penrhyn Stanley: His Life, Work, and Teachers.* Boston: Cupples, Upham and Company, 1885.

Oliver, Rev. W. P., *The Negro in Nova Scotia,* Journal of Education, Vol. 13, No.2, February 1964.

Pachai, Bridglal, *Beneath the Clouds of the Promised Land: The Survival of Nova Scotia's Blacks Volume II: 1800-1989,* Lancelot Press, Halifax, Nova Scotia, 1990.

Pachai, Bridglal, *Peoples of Maritimes Series: Blacks.* Nimbus Publishing Ltd., Halifax, Nova Scotia, 1997.

Payzant, Joan M. *Halifax: Cornerstone of Canada.* Halifax: Windsor Publications, Inc. 1985.

Payzant, Joan M. *Second to None: A History of Public Education in Dartmouth, Nova Scotia.* Dartmouth, Nova Scotia: The Dartmouth historical Association, 1991.

Personnel of Harbour Commission. Port of Vancouver British Columbia, Vancouver Harbour Commission, 1932.

Quarles, Benjamin, *Black Abolitionists.* Oxford University Press, New York, U. S. A., 1969.

Regan, John W. *Sketches and Traditions of the Northwest Arm.* Halifax, Nova Scotia: McAlpine Publishing Company, Ltd., 1909.

Report of Board of School Commissioners for the City of Halifax for the Year Ending 31st October, 1911. Weeks Printing Co., Ltd., Halifax, Nova Scotia, 1912.

Report of Board of School Commissioners for the City of Halifax for the Year Ending 31st October, 1930.

Report of Board of School Commissioners for the City of Halifax for the Year Ending 31st October, 1939.

Riendeau, Roger et al. *An Enduring Heritage: Black Contributions to Early Ontario.* Dunduan Press Limited, Toronto, Ontario, 1984.

Robbins, Arlie C., *Legacy to Buxton.* Chatham, Ideal Printing, Chatham, Ontario, Canada, 1983.

Robinson, Ernest Fraser. *The Halifax Disaster December 6, 1917.* Vanwell Publishing Limited, St. Catharines, Ontario, Canada, 1987.

Raddall, Thomas H. *Halifax: Warden of the North.* Doubleday & Company, Inc., Garden City, New York, U. S. A., 1965.

Rogers, Joesph S, Photographer. *Rogers' Photographic Advertising Album.* Halifax, 1871 (Reprinted Publications Committee Heritage Trust of Nova Scotia, 1970.

Ross, Alexander Malton. *Memories of a Reformer (1832-1892).* Toronto: Hunter, Rose & Company, 1893.

Ruck, Calvin W. *The Black Battalion 1916-1920: Canada's Best Kept Secret.* Halifax, Nova Scotia: Nimbus Publishing Ltd., 1987.

Rust, Edna and Pat Jr., *Pat Rusts' Illustrated History of the Black Athlete,* Doubleday & Company, Inc., Garden City, New York, U. S. A., 1985.

Saunders, Charles. *Black and Bluenose: The Contemporary History of a Community,* Pottersfield Press: Laurencetown Beach, Nova Scotia, 1999.

Saunders, Charles R. *Share & Care The Story of the Nova Scotia Home for Colored Children.* Nimbus Publishing Limited, Halifax, Nova Scotia, Canada,1994.

Schrodt, Redmond, Bakar. *Sport Canadians,* Executive Sports Publications Ltd., Edmonton, 1980.

Schmidt, Rene. *Canadian Disasters.* Scholastic Canada Ltd., Richmond Hill, Ontario, 1986.

Sea Tales: The Halifax Explosion, A&E Television Networks, New York, New York, 1997 (Video 50-minutes).

Shand, Gwendolyn V. *Adult Education Among the Negroes of Nova Scotia.* Halifax, N. S., Dalhousie University, 1961.

Spray, W. A. *The Blacks in New Brunswick,* Brunswick University Press, Saint John, Canada, 1972.

Stowe, Harriet Beecher, *Uncle Tom's Cabin: A Picture of Slave Life in America. The Ruby Series.* London: Routledge and Sons, 1852.

Stephenson, Gordon, M.T.P.I.C., *A Redevelopment Study of Halifax, Nova Scotia (including Supplementary Volume),* The Corporation of the City of Halifax, Nova Scotia, 1957.

Thomson, Colin A. *Blacks in Deep Snow Black Pioneers in Canada.* J.M. Dent & Sons, Don Mills, Ontario, Canada, 1979.

Tobin, Jacquline L. & Raymond G. Dobard, Ph. D. *Hidden in Plain View: A Secret History of Quilts and the Underground Railroad.* First Anchor Books, New York, NY, 2000.

Tulloch, Headley, *Black Canadians: A Long Line of Fighters.* NC Press Limited, Toronto, 1975.

Ullman, Victor, *Look to the North Star: A Life of William King.* Beacon Press, Boston, Mass., 1969.

Vaughan, Garth, *The Puck Starts Here,* Goose Lane Editions & Four East Publications, Fredericton, New Brunswick,1996.

Walker, James W. St. G., *The Black Loyalists, The Search for the Promised Land in Nova Scotia and Sierra Leoni, 1789-1878.* Africana Publishing Company, New York, 1976.

Washington, Prof. Booker T. *A New Negro for A New Century: An Accurate and Up-to-Date Record of the Upward Struggles of the Negro Race.* Chicago: American Publishing House, 1899.

Washington, Booker T., *Up From Slavery,* Heritage Press, Norwalk, Connecticut, 1970.

Washington, Booker T., Editor. *Tuskegee & Its People: Their Ideals and Achievements.* D. Appleton and Company, New York, 1905.

Washington, Booker T. *Working With the Hands: Being a Sequel to "Up From Slavery" Covering the Author's Experiences in Industrial Training at Tuskegee.* Doubleday, Page & Company, New York, 1904.

Watson, T. & D. D. Smith. *The Slave in Canada. Collections of the Nova Scotia Historical Society, for the Years 1896-98. Volume X.* Nova Scotia Printing Company, Halifax, Nova Scotia, 1899.

Wedderburn, H.A.J., *From Slavery to the Ghetto the Story of the Negro in the Maritimes.* A paper presented to the New Brunswick Human Rights Commission, March 25-26, 1968.

Wesley, Charles H. *International Library of Negro Life and History: In Freedom's Footsteps. From the African Background to the Civil War.* Publishers Company, Inc., New York, 1969.

Winks, Robin W., *Negro School Segregation in Ontario and Nova Scotia.* The Canadian Historical Review, Volume L. No. 2, 1969.

Winks, Robin. *The Blacks in Canada: A History.* McGill-Queens University Press, Montreal, Quebec, Canada, 1971.

Worldwarone.com Website.

Young, A. J. "Sandy". *Beyond Heroes A Sport History of Nova Scotia. Vol. 2.* Lancelot Press: Hantsport, Nova Scotia, 1981.

ABOUT THE AUTHORS

George Robert Fosty is a Canadian historian and documentary filmmaker currently living in New York City. He was born in 1960 in Prince Rupert, British Columbia, Canada. In 1980, he received a Diploma in International Law from The London City Polytechnic, London, England. He obtained his Bachelor of Arts in History from the University of Hawaii at Hilo in 1985. In 1991 he was awarded a Master of Arts in History from Midwestern State University, Wichita Falls, Texas. From September 1990 to November 1991 he worked as a Military Historian (GS-7) within the United States Office of Personal Management under special contract to the United States Department of Defense and the United States Air Force, Sheppard AFB, Texas.

While at Sheppard he authored numerous articles on the USAF, helped create two temporary museums (in conjunction with Sheppard 50th Anniversary celebrations); served as a historical consultant on three locally produced television documentaries; and co-authored the award-winning book: *Sustaining the Wings: A Fifty Year History of Sheppard AFB*. He is the co-author of *Splendid is the Sun: The 5,000 Year History of Hockey*.

Darril W. Fosty is a Canadian historian and documentary filmmaker currently living in York Beach, Maine. Though he was born in Terrace, British Columbia, Canada in 1968, he spent much of his youth in Kamloops, British Columbia. He studied History and Journalism at Western Washington University in Bellingham, Washington completing his Bachelor of Arts degree in 1992 with a concentration in North American, Native North American, and Post-French Revolutionary European history.

He is the co-author of *Splendid is the Sun: The 5,000 Year History of Hockey*.

262

SPECIAL THANKS

It has taken seven years to complete this book. In addition to our immediate families, we would like to thank the following people for their kind assistance and support during the course of this project:

David Erste, Stephen Vance, Joe Francis, Bret Talbot, Dennis Sita, Mary Maharg, John Johnson, Harvey Rubin, Francine Goodman Esq., Arleen Tortorelli, Ken Rodan, Edye Weissler, Torkia Nzidee, Jeff Eigen, David Crow, Pratibha Patel, Paul Patskou, Doug Robertson, Esq., Dan Amman, Roger Schuerger, Michael Kessel, Esq., David Freeman, Leslie Bauchelle, Michael Schorr, Laurence Weeks, Stan "Chook" Maxwell, Duane Snipe, Evan Dobson, Ken Greenwood, Esq., Noemi Fascullo, Susan Ginch, Rachael Dean, Craig Campbell, Dr. Garth Vaughan, Dr. Henry Bishop, Regina Bishop, Howard Dill and Family, Lori Slatzer, Bruce Waldinger, Debbie Reid, Penny L. Lighthall, Marco Campanelli, Bruce Bennett, Lance Rosen, Jeff Klassen, Kathy Meagher, Jason Hagberg, Murphy Shewchuck, Mary McDonough, Phil Piazza, David Saito, Mark Wilson, Esq., John Jelley, Dawn Jelley, Susan Jelley, John Conrad, Ruthann Libard, Ivan Harris, Prof. Robin W. Winks, Crawford Killian, Stephen Bass, Elizabeth Avon-Braun, Xiang Hong, Fred and Ann P. Buscaglia, Anthony Fletcher, Esq., Rana Dershowitz, Esq., Kelli Bagley, David Dahl, Al Peterson, Rebecca Ruddle, Bobby Bryde, Kevin Greenstein, Sanford Wexler, Katrina Bailey, David Alpine, Basil M. Tomlinson, John Thorn, Dan Diamond.

OTHER BOOKS BY
GEORGE & DARRIL FOSTY

SPLENDID IS THE SUN:
THE 5,000-YEAR HISTORY OF HOCKEY.

Named the Book-of-the-Month in October 2003 by England's A to Z Encyclopedia of Hockey! Praised by America's Inside Hockey experts as being hockey's equivalent to Darwin's Theory on Evolution! The only ice hockey history book ever to be reviewed by the Syrian media! Six years in the making, over 6,000 historic hockey sources identified worldwide in 48 countries and 13 languages, utilizing the research skills of three professional historians, it is quite simply the most detailed and controversial historic account on hockey ever written. A book which rewrites Canadian and world hockey history. A must read for any sports fan.

Buy a copy today at:
www.stryker-indigo.com or www.splendidisthesun.com

264